Blender for Beginners
Part 2

Third Edition

Animate, light, and render in Blender 4.5 to create polished, optimized, and professional 3D scenes

3D Tudor (Neil Ian Bettison)
Vanessa Haralambous

Blender for Beginners
Part 2
Third Edition

Copyright © 2025 Packt Publishing

Portfolio Director: Rohit Rajkumar
Relationship Lead: Kaustubh Manglurkar
Project Manager: Sandip Tadge
Content Engineer: Anuradha Joglekar
Technical Editor: Tejas Vijay Mhasvekar
Copy Editor: Safis Editing
Indexer: Tejas Soni
Proofreader: Anuradha Joglekar
Production Designer: Shantanu Zagade
Growth Lead: Lee Booth
Marketing Owner: Nivedita Pandey

First edition: June 2012
Second edition: August 2014
Third edition: November 2025

Production reference: 1261125

Published by Packt Publishing Ltd.
Grosvenor House
11 St Paul's Square
Birmingham
B3 1RB, UK.

ISBN 978-1-80638-199-9

www.packtpub.com

We would like to dedicate this book to our two daughters who we hold most dear, to Luke, and all the people, seen and unseen, who helped put this book together.

— Vanessa & Neil

Contributors

About the authors

3D Tudor is an online course creator team publishing courses on 3D modeling, game design, and animation. Founded and led by **Neil I. Bettison** in 2019, 3D Tudor brings with it over 10 years of specialist experience. The focus of 3D Tudor is on teaching 3D modeling and animation through free and accessible software, including Blender and Unreal Engine 5, to over 250,000 students from all backgrounds. The team publishes courses, 3D models, and game props, and also runs a YouTube channel where free Blender-to–Unreal Engine 5 environment tutorials are posted. The 3D Tudor headquarters are in Paphos, Cyprus, and Neil holds a Computer Games Art BA (Hons) degree from the University for the Creative Arts.

Vanessa A. B Haralambous is an academic writing specialist with over 10 years of experience. Since 2010, she has taught academic writing and proofreading techniques to university students from different levels and disciplines, including the humanities and arts. Between 2019 and 2020, Vanessa published two courses on academic writing for university students. Vanessa offers ad hoc copywriting support to 3D Tudor and holds a Psychology with Criminology BSc (Hons) degree and a Forensic Psychology MSc degree.

I would like to extend my thanks to Vanessa and Vanessa would like to extend her thanks to me (pun intended!) for working together to write the book around us both looking after the girls and keeping them off the keyboard. Because let's face it; they are far too young to be keyboard warriors. We would like to wholeheartedly thank our partner in 3D Tudor and real friend for many reasons he no longer needs to prove, Lukas Partaukas – the technical genius behind image creation and fact-checking for this book. Special thanks to the different editors who worked with us while we wrote this book, including Hayden Edwards, Rashi Dubey and Anuradha Vishwas Joglekar - for their valuable input and time reviewing this book. Also, extending our dearest thanks to the entire Packt team for their support during the course of writing this book.

About the reviewers

Skylar Jetton is a multidisciplinary artist whose career has spanned professional ballet, manga illustration, and VR technology. Today, he is the Creative Director of Spookhaus, where he guides narrative and art direction while creating photorealistic 3D characters for film and games. He specializes in Look Development using Maya, Blender, Unreal Engine, Mari, and the Substance Suite. The author of a book on ballet technique, he now spends his free time composing orchestral scores and playing narrative-heavy video games. He is based out of Los Angeles, California.

I would like to sincerely thank Namita for inviting me onto this project and welcoming me into the Packt Publishing family. My gratitude also goes to Sonam and Rashi for their kindness, incredible support, and expert guidance throughout the editing process.

Jane Suteerawanit is a Senior Character Artist at Gameloft Brisbane. Originally from Perth, she holds a Bachelor's in Animation and Game Design from Curtin University, where she earned the Best Portfolio Award and Academic Award for high achievement. Her career began with an internship at Landshark Games in Singapore, creating low-poly characters and assets. In 2021, she joined Flying Bark Productions, contributing to *100% Wolf: The Book of Hath* on ABC ME. Her recent game credits include *My Little Pony: Mane Merge (2022)* and *Carmen Sandiego (2025)*, where she modeled the iconic title character.

Jane also previously contributed as a reviewer on *Low Poly 3D Modeling in Blender* by Samuel Sullins.

Table of Contents

Chapter 5: Introducing Blender's Rendering Engines: A Comprehensive Exploration   115

Preface

When you arrive at *Part 2* of *Blender for Beginners*, you are no longer someone who has just opened Blender and wondered where the cube has gone. You have moved past the first panic of navigating in 3D, you know how to get around the 3D Viewport without losing your camera, and you have a few finished props or small scenes under your belt. That is a big deal. Most people never get this far.

Part 2 is where we start treating you less like a passenger and more like a junior pilot. You will still get plenty of guidance, but now the focus shifts from "learning where things are" to "making those things move, respond, and render properly." This is the half of the book where your scenes stop being static and start to feel alive.

Part 1 of *Blender for Beginners* was about building things. *Part 2* is about running them. By the end of *Part 1*, your files will be organized, your models will hold up when you add light, and you will have the sort of clean assets that are actually ready to animate or send to a client, not just "nice screenshots".

Part 2 picks up from there and moves you into motion, systems, and final look-dev:

- You will animate with keyframes, interpolation, and the graph editor, and you will add simple rigs, constraints, and an approachable first look at inverse kinematics so posing feels natural instead of fiddly.

- You will explore beginner-friendly Geometry Nodes with practical mini-projects: scattering, instancing, and very simple generators, always with an eye on performance so your machine does not melt.

- You will light for readability, manage exposure and shadows, and make informed choices between Eevee and Cycles depending on the shot.

- You will build reusable compositing stacks driven by AOVs, add fast surface variation with vertex painting and light texture-paint passes, and then finish with optimization: instancing, LODs, Simplify, and tidy asset management for clean hand-offs.

Part 2 assumes that you either have worked through *Part 1* or that you already have a similar level of comfort with Blender basics. If you feel shaky on navigation, object and edit modes, or simple modelling and materials, it is worth going back and shoring that up before charging ahead here. You will enjoy this part a lot more if you are not fighting the fundamentals at the same time.

My advice is to treat each chapter in *Part 2* as a self-contained upgrade to your existing skills: When you learn collections and scene organization, go back to one of your older projects and clean it up. When you learn animation and rigging, add a simple movement or pose cycle to an asset you care about, not a throwaway cube. When you learn lighting, re-light one of your earlier models and compare the old and new renders side by side.

I will point out common beginner traps, give you honest time-saving tips, and occasionally tell you to put the kettle on and come back with fresh eyes when something is being stubborn. There is no point pretending that everything in 3D is quick and easy. Some parts are fiddly. The difference is that now you will have a clear path through that fiddly bit, instead of guessing.

If *Part 1* was about proving to yourself that you can do 3D at all, *Part 2* is about proving that you can finish things properly. So take your time, follow the chapters in order, and give each exercise a fair shot. Do not worry if your first animations look a bit stiff, or if your first lighting setups are a bit flat. That is normal. The important thing is that you keep going, keep adjusting, and keep finishing. Thank you for coming this far with Blender for Beginners. I hope this second part helps you push your skills to the point where you start to recognize your own work and think, "Yes, that actually looks like something I would like to play, watch, or use."

Until next time, happy modeling, everyone!

– 3D Tudor (Neil Bettison) & Vanessa Haralambous

Who this book is for

If you are a video games enthusiast looking to gain experience in 3D modelling, game design, and animation for game props, assets, and environments, this is the book for you. Character artists, game designers, motion graphics designers, animators, environment artists, or other technical artists would also benefit from this book. 3D modelling artists already familiar with video game assets, prop, and environment design will be able to learn new workflows that maximize their productivity using Blender.

This book teaches 3D modelling techniques using Blender - a type of free, open-source software. From familiarizing you with the user interface to all kinds of digital creations, taken together, *Parts 1* and *2* of *Blender for Beginners* will take you on a journey up and including rendering your 3D art for your portfolio.

What this book covers

Chapter 1, Rigging and Weight Painting for Beginners, teaches how to make your models move in a controlled way. You will create basic armatures, bind meshes with automatic weights, adjust those weights where deformation breaks, and add simple IK chains so posing feels natural instead of painful.

Chapter 2, Mastering the Basics of Blender Geometry Nodes, gives a friendly introduction to procedural workflows. You will learn how Geometry Nodes graphs are structured, how data flows through them, and how to build simple setups for scattering, instancing, and modifying geometry in ways that would be tedious by hand.

Chapter 3, Unlocking Creativity with Blender Texture Painting, gives you the skills to paint directly onto your models. You will set up texture paint slots, choose and customize brushes, work with stencils and masks, and add stylized surface detail, wear, and variation that would be difficult to achieve with flat, procedural materials alone.

Chapter 4, Releasing Colorful Creativity with Vertex Painting in Blender, explores vertex colors as a lightweight, engine-friendly way to add life to your assets. You will paint color information straight onto vertices and use it inside your materials to drive gradients, dirt, edge highlights, and subtle variation without using extra textures.

Chapter 5, Introducing Blender's Rendering Engines: A Comprehensive Exploration, looks under the hood of Eevee and Cycles. You will compare how each engine handles light and shadows, adjust sample counts and noise controls, tune light path settings, and make sensible decisions about which engine to use for diverse types of projects.

Chapter 6, Enhancing Realism in Blender: Mastering Light Linking, Light Portals, and the Shadow Catcher, refines your lighting toolkit. You will control which objects each light affects, guide indirect light with portals, and use the shadow catcher to integrate 3D elements into backgrounds or plates, pushing realism without overcomplicating your scenes.

Chapter 7, Guiding You through Compositing in Blender, teaches you how to polish your renders after they leave the 3D view. You will work in the Compositor with render passes, masks, and common nodes such as color correction, glare, and blur, building reusable stacks that let you enhance images without re-rendering entire sequences every time.

Chapter 8, Optimizing Blender for Success, focuses on performance and finishing. You will use tools such as instancing, linked duplicates, LODs, and the Simplify panel to keep large scenes responsive, and you will adopt naming, organization, and export habits that make your work easier to hand off to game engines, clients, or Future You.

To get the most out of this book

Part 2 assumes you are no longer at the "what does this button do?" stage. Before you start this half of the book, it is worth checking that your foundations are in place.

What we assume you already know For *Part 2*, I am assuming at least one of the following is true:

- You have worked through *Part 1* of this book, or
- You already have equivalent experience in Blender from courses, tutorials, or production work.

That means you should already be comfortable with:

- Navigating the viewport, framing objects, and working in different views. Switching between Object and Edit Mode and using core modelling tools (Move, Rotate, Scale, Extrude, Inset, Bevel, Loop Cut, etc.).
- Organizing scenes with collections and the Outliner at a basic level. Creating simple materials with the Principled BSDF and plugging in basic textures.
- Unwrapping UVs for straightforward objects and recognizing obvious stretching.
- Creating and playing back basic keyframe animations on objects or cameras.

If any of those feel very shaky, it is absolutely worth revisiting *Part 1* or doing a focused refresh before jumping into *Part 2*. The chapters here move faster and assume you are not fighting the interface anymore.

You do not need to be:

- An expert rigger, animator, or technical artist.
- Fully comfortable with Geometry Nodes yet (we introduce it gently).
- An advanced compositor or lighting artist.

Those are exactly the areas *Part 2* is here to grow. What you need installed to work through *Part 2*, you will need everything from *Part 1*, and the technical specifications we describe in full in *Chapter 1* of both parts.

Download the color images

We also provide a PDF file that has color images of the screenshots/diagrams used in this book. You can download it here: `https://packt.link/gbp/9781806381999`.

This book contains long screenshots captured to provide you with an overview of the entire Blender interface. As a result, the text on these images may appear small at 100% zoom. We recommend referring to the graphics bundle for the ease of understanding.

Conventions used

There are a number of text conventions used throughout this book.

`CodeInText`: Indicates code words in text, database table names, folder names, filenames, file extensions, pathnames, dummy URLs, user input, and Twitter handles. For example: "For Blender's **Symmetrize** function to work properly, the bones on one side of the rig must already be labeled with `.L` and `.R` to keep track of which side is which, left or right."

Bold: Indicates a new term, an important word, or words that you see on the screen. For instance, words in menus or dialog boxes appear in the text like this. For example: "Go to the **Add** menu, select **Armature**, and then **Single Bone**."

Warnings or important notes appear like this.

Tips and tricks appear like this.

Get in touch

Feedback from our readers is always welcome.

General feedback: If you have questions about any aspect of this book or have any general feedback, please email us at customercare@packt.com and mention the book's title in the subject of your message. If you have feedback on content, you can email the authors at bettison.gamedesign@gmail.com or vanessa.haralambous@gmail.com.

Errata: Although we have taken every care to ensure the accuracy of our content, mistakes do happen. If you have found a mistake in this book, we would be grateful if you reported this to us. Please visit http://www.packt.com/submit-errata, click **Submit Errata**, and fill in the form.

Piracy: If you come across any illegal copies of our works in any form on the internet, we would be grateful if you would provide us with the location address or website name. Please contact us at copyright@packt.com with a link to the material.

If you are interested in becoming an author: If there is a topic that you have expertise in and you are interested in either writing or contributing to a book, please visit http://authors.packt.com/.

Share your thoughts

Once you've read *Blender for Beginners, Part 2*, we'd love to hear your thoughts! Scan the QR code below to go straight to the Amazon review page for this book and share your feedback.

https://packt.link/r/1806381990

Your review is important to us and the tech community and will help us make sure we're delivering excellent quality content.

Free Benefits with Your Book

This book comes with free benefits to support your learning. Activate them now for instant access (see the "*How to Unlock*" section for instructions).

Here's a quick overview of what you can instantly unlock with your purchase:

PDF and ePub Copies	Next-Gen Web-Based Reader

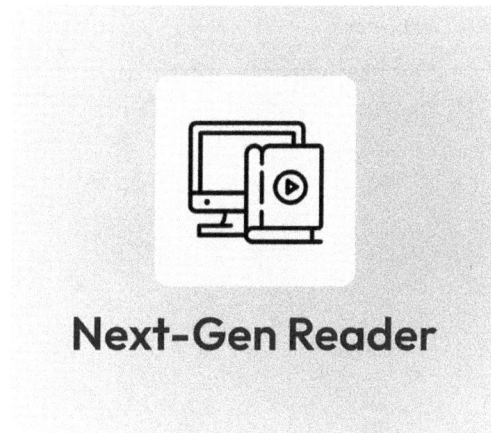

Free PDF and ePub versions

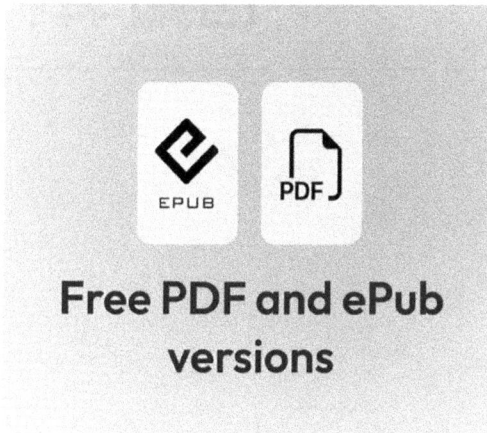

Next-Gen Reader

- Access a DRM-free PDF copy of this book to read anywhere, on any device.
- Use a DRM-free ePub version with your favorite e-reader.

- **Multi-device progress sync:** Pick up where you left off, on any device.
- **Highlighting and notetaking:** Capture ideas and turn reading into lasting knowledge.
- **Bookmarking:** Save and revisit key sections whenever you need them.
- **Dark mode:** Reduce eye strain by switching to dark or sepia themes.

How to Unlock

UNLOCK NOW

Scan the QR code (or go to packtpub.com/unlock). Search for this book by name, confirm the edition, and then follow the steps on the page.

Note: Keep your invoice handy. Purchases made directly from Packt don't require one.

1

Rigging and Weight Painting for Beginners

You wrapped up *Part 1* of *Blender for Beginners* with the basics sorted: clean modelling, sensible UVs, materials that do as they are told, and a first wobble into animation in *Chapter 16*. Lovely stuff. Now for *Part 2*, where we swap training wheels for actual gears. First stop: **rigging and weight painting**: the difference between a character that moves and a character that moves without falling apart like a cheap deckchair.

Think of rigging as building a skeleton inside your mesh. This skeleton, called an armature in Blender, is made up of interconnected bones that define how different parts of the model will move. Every bone in your model is a lever, controlling the movement of specific parts of the model. By setting up the hierarchy and constraints of these bones, you will make up the rules for how the bones interact with each other.

Once your skeleton is in place, the next step is weight painting. Weight painting adjusts how much each part of your character's outer model responds to the movement of each bone within the rig. Weight painting is there to make sure that the movements appear smooth and realistic so that everyone believes your character is real.

By learning the basics of rigging and weight painting, you can animate a wide variety of characters, whether you want to create a brave character for a video game or a creature for a movie. This chapter is designed to help you understand these essential skills and guide you through your first attempt at rigging and weight painting.

So, in this chapter, we will cover the following topics:

- Understanding rigging in Blender
- Starting with weight painting
- Advanced rigging techniques
- Troubleshooting common rigging and weight painting issues
- Bringing it all together: rigging and weight painting a complete character

Free Benefits with Your Book

Your purchase includes a free PDF copy of this book along with other exclusive benefits. Check the *Free Benefits with Your Book* section in the Preface to unlock them instantly and maximize your learning experience.

Technical requirements

As for **Blender 4.5 LTS (Long-Term Support)**, the general requirements include the following:

- macOS: minimum now ~11.2+ (Apple Silicon supported natively).
- Linux: glibc baseline rises from ~2.17 to ~2.28+
- CPU: instruction set reference updated from SSE2 to SSE4.2 (newer CPUs)
- RAM: practical minimum 8 GB (32 GB recommended for heavy scenes)
- GPU/OpenGL: OpenGL 4.3; VRAM 2 GB+ (more recommended)
- GPU backends: include Metal (macOS), AMD HIP, Intel oneAPI, alongside CUDA/OptiX
- Practical notes: Full HD display recommended; app footprint ≈1 GB; SSD recommended

Understanding rigging in Blender

Rigging turns static 3D models into characters that can move. You do that by adding a digital skeleton, called an **armature**. Each bone is like a control point for your model, letting you move and pose it in realistic ways. These bones are arranged in a hierarchy, which means they are connected in a way that moving one bone will move others linked to it. For example, if you move the upper arm bone, the lower arm and hand bones will move too, just like in a real arm. This setup helps make your model's movements look natural. This is shown in *Figure 1.1*.

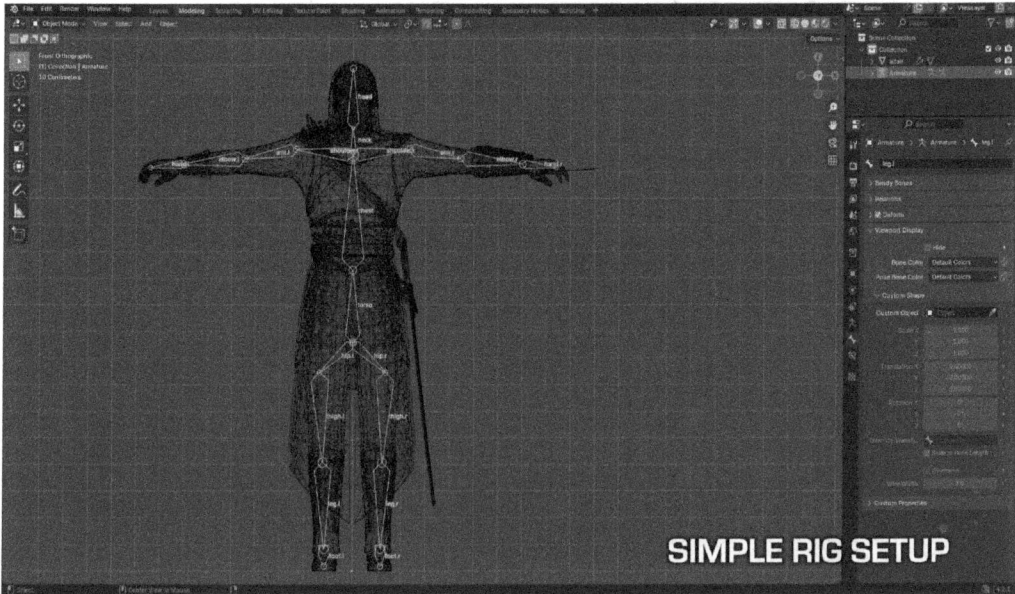

Figure 1.1: Armature hierarchical order example

For example, the top of one of the hierarchies involved in this armature would be the shoulder. This would control the movement of the joint for the arm, allowing it to rotate realistically.

Bones included in an armature are invisible in the final render but are crucial for animation. They define how parts of the mesh move in relation to each other.

To create your first armature, follow these steps:

1. Double-check that your 3D model is ready (i.e., fully designed and detailed, as in all the parts that you want to animate are in place), and that you are in **Object Mode**.

2. Go to the **Add** menu, select **Armature**, and then **Single Bone**. A single bone will appear in your 3D Viewport, usually at the center of your grid, as in *Figure 1.2*.

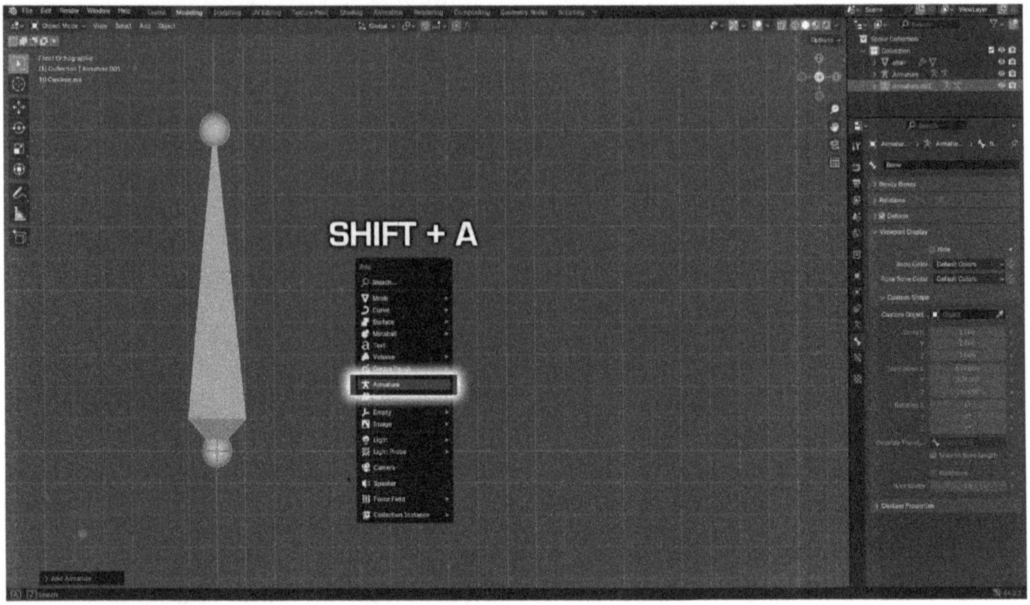

Figure 1.2: First steps of adding an armature in Blender

3. Switch to **Edit Mode** to adjust your armature. Here, you can extrude new bones from the existing ones by selecting the tip and pressing *E*. You are effectively building out the skeleton to fit inside your model, as in *Figure 1.3*.

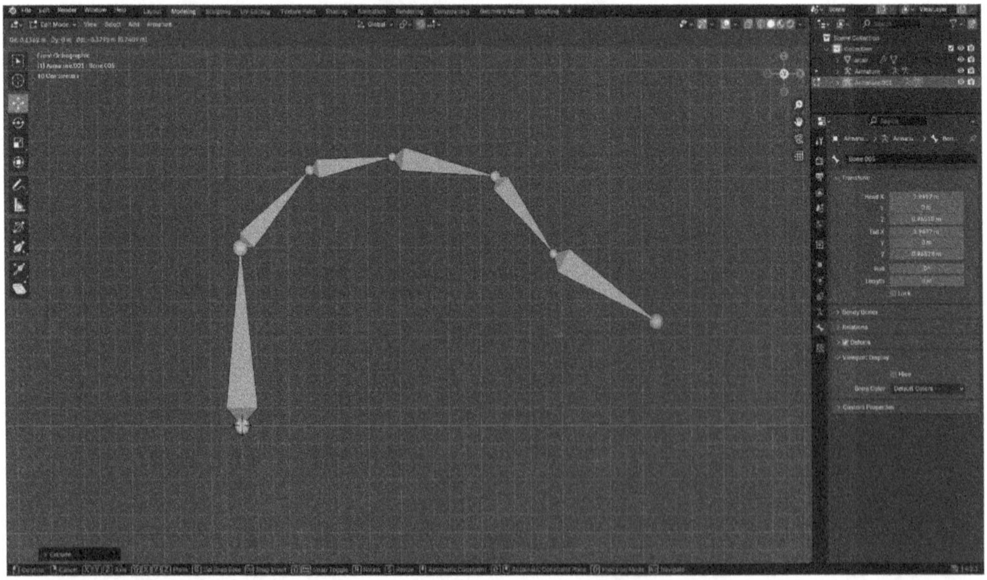

Figure 1.3: Building out a skeleton inside your model

4. To see the armature through your model, switch to the **Object Data Properties** tab for the armature and enable **In Front** under the **Viewport Display** section. You should have something like *Figure 1.4*.

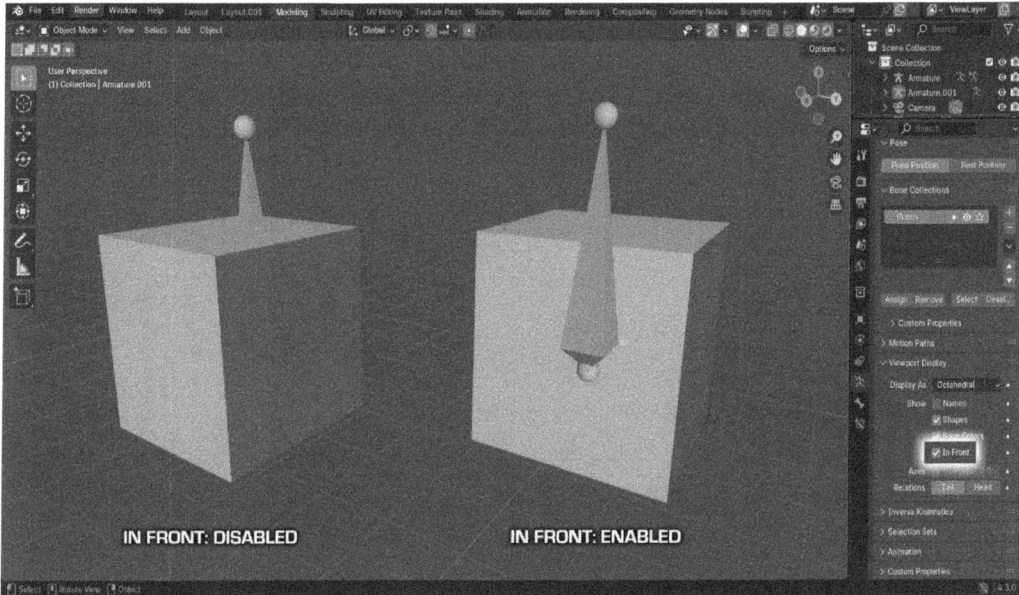

Figure 1.4: Checking that you enabled the In Front armature settings

After creating the armature, the next step involves setting up your bone properties, defining how each bone will behave and interact with the mesh during animation. In the next section, we will discuss bone properties and their significance in detail.

Bone properties and their significance

Each bone in an armature can be customized with key rigging techniques that influence how it interacts with the mesh and other bones. Key properties that can be adjusted to control how each bone behaves and interacts within the rig include the following:

- Parenting, as in when one bone (i.e., the child) is linked to another bone (i.e., the parent) so that moving or rotating the parent automatically moves or rotates the child. Think of it like a parent and child: if the parent moves or rotates, the child follows along. This is super handy for creating animations where different parts need to move together, such as limbs or objects in a scene.

- Bones can be parented to each other so that you can build up on that hierarchy we talked about earlier, and in *Figure 1.1*. This means moving a parent bone will also move its children. This might sound quirky, but it is essential for creating natural limb movements.
- Proper naming is crucial for organization, especially if your **rig** (i.e., the system of bones and controls) becomes complicated. Clear naming is your best friend here. Name your bones with something clear, such as LeftArm or RightLeg, rather than Bone.001 through Bone.100. Naming your bones the right way will save you from a bone identity crisis later.

> **Tip**
>
> Setting up a clean and functional rig is a bit like organizing a wild party where every guest (i.e., bone) needs to know where to go and what to do.

- Last but not least, **constraints** can be applied to bones to limit their movements or make them follow other objects. This is useful for complex animations. There are various types of constraints available in Blender with specialized roles, such as the following:
  - **Inverse Kinematics (IK):** Makes sure that the end of a chain of bones reaches a specific target. This is often used for legs and arms to keep feet or hands in place while the rest of the limb moves. We will talk about that in depth in the *Advanced rigging techniques* section later in this chapter.
  - **Copy Location/Rotation:** Makes a bone copy the position or rotation of another bone or object. This is useful for synchronizing movements between different parts of the rig.

In an example project, apply an **IK** constraint to the character's hand bone so that it follows the neck of the guitar. This will make sure that as the guitar moves, the hand follows smoothly, mimicking realistic playing motions.

> **Note**
>
> Another common approach is to make the **IK** control bone a child bone of the guitar neck bone. This way, the hand naturally follows the guitar's movement without losing the **IK** control of the arm. You can also keyframe the influence more easily, which gives you extra flexibility if you want to switch between constrained and free movement.

As rigs get more complex, two common pitfalls to watch out for are cyclic dependencies and messy controller setups, both of which can cause major headaches if left unchecked:

- Cyclic dependencies, where one bone ends up driving another that circles back to the first, can break rigs in unexpected ways. Blender's evaluation system needs a clear, one-way chain; otherwise, motion becomes unpredictable, or worse, the rig breaks (https://www. youtube.com/watch?v=x74nBaxklis). If you accidentally set up a bone that influences its own controller (e.g., via an **IK** chain), you have built a dependency loop. To avoid that, make sure constraints flow only in one consistent direction.

- Similarly, when using bones as controllers, for animators to manipulate, you often want them separate from your main deform bones. This means separating the control rig bones from the skeleton that deforms the mesh. You can drive deformations via drivers or **Child Of** constraints, keeping your animation logic clean, flexible, and easy to debug, without messing with the actual rig functionality (https://code.blender.org/2015/03/more-dependency-graph-tricks/).

Parenting your mesh to the armature

The final step in the rigging process is to connect your mesh to the armature:

1. In **Object Mode**, select your mesh, and then *Shift-click* to select your armature. The armature should be the active selection (highlighted in a lighter color on the left, as in *Figure 1.5*).

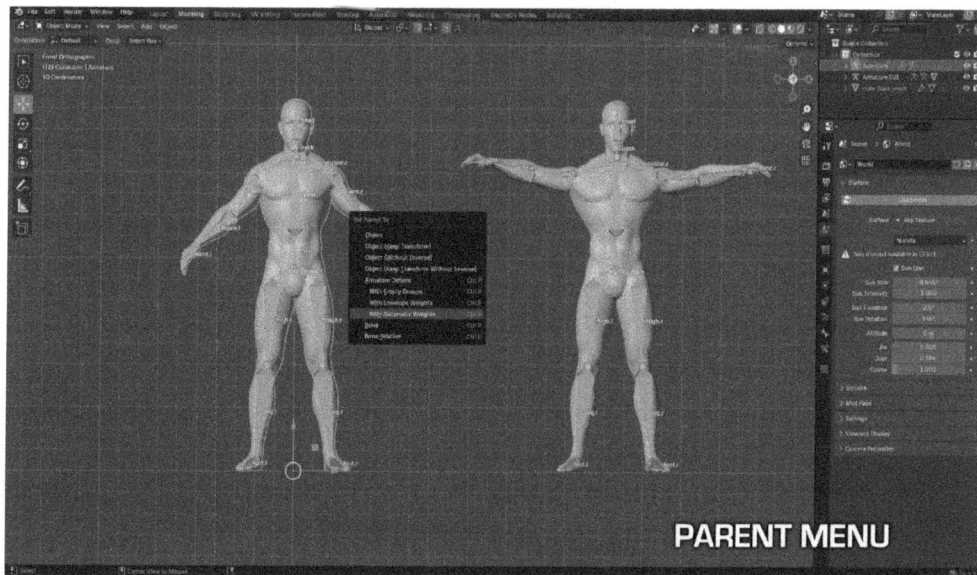

Figure 1.5: Armature as the active selection in Blender

2. Press *Ctrl + P* to bring up the **Parenting** menu and choose **With Automatic Weights**. Blender will attempt to automatically assign weights to the mesh based on how close the bones are to each other.

3. Press *Ctrl + Tab* to switch between **Object Mode** and **Pose Mode**, select a bone, and rotate it. If everything is set up correctly, the mesh should deform in response to the bone movement, as seen in the right character of *Figure 1.5*.

4. Keep your deform bones and your mechanical bones (e.g., **IK** targets) in separate corners. This keeps your rig from turning into a bone jumble that is harder to animate than a cat on a caffeine buzz.

Rigging is a key step in making your 3D models move in Blender. It can be as straightforward or as detailed as your project needs. The basics, such as organizing bones in a certain order, naming them properly, and connecting them correctly to the model, are, however, non-negotiable. As you keep practicing these basic rigging techniques, you will get better and be able to handle more complex animations.

Now, let's move on to the next logical step, weight painting.

Starting with weight painting

Weight painting is also a key part of the rigging and animation workflow in Blender. It is the bridge between your model's armature (i.e., skeleton) and its mesh (i.e., skin). When a bone moves, the mesh moves with it. Weight painting determines how strongly each vertex of the mesh follows that bone. Without weight painting, movements can appear stiff or unnatural because the mesh may not deform as expected.

Preparing your model for weight painting

Before you start weight painting, it is important to make sure your model is ready by going through this checklist:

*   **Complete the rigging process**: Your model should already be rigged with an armature. The mesh should be parented to this armature using automatic weights.

*   **Parenting checks**: The mesh needs to be parented to the armature using **With Automatic Weights**. In **Object Mode**, select the mesh, then select the armature. Press *Ctrl + P* and choose **Set Parent to** and then **With Automatic Weights**. This will generate a base weight paint for the mesh, assigning mesh parts to the closest bones automatically.

*   **Check the mesh topology**: Make sure your mesh has a clean topology with enough subdivisions so that you can make smooth deformations.

Tip

Add extra edge loops at joints wherever your mesh needs to bend: elbows, knees, and shoulders. These loops spread the deformation across a wider area, which keeps the bend smooth instead of turning your mesh into a crumpled crisp packet. Also, think about bone placement. Put them too far from the pivot and you get warping, too close and the movement looks stiff and unnatural. Careful positioning, especially around limbs and facial rigs, makes the difference between fluid movement and something that looks like it belongs in a low-budget horror game.

- **Apply all modifiers**: Except for the **Armature** modifier, apply any other modifiers to your mesh to avoid unexpected results during weight painting.

Once your model is prepared, you can start weight painting.

Basic weight painting techniques

To start weight painting, follow these steps:

1. Select your mesh and switch to **Weight Paint** mode (*Figure 1.6*).

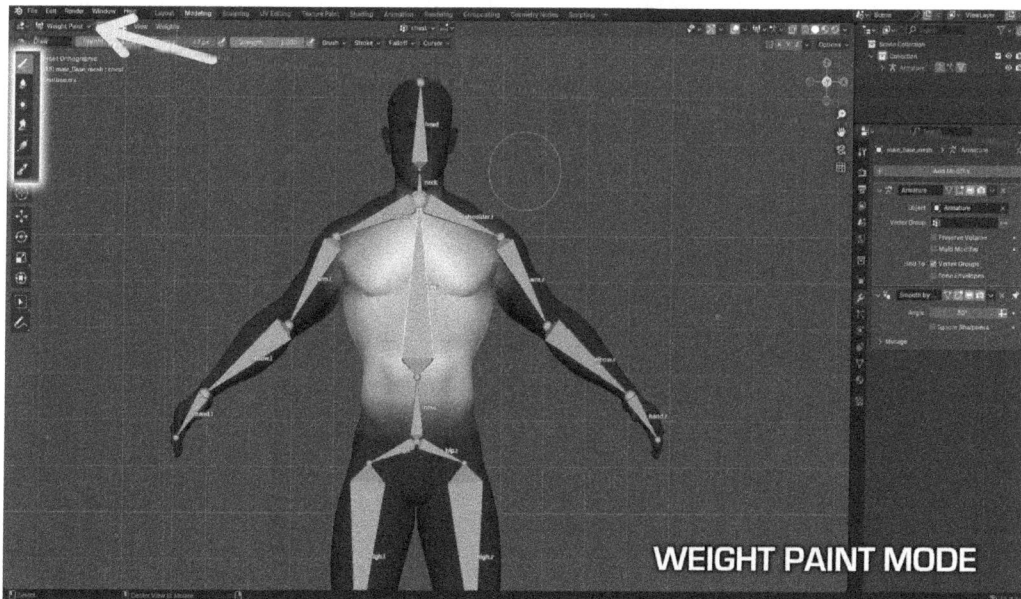

Figure 1.6: Entering Weight Paint mode

Once you are in **Weight Paint** mode, you will notice that the process relies on color coding to show how bones will influence the mesh. Weight painting is based on color coding and makes it so that bones bend realistically at joints, such as knees, elbows, and fingers. You will see that there is a heatmap indicating the weight distribution, with the colors ranging from blue to red:

- **Blue**: Represents areas with no influence from the bone. This means that the bone will not affect these parts of the mesh.
- **Green/yellow/orange**: Indicates varying levels of influence. Green areas have a small influence, while yellow and orange areas have a moderate influence.
- **Red**: Represents areas with full influence from the bone. This means that the bone will fully control these parts of the mesh.

For example, consider the human torso in *Figure 1.6*. The red areas on the heatmap highlight parts of the torso, such as the chest, that move the most when connected bones are animated. The blue areas, such as the sides of the torso, do not move much.

2. To make sure your weight painting is accurate and avoids unexpected issues, it is important to enable certain settings:

   - Go to the **Options** tab, located at the top right if you are in **Weight Paint** mode, and enable **Auto Normalize**. This makes sure that the total weight for each vertex across all bones remains consistent, preventing unexpected deformations. For example, if a vertex is accidentally assigned too much weight, exceeding 100% when you combine it across different bones, then **Auto Normalize** automatically adjusts the weights. This makes sure that their total adds up to 100%. This means that your mesh deforms correctly when you animate it.
   - Alternatively, go to **Weights**, and then select **Normalize All**.

3. In **Weight Paint** mode, select different bones by either clicking on them in the 3D Viewport or selecting them from the **Armature** hierarchy. The mesh will update to show the weights for the selected bone.

> Note
>
> You cannot select bones in the 3D Viewport with **Weight Paint** mode active in newer versions, but you can still select them in the Outliner or from **Vertex Groups** in the **Data** tab in the **Properties** panel.

4. Use the **Brush** tools to paint weights onto the mesh. To do that, you need to go to **Blend** mode for the brush, and you can access it from the tool side panel or the drop-down menu at the top of the 3D Viewport. The **Add** brush increases the influence of the selected bone on the mesh, and the **Subtract** brush decreases it. You can also use the brush's **Size** and **Strength** settings as you want.

With these steps, you now have the tools to start weight painting and make sure your 3D models have accurate deformations. From enabling **Auto Normalize** to using the **Brush** tools for precise control, I showed you how to animate smooth and natural movements. Remember, the more care you put into this step, the easier it will be to refine your model later.

Now that you have mastered the basics, it is time to move on to fine-tuning your weights. In the next section, we will dive deeper into smoothing transitions, mirroring weight painting, and testing your rig to see whether it moves as in real life.

Fine-tuning weights for realistic deformation

Refining weights in your 3D models might seem long and tedious. One of our technical reviewers summed this up best: *"I've lost years off my life to skinning alone."* And honestly, they are not wrong. Weight painting can test anyone's patience, but stick with it. Trust me, the payoff in animation realism is worth it, so bear with it. Let's dive into how you can fine-tune the weights on your model to create that lifelike movement:

1. Use the **Smooth** brush to even out harsh transitions between weighted areas, such as around joints, for more natural bending.

> **Note**
>
> You might want to use **Smooth** on the shoulders of a humanoid model because it helps the arm movements look more fluid and less mechanical. It is also useful if you are modeling a snake, where a smooth transition along the entire body is what you need for realistic slithering movements.

2. If your model is symmetrical, use the **Mirror** option to mirror your weight painting from one side to the other. This is ideal if you are modeling a bipedal robot, for example, because you can make sure that both arms and legs have symmetrical weights for your animation to be balanced.

3. Switch to **Pose Mode** from time to time to test how your mesh deforms based on how the armature moves. Pay close attention to problem areas and adjust the weights as needed. You might have problems in this area if the elbows or knees pinch unnaturally when they bend, as in *Figure 1.7*.

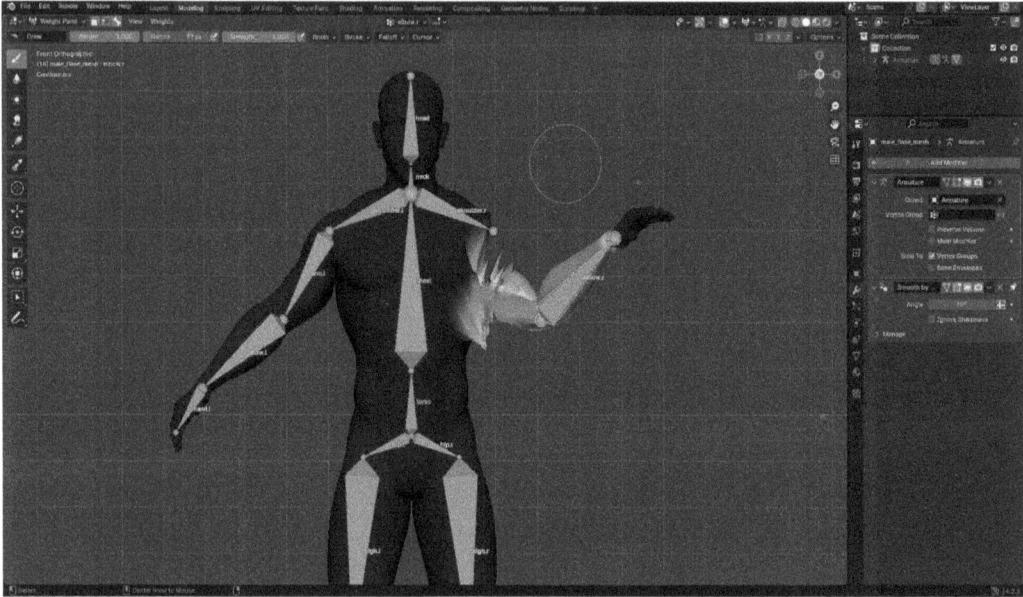

Figure 1.7: Unnatural pinching in problem areas during weight painting

If this happens, you should look at the weight distribution in these joints again and use the **Smooth** or **Add** brushes to adjust the influence of nearby bones.

4. For long bones or areas that need a gradual change in influence, use the **Gradient** tool. It will help you make sure that the movement flows naturally from one segment to the next without sudden jumps in deformation.

Tip

Always remember to regularly test your rig. It is like giving it a quick test drive to catch any odd squeaks or rattles. Pose your character in all sorts of ways to make sure everything moves just right. Catching problems early means you will not have to backtrack later.

Now that you know about basic weight painting techniques, we will talk about advanced techniques. I will introduce you to **Inverse Kinematics (IK)**, which we will use for more natural movement. You will also find out about how to set up pole targets and **IK** constraints to refine how limbs bend, combining the movements of multiple bones into a single movement.

Advanced rigging techniques

In rigging, **Forward Kinematics (FK)** and IK are two essential tools, each with its own approach to controlling bone chains. With FK, you animate by rotating each bone in the chain one at a time, starting from the base and working your way to the tip. This gives you full control but can be time-consuming, especially if you are working on complex movements.

IK, on the other hand, simplifies this process by letting you move just one endpoint: the last bone in the chain. With IK, you move the endpoint, and IK figures out the best angles for the other bones. You can see it better in *Figure 1.8*.

Figure 1.8: Basic IK of lowering chain before (top right) and after (bottom right) in Stylized Crystal Tower Modular Pack, by 3D Tudor

To set up an **IK** chain in Blender, follow the next steps:

1. Select the bone that will serve as the end effector. This is the bone at the end of the chain that you will control directly.

2. While in **Pose Mode**, go to the **Bone Constraints** tab (a blue chain icon located just below the **Bone Properties** tab in **Properties Editor**), add an **Inverse Kinematics** constraint. This tells Blender that you want to use IK for this bone chain.

3. Tell Blender how long your chain is so that it can determine how many bones back from the end effector the **IK** effect will influence. For example, if you are working on animating a leg, you would want three bones because this typically includes the thigh, shin, and foot, allowing the entire leg to move realistically based on where the foot is at any one time. By specifying the chain length, you ensure that the IK combines the movements of these bones to create a natural motion.

One major advantage of using IK is that it simplifies the animation process. By focusing on controlling just the endpoint of a bone chain, you are combining the movement of all bones in the chain into one single action.

Another benefit of IK is that when you set a target for the end bone, IK works out the most realistic way the joints should bend to reach that point. This is especially useful for complex movements such as walking. However, if you want to create a specific gait style, such as for a character who is limping on one leg, you will want to use FK instead because it gives you detailed control over each joint's rotation.

Overall, IK reduces your workload by doing complex calculations automatically, so you can focus on other parts of your project. This makes it easier for you to bring your characters to life with less technical hassle.

While this chapter keeps things beginner-friendly, it is worth flagging a few advanced rigging and weight painting techniques that can help when you start tackling more complex characters or stubborn deformation issues:

*   Stuck on problematic bends such as armpits or knees? Those stubborn mesh stretches often stem from topology and transition issues, areas where weight influence drops off too abruptly. Blender's manual offers a solid grounding in **Weight Paint** tools and armature setup, including tips to finesse bending at joints (https://docs.blender.org/manual/en/latest/animation/armatures/index.html).

- For real-world fixes, *Blender Artists* has practical advice, such as using a **Corrective Smooth** modifier targeted with a vertex group to clean up armpit deformations (`https://blenderartists.org/t/clothes-weight-paint-strange-deformation-please-help/1358539/4`).

- Thinking about rigging faces or clothing with separate armatures? You're not alone. Creating secondary armatures, such as for facial expressions, can enhance flexibility without disturbing your main rig (`https://studio.blender.org/blog/proposal-facial-rigging-with-shape-keys/`).

In the next subsections, we are going to dive into some cool stuff. First, I will show you how to set up a pole target and **IK** constraints to ensure your character's joints, such as knees and elbows, bend correctly. Second, instead of boring standard bones, I will tell you all about using custom bone shapes that make rigging a lot easier to handle. You will also learn how to use small bones or shape keys to animate your character's face, capturing all those subtle emotions. By the end, you will combine these techniques to make your characters move and express themselves naturally.

Setting up pole targets and IK constraints

A **pole target** is like your secret sauce to making the perfect bowl of ramen when you are using IK in your rigging. Pole targets help make sure the joints in your IK chain bend the right way, which is super important for getting limbs to look just how you want them to.

Think about when you are animating something, such as a knee or an elbow: you want it to move like it really would. A pole target guides the middle joint in your IK setup, such as the knee in a leg. It tells the joint which direction to point, which helps stop it from bending weirdly or flipping the wrong way. When you are working on animations where your character is walking, jumping, or doing any sort of action, having this kind of control lets you make the movements look more real and match exactly what you are going for.

To create a pole target, add an empty or a small bone outside your character to serve as a pole target, as in *Figure 1.9*.

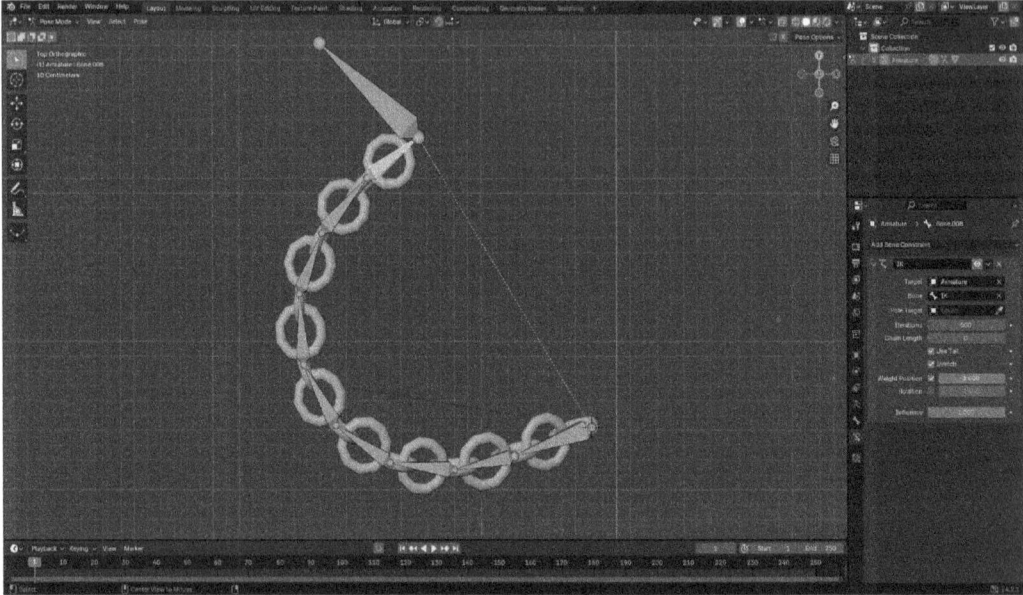

Figure 1.9: Example pole target for a chain animation

This target helps manage how bones in a chain, such as a mechanical arm or tail, interact and bend. When you assign a pole target to the **IK** constraint, it controls the rotation and direction of the middle bones in the chain. This is essential for smooth and predictable bending, especially if your planned movement involves multiple bones.

Another plus is that it makes it easier to control how the chain behaves during animation. For example, in a project with multiple characters, a pole target will make sure each character's movements look coordinated and fluid, preventing awkward joint positions in complex scenes.

Note

When you are using pole targets, you need to make sure you configure the **IK** constraints. In the **IK** constraint settings for your end effector, choose the pole target and adjust the pole angle until the limb aligns correctly. This will make sure that your character's joints bend naturally, based on the pole target position.

Custom bone shapes for enhanced control

Instead of sticking with the standard bone visuals, custom bone shapes let you replace them with any shape that makes sense for the control you are working on. This makes your rigging work smoother and more intuitive. If you are rigging a dragon, for example, why not use wing-shaped icons for the wing bones? It is a lot more fun and keeps things clear when you are knee-deep in animation land.

Using custom bone shapes is a visual upgrade that not only makes your rig look cooler but also makes it much easier to understand and use, especially when you are dealing with lots of different parts.

To create and apply custom bone shapes, follow the next steps:

1. Design a mesh shape that represents the control you are rigging, such as a circle for a foot control. Let us say that you are animating a character, and you need to control the character's foot.

2. Select the bone you want to customize. In our example, that would be the character's foot.

3. Go to the **Bone Properties** tab, and under **Viewport Display**, choose your custom shape from the **Custom Object** dropdown, let's say a circle. The bone will now change into a circle in the 3D Viewport, making it easier to select and understand what it is there for. You can see how that looks in *Figure 1.10*.

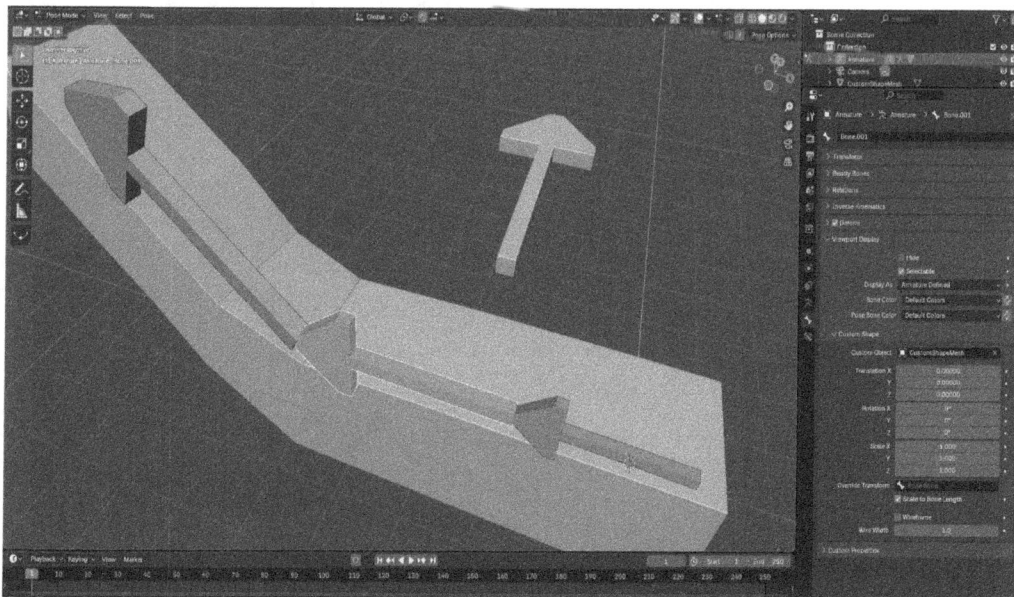

Figure 1.10: Foot IK set up with custom IK shape through Bone Properties

Rigging facial expressions

Facial rigging is all about bringing characters to life by animating their faces. It can be used to capture subtle emotional cues from a sly smirk to a full-blown sob fest, or even a brow-furrowing moment of epic confusion. Here's how you can get started with bone-based facial rigging and shape keys:

1. Begin by placing small bones around key areas of the face, such as the eyebrows, eyes, and mouth. These bones will act as control points to manipulate facial expressions.

2. Move these bones directly to create basic expressions such as anger, surprise, or sadness. For example, raising the bones around the eyebrows can make the character look surprised.

3. To make controlling these bones more intuitive, you can change how they appear in the 3D Viewport. Instead of using custom mesh objects, a quick and flexible method is to switch the bone display type to **B-Bone**, which gives each bone a more visible, controllable shape. This is super useful for facial rigs. To do this, follow these steps:

   a. Go to the **Object Data Properties** tab (green stickman icon), open the **Viewport Display** panel, and change the **Display As** setting to **B-Bone**. This will visually thicken the bones in the 3D Viewport, making it easier to select and manipulate them, as shown in *Figure 1.11*.

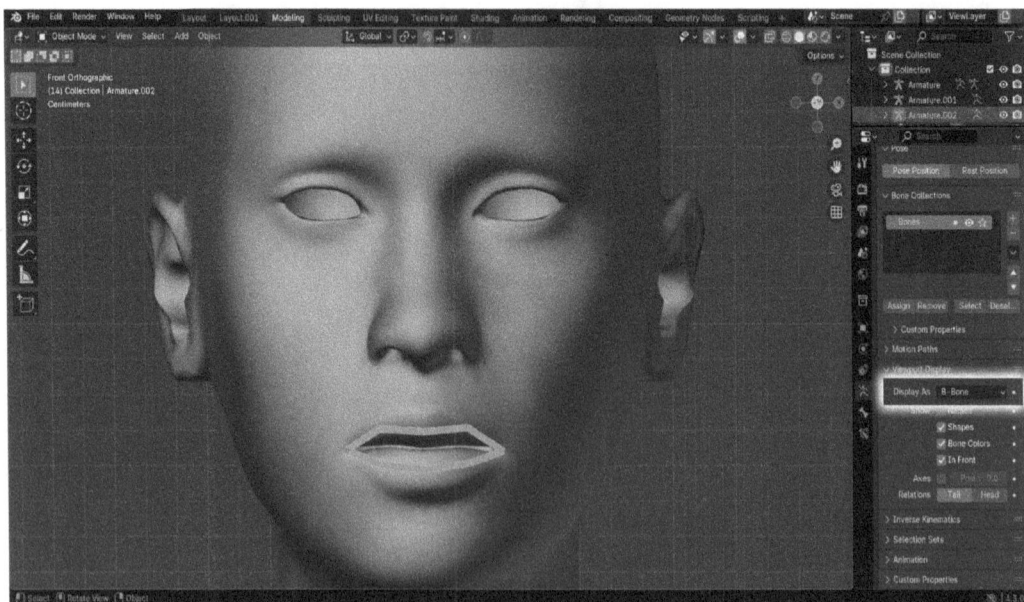

Figure 1.11: Using a custom shape for mouth control

b. To make controlling these bones more intuitive, you can change how they appear in the 3D Viewport. Blender actually gives you two different places to do this:

1. Go to **Object Data Properties** and select **Viewport Display**. This controls the global appearance of the entire armature. Here, you can switch how bones are drawn (B-bones, sticks, or envelopes) and toggle things such as names or axes.

Note

If a bone has a custom object assigned, or its **Display As** setting is not set to **Armature Defined**, it will ignore the global settings from **Object Data Properties**. This is useful for overriding visuals on a bone-by-bone basis, giving you intuitive rig controls while still preserving the global rules for the rest of the skeleton.

2. Go to **Bone Properties** and choose **Viewport Display**. This lets you customize individual bones. You can assign a custom object (such as a mesh control shape), change bone color, or adjust visibility, as in *Figure 1.12*.

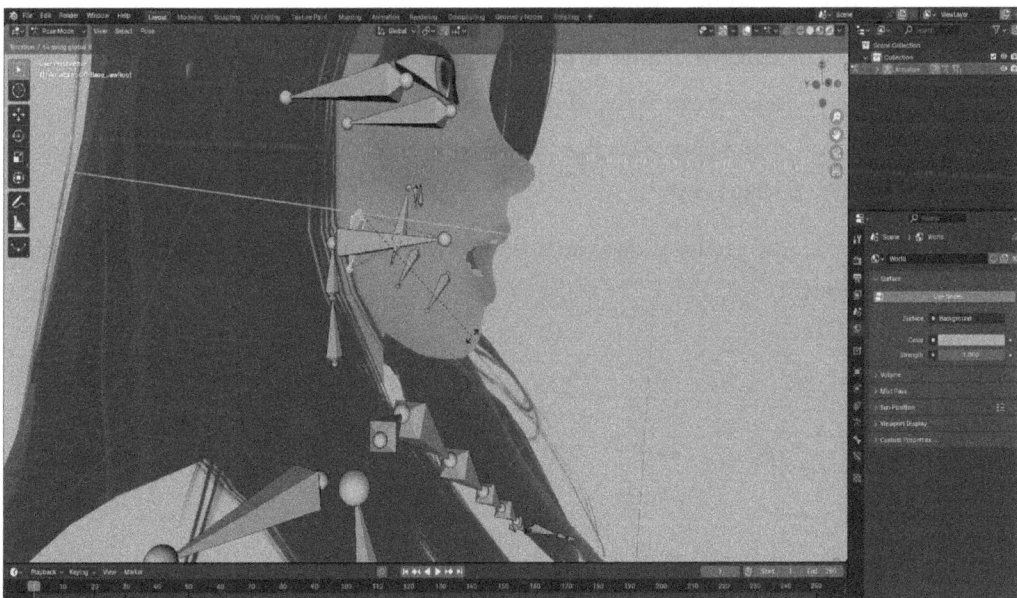

Figure 1.12: Changing bone properties on a mouth bone

4. Facial animation in Blender can be tackled in several ways, each with its own strengths depending on the style of character and the animator's workflow:

    a. **Bone-based controls:**

- Use bones as handles to drive expressions.
- For example, rotate a mouth-corner bone to form a smile.
- These are best for rig-based workflows and animators who like real-time pose manipulation.

    b. **Shape keys:**

- Sculpt expressions directly into the mesh.
- Start with a **Basis** shape key (default state).
- Add extra keys for poses such as smiling, frowning, or blinking.
- Animate between them using the **Value** slider for smooth interpolation.
- This works especially well for stylized or cartoon characters that need exaggerated deformations.

    c. **Hybrid method – drivers:**

- Link bone movement to shape key values using drivers.
- A bone can then indirectly control a shape key.
- Combines animator-friendly rig controls with the fine deformation of shape keys.

As shown in *Figure 1.13*, this setup allows you to fine-tune expression intensity and blend multiple emotions with ease.

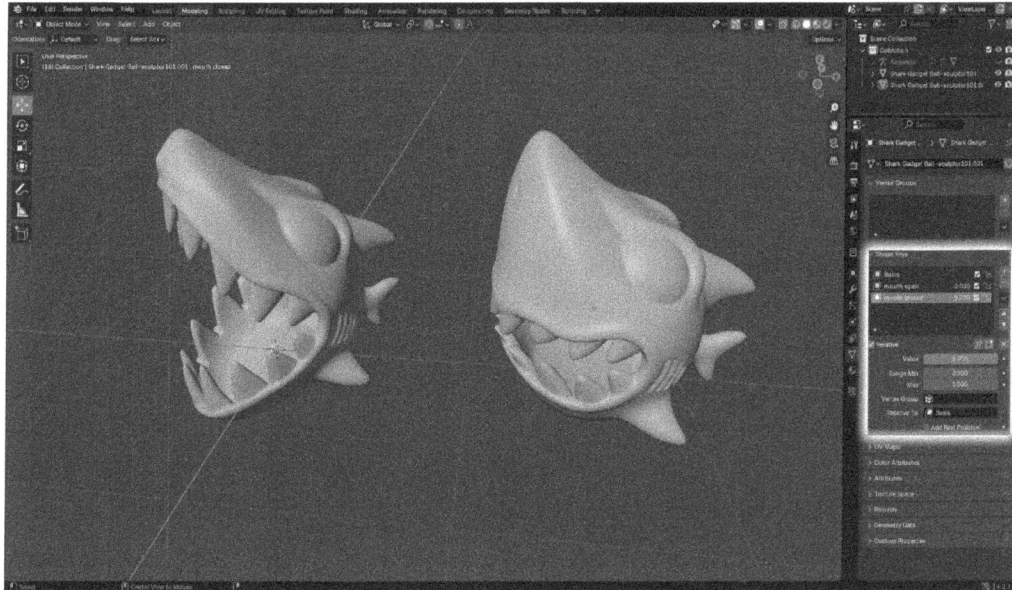

Figure 1.13: Shape Keys sliders in Blender

Tip

For very detailed projects, such as a feature film or a video game with complex characters, it is best to use both methods. Use bone-based controls for the big movements, such as opening the mouth or raising the eyebrows. Then, use shape keys for the finer details, such as wrinkles when the character frowns or subtle smiles. This will give you tons of flexibility to get the expressions just right.

We all have a friend who claims they can dance, and then suddenly, they bust out moves so wild, it is like watching a spaghetti noodle in a windstorm. Along the same line, sometimes, moving from setting up these awesome rigs to animating your character can hit a snag, especially when you start weight painting.

Now, we will look at some common problems you might run into, such as parts of your character not moving properly or looking weird when they bend. We will also go over how to fix these issues, so everything moves smoothly and looks great. Whether it is a shoulder that does not bend right or a knee that is acting up, knowing how to sort out these issues will make your animations look much better.

Troubleshooting common rigging and weight painting issues

Rigging and weight painting in Blender are your go-to tricks to bring your characters to life. Regardless, even seasoned animators can run into trouble sometimes. Here, we will cover some typical headaches you might run into while working on your models and give you tips to keep your rigs running smoothly. And remember, even though it can get a bit hairy, try not to lose your cool. With every problem that crops up, you are just leveling up your animation game!

Dealing with weight painting challenges

Weight painting is key to making sure your character's mesh moves naturally, like real muscles and skin. But sometimes, you might run into issues such as uneven deformations, or parts of the mesh might not be moving the way you expected.

Let us assume the following scenario: you notice some uneven deformations, where parts of your mesh are acting weirdly or too dramatically, as in *Figure 1.14*.

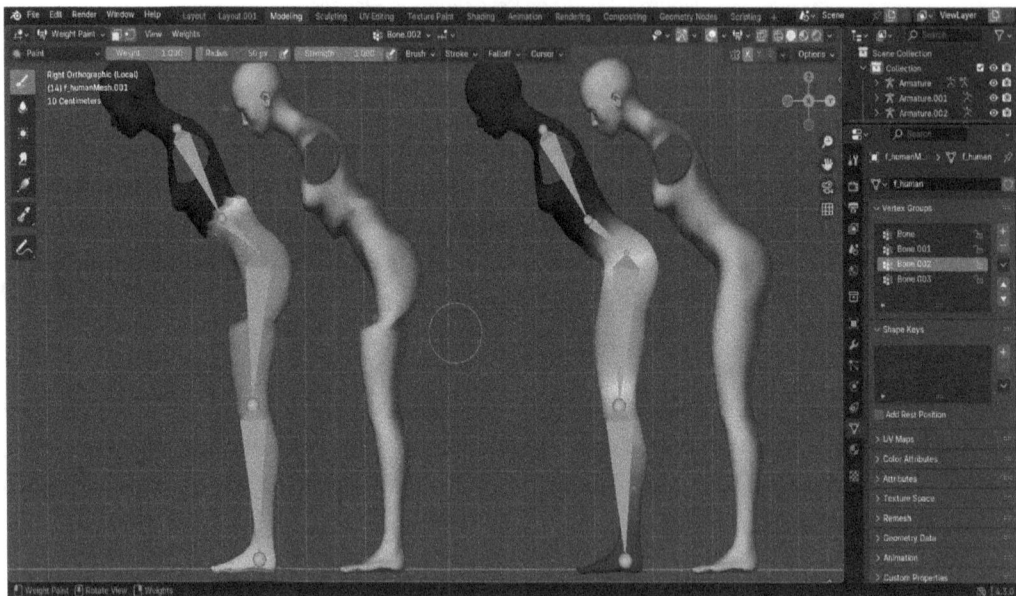

Figure 1.14: Uneven deformations in a mesh (left) and using the Smooth brush to evenly spread weights (right)

You can smooth things out using the **Smooth** brush in **Weight Paint** mode. The **Smooth** brush will spread the weights evenly across the tricky areas. Make sure you turn on **Auto Normalize**, too. This keeps the total weight for all bones at **1.0**, so no single bone throws everything off balance, as shown in *Figure 1.14*.

If you find some mesh parts not moving as they should, it is probably because the vertices are not weighted right to the bones. To solve this issue, pick the bone that is not behaving right in **Pose Mode**, then switch over to **Weight Paint** mode. There, you can adjust the weights with the **Add** or **Subtract** brushes to get the influence just perfect. It is a good idea to assign weight data directly onto selected vertices, especially on harder-to-reach spots, as shown in *Figure 1.15*.

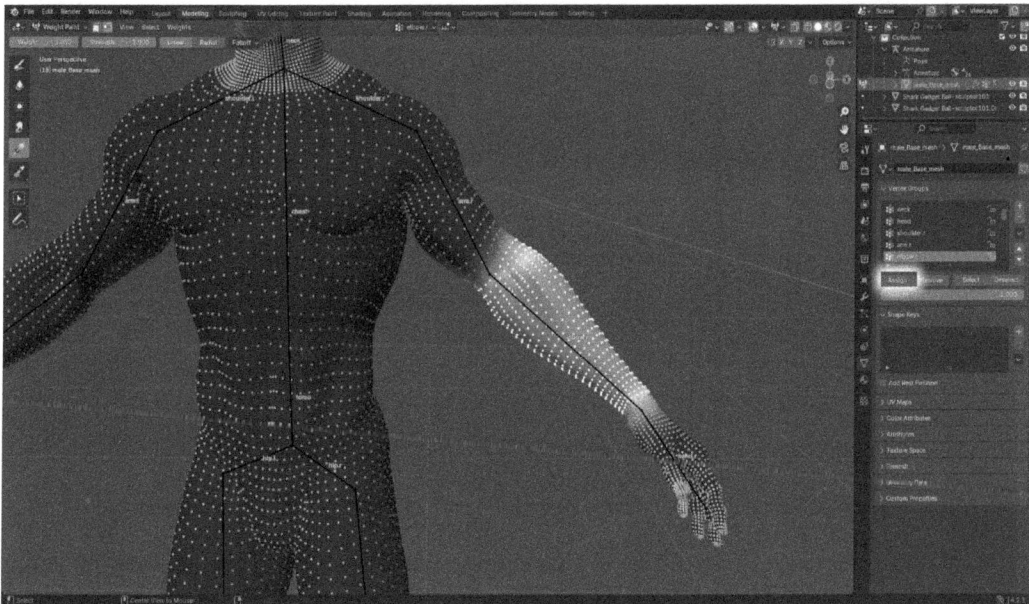

Figure 1.15: Selecting vertices in Weight Paint mode

This way, you will get real-time feedback about how your changes help the mesh move better. By tweaking weights and checking your progress, you can dial in those natural-looking movements.

Adjusting problematic bones and weights

If you are working on a character in Blender and notice some weird deformations happening, or if the **Automatic Weights** are not quite cutting it, you are not alone. It happens a lot, especially with specific bones acting up or the weights needing some fine-tuning.

Sometimes, parts of your mesh might start following multiple bones even though you have not set them to, and this makes things look wonky (e.g., parts stretching or moving unexpectedly). To fix this, grab the **Subtract** brush and start removing the influence from those unintended bones. If you want to make the transition between weighted areas smoother, try using the **Weight Gradient** tool. This tool is super helpful for blending weights nicely, so that you do not get those harsh, unnatural lines, as in *Figure 1.16*.

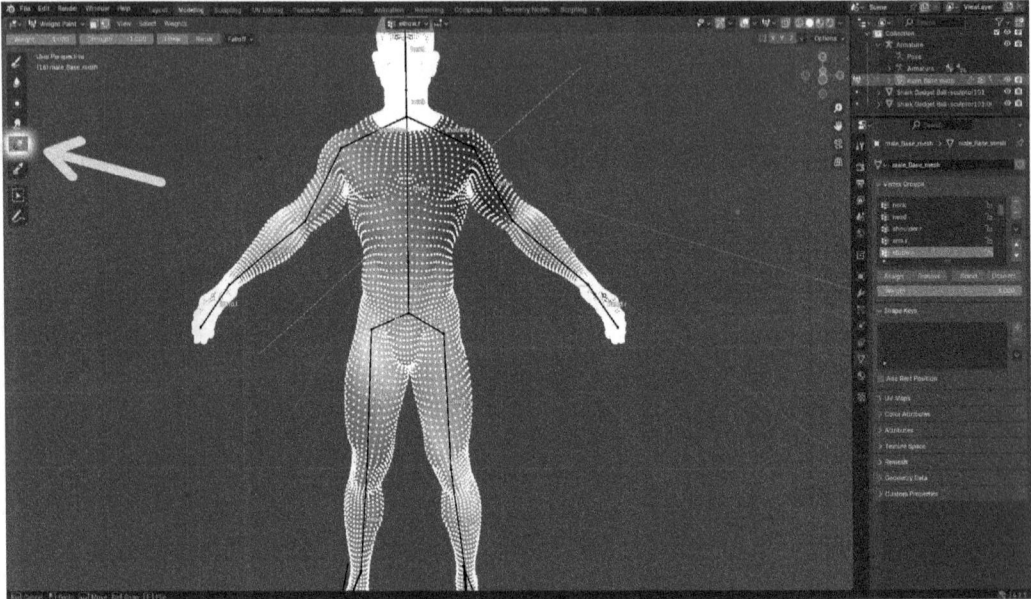

Figure 1.16: Before (left) and after (right) using the Weight Gradient tool in Blender

Now, getting areas such as shoulders or hips to move naturally can be a bit of a puzzle. These spots can be tricky because they need to move smoothly with the rest of the body. A good thing to remember is that the way you set up weights can change depending on the mesh: for example, if the shoulders are really broad or narrow, you will need to tweak things differently. It mostly comes down to practice, but a good tip is to move the joint around while you're adjusting the weights. That way, you can see how it bends and make sure it looks right.

A good trick is to dial back the influence of the bones around them and boost the influence of the main bone that should control that area. For example, if you are working on a character who is about to punch someone, tweaking the shoulder weights will make the whole action look more fluid and realistic.

Symmetrizing your rig for efficiency

Having a symmetrical build is a must-have when it comes to building characters. Let us dive into how you can make your rigging symmetrical. First up, when you are in **Edit Mode**, pick the bones you want to mirror. Then, go to the **Armature** menu and choose the **Symmetrize** function. Blender's pretty smart here: it automatically creates a mirrored copy of your selected bones. For Blender's **Symmetrize** function to work properly, the bones on one side of the rig must already be labeled with .L and .R to keep track of which side is which, left or right. That is it; problem solved, all you had to do was know how!

Now, symmetry is also important in weight painting. After you finish making sure your armature is mirrored, you need to make sure the weight painting matches up. Switch over to **Weight Paint** mode and look for the **Mirror** option in your **Brush** settings. This will let you apply weights so that they are the same on both sides of the X axis. This is not a step you can miss since making your weight painting symmetrical makes sure your character deforms the same way on both sides, giving you that consistent, natural look.

Fixing rigging and weight painting problems is part and parcel of making animations. By handling common issues, tweaking tricky spots, making sure everything is symmetrical, and keeping your rig tidy, you can create smooth and realistic animations. Remember, rigging and weight painting need you to try different things and make improvements here and there, over time. As we wrap up this section, we are setting the stage to dive deeper into rigging and weight painting a complete character in Blender. This next section is all about putting everything you have learned into action.

Bringing it all together: rigging and weight painting a complete character

Rigging and weight painting a complete character in Blender is a detailed process that blends technical skill with a vision of what you want to portray.

Start by really digging into what your character needs to do. Will they be jumping, or running, or will they be showing off detailed facial expressions? Asking yourself these questions is your first step to planning a suitable rig. For example, if I planned to animate someone who is clearly showing micro-expressions of disgust, I would concentrate on detailed facial rigging, especially around the eyes and mouth. The difference lies in what the rig is made for, whether that is broad and dynamic for physical actions, such as flight, or fine and precise for subtle emotional expressions.

The next item on your agenda should be deciding how complex your rig should be based on these movements you planned. A simple humanoid might only need basic bones, but a fantastical creature with wings and a tail will require a lot more to capture all those secondary motions and expressions that humans simply do not have. Before you dive into Blender, take some time to sketch out your armature. This visual plan will help you keep track of all the necessary bones and ensure you do not miss anything important.

Once your armature is set, move on to weight painting to define how much influence each bone has on the mesh. This step is crucial to make sure the character deforms correctly when animated. Proper weight painting helps blend movements naturally and avoids awkward deformations.

If your character needs to perform highly detailed actions, think about using multiple armatures. Start with a main armature for the basic structure, such as limbs and torso, and then add secondary armatures for the finer details, such as facial expressions and clothing. Make sure these armatures work well together, allowing for smooth and coordinated movements without losing any detail.

I imagine this working well with a project where a character needs to manipulate complex tools or interact with various objects. The environment that comes to my mind as I write this is *"Blender 3 to Unreal Engine 5 Dungeon Modular Kitbash"* (*Figure 1.17*), where you get to build a medieval dungeon. Proper rigging makes sure that the character's movements look natural and seamless within such a detailed environment.

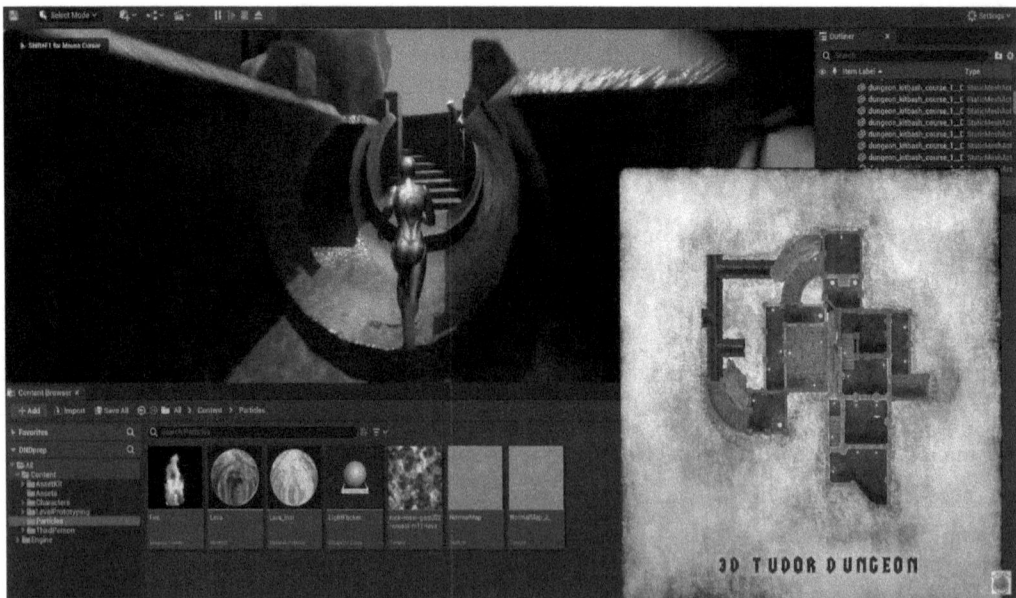

Figure 1.17: Visualizing the environment in "Blender 3 to Unreal Engine 5 Dungeon Modular Kitbash" by 3D Tudor

In this scenario, multiple armatures would help separate the main body movements from the intricate hand manipulations of tools that help players interact with the environment. After planning and layering your armatures, continue with detailed weight painting to make sure that all the bones influence the mesh the way you wanted them to.

Now, add the assets from *Blender to Unreal Engine Become a Dungeon Prop Artist* (*Figure 1.18*), and you have the perfect opportunity to put this idea into action. This project provides exactly the kind of complex tools we discussed.

Figure 1.18: Complex tools and interactable assets in Blender to Unreal Engine Become a Dungeon Prop Artist, by 3D Tudor

With the basics nailed down to a T, you are ready to tackle more detailed movements and interactions for your character. Next up, we will look at how to use multiple armatures to get even better control, whether it is for big movements or small, detailed ones. Let us jump into how to set them up and make everything work together smoothly for realistic animation.

Layering multiple armatures for detailed control

When rigging and weight painting a character, achieving detailed control over your character's movements sometimes needs you to use multiple armatures. This approach ensures both broad and intricate movements are handled smoothly and realistically. Here's how to effectively layer multiple armatures:

1. **Main armature for basic structure**: Start with a main armature that controls the overall structure of the character, including limbs and torso.

2. **Secondary armatures for details**: Create additional armatures for facial expressions, clothing, or other detailed movements. These can be parented to the main armature or specific bones within it.

3. **Integrating armatures**: Ensure that your multiple armatures work together seamlessly. This is a must-have for coordinated movements without losing the intricate detail you were given the secondary armatures. Parenting secondary armatures to the main one makes movements coordinated without compromising the detail provided by the additional armatures.

By layering multiple armatures, you can better manage complex interactions and detailed movements, making your character's actions look more natural and believable.

Finalizing your rig: a checklist

After setting up your rig and weight painting, you need to finalize and refine your setup to ensure everything works as intended. Use this checklist to triple-check that your character is fully prepared for animation:

-   **Name and organize well**: Check that all bones are correctly named and organized within the **Armature** hierarchy. This simplifies animation and rig maintenance.

-   **Check your weight painting**: Make sure all mesh parts deform correctly in relation to their corresponding bones. Pay extra attention to areas with detailed movements.

-   **Test all movements**: Pose your character in various positions to test the full range of motion. Ensure that movements look natural and that there are no unexpected mesh deformations.

-   **Check custom bone shapes**: If you have used custom bone shapes for controllers, make sure they are correctly linked to their respective bones and that it makes sense to use them.

-   **Review constraints and drivers**: Double-check any constraints or drivers you have applied to the rig to make sure that they are working as intended and that they are making the rig better and easier to use.

This checklist will help you make sure your rig is solid, well-organized, and ready for animation. Getting the rig and weight painting right means your character will move smoothly and look realistic, just like you imagined.

Summary

And there you have it! After trekking through the world of rigging and weight painting in Blender, you are now armed with the tools to make any static model come to life. Remember how we started?

We kicked off with rigging basics, essentially playing puppeteer and setting up the bone structure. Then, we shifted gears into weight painting, which is kind of like telling your model's skin not to freak out when it moves. We also navigated through some advanced rigging techniques: those are your tools for when you need your characters to perform more than just the basics.

Of course, there were bumps along the way. Troubleshooting rigging and weight painting issues and solving these mysteries are part of the fun of being a 3D artist and animator. By now, you should feel more prepared to take on your projects, and you have a solid foundation to research rigging more using other sources.

Up next, we are looking at the fresh fish in our waters, **Geometry** nodes. Rigging and weight painting allowed you to animate your models. **Geometry** nodes will give you powerful tools to create complex, procedural designs and effects. Get ready to expand your creativity with this exciting feature in Blender that is just getting started!

Further reading

- If you are looking to get really good at rigging and animation, you have to check out *The Ultimate Guide to Blender 3D Rigging & Animation* (https://www.udemy.com/course/blender-3d-rigging-animation/?referralCode=39A1E0B8F07B474DFE0F). It covers everything from basic stuff, such as simple animations, all the way to more advanced things, such as walk cycles, tank tracks, animated flames, and even crazy adventure scenes with traps. Whether you are working on characters or props, this course gives you all the tools and tips you need to bring your projects to life. Definitely worth it!

- If you want to see how IK works, *Stylized Crystal Tower Modular Pack* (https://3dtudor.gumroad.com/l/blender-unreal-engine-stylized-tower) is a great place to start.

- If you want to learn more about rigging and weight painting, *Blender 3 to Unreal Engine 5 Dungeon Modular Kitbash* (https://www.udemy.com/course/blender-3-to-unreal-engine-5-kitbash/?referralCode=3F43CC836F2DD9A7178D) is a fantastic resource. You can use the environment you will create as a space to practice animation, even though that is not covered in the course, so that your character deforms correctly with natural movements and without awkward distortions.

- *Blender to Unreal Engine Become a Dungeon Prop Artist* (https://www.udemy.com/course/blender-to-unreal-engine-become-a-dungeon-prop-artist/?referralCode=979CA6D3C71A4B2BB8CD) is a great follow-up. Using the assets created in the course, you can practice detailed weight painting to ensure the bones influence the mesh precisely as intended.

Subscribe to Game Dev Assembly!

We are excited to introduce **Game Dev Assembly**, our brand-new newsletter dedicated to everything game development. Whether you're coding, designing, animating, or managing a studio, we've got insights, trends, and expert advice to help you create, innovate, and thrive. Sign up now and get exciting benefits.

https://packt.link/gamedev-newsletter

Get This Book's PDF Version and Exclusive Extras

UNLOCK NOW

Scan the QR code (or go to packtpub.com/unlock). Search for this book by name, confirm the edition, and then follow the steps on the page.

Note: Keep your invoice handy. Purchases made directly from Packt don't require one.

2

Mastering the Basics of Blender Geometry Nodes

This chapter will introduce you to one of Blender's standout features: **geometry nodes**. Geometry nodes let you create, change, and visualize shapes and designs in new ways. Think of it as using building blocks, or **nodes**, that you can connect in different ways to make complex scenes or effects.

One of the big advantages of using geometry nodes is how they can speed up the process of making detailed models, patterns, and animations. You can do things quickly that would usually take a lot longer if you were doing them by hand. This can be anything from adding trees to a forest to building detailed parts of a building. You can also use geometry nodes to procedurally generate content for your environments, such as jungle foliage and terrain (see *Figure 2.1*).

Figure 2.1: Blender 4 Jungle Terrain Geometry Node by 3D Tudor

This chapter starts by explaining the basics of geometry nodes so you can understand the fundamental concepts, such as how nodes work and what they can do. Then, you will dive into your first geometry node setup, where you will get hands-on experience by creating something simple, such as a basic pattern or shape.

After that, we will show how to customize geometry nodes with group inputs and explore fundamental nodes. Finally, you will learn about modifying geometry with nodes, and you will see how to simplify your setups and improve performance, such as reducing the lag when working with complex scenes.

All in all, this chapter will be your guide to using geometry nodes effectively. By the end, you should have a good foundational knowledge and be ready to start experimenting on your own.

So, in this chapter, we will cover the following topics:

- Explaining the basics of geometry nodes
- Trying out your first geometry node setup
- Customizing geometry nodes with **Group Inputs**
- Exploring fundamental geometry nodes

- Modifying geometry with nodes
- Enhancing your node networks

Technical requirements

As for **Blender 4.5 LTS (Long-Term Support)**, the general requirements include a macOS 11.2 or newer (Apple Silicon supported natively) operating system, or a Linux (64-bit, glibc 2.28 or newer) operating system. Blender now requires a CPU with the SSE4.2 instruction set, at least 8 GB of RAM (32 GB recommended for heavy scenes), and a GPU supporting OpenGL 4.3 with a minimum of 2 GB of VRAM.

For a full list of technical requirements, please refer back to *Chapter 1* of this part.

Explaining the basics of geometry nodes

Normally, if you wanted to change something about your model, you would have to push and pull it into shape yourself, right? Well, geometry nodes give you a lot of freedom and control over what you create.

At their core, geometry nodes are a procedural modeling system within Blender. Unlike traditional modeling, where each action directly affects the geometry of an object, procedural modeling uses a set of rules or operations, defined by nodes, to generate and manipulate geometry through their relationship. These nodes are then linked together in what is called a node tree. This tree outlines the order and combination of operations that will be applied to your model.

Geometry nodes are specialist tools for specialist situations, such as when you want to create repetitive patterns. For example, if you are designing an environment and want to add lots of trees and plants quickly, geometry nodes can be a huge time-saver. Then, say you made a tree but later decided it should be taller, or perhaps you wanted more trees. Instead of remaking everything from scratch, you just tweak a few commands, and voilà, your scene updates automatically. This is a bit like our *Blender 4 Grass & Flowers (Meadow) Procedural Geometry Node*, where you can generate meadows exactly like that (see *Figure 2.2*).

Figure 2.2: Procedurally generated foliage with Blender 4 Grass & Flowers (Meadow) Procedural Geometry Node by 3D Tudor

With geometry nodes, you can send instructions to Blender to make something change in your model (e.g., shape, size, scale, etc.) without using any modeling tools on it. It is the closest you will get to coding without coding, if I can say that. Geometry nodes will tell your original shape, whether that is a primitive or something you have been working on already, to grow or change shape without touching it directly. For example, with our *Blender 4 Procedural Stairs Geometry Node* (see *Figure 2.3*), you can set up a system that automatically generates stairs, like so:

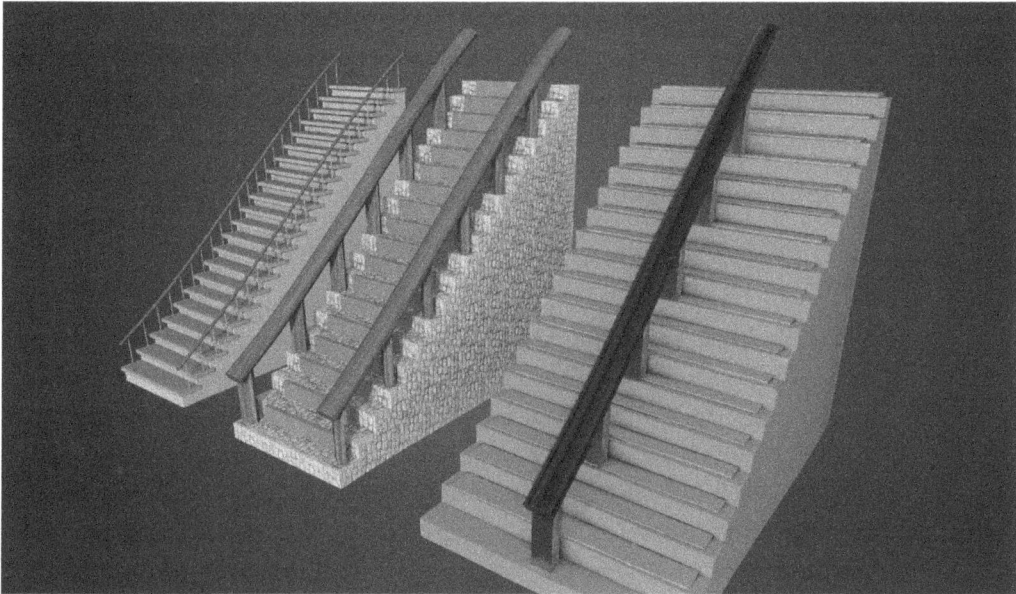

Figure 2.3: Customizability in Blender 4 Procedural Stairs Geometry Node by 3D Tudor

You can adjust the step width, height, and depth to fit the specific needs of your scene. This means if you are creating a scene that requires a grand staircase with wide, shallow steps, you can easily configure your node setup to produce that. Alternatively, for a more cramped space, such as what you might find in sprawling mega-cities, you might opt for narrower and steeper steps.

But, like any tool, geometry nodes have their pros and cons. On the positive side, they can save you a lot of time on repetitive tasks and let you make changes without messing up your original model. Plus, the beauty of the geometry node system lies in its non-destructive nature; changes can be made at any stage without permanently altering the original geometry. For example, if you are in the middle of creating a procedural landscape, you might want to adjust the height of the hills to make them more dramatic. By changing the value of the **Height** parameter in a **Displace** node to increase from a lower value to a higher one, you will see that the terrain becomes more rugged and elevated, without affecting the base geometry of the plane.

On the downside, geometry nodes can be tough if you are a beginner because their interface is complex. Geometry nodes can also slow down your computer if your node setup is too convoluted. Even though geometry nodes are versatile, there might be times when you need to do some things by hand.

By understanding these foundational concepts and familiarizing yourself with the **Geometry Node** editor, you are on your way to unlocking the creative potential of procedural modeling. Remember, the key to mastering geometry nodes is experimentation and practice. Do not be afraid of trying different things out and failing along the way!

Let us try setting up your first geometry node together.

> Note
>
> While this chapter primarily focuses on instancing as an easy entry point to geometry nodes, the same node system can power much more advanced workflows. You can use geometry nodes for procedural modeling, whether that's building complex structures via Boolean operations or scattering intricate details across a mesh. For example, the **Mesh Boolean Node** lets you join, cut, or subtract shapes, just like the **Boolean** modifier but inside a procedural node setup (`https://docs.blender.org/manual/en/latest/modeling/geometry_nodes/mesh/operations/mesh_boolean.html`).

Trying out your first geometry node setup

With Blender ready and loaded, we will work on understanding geometry nodes with a simple setup. But before you start, I need to talk to you about some basic concepts. Let us dot the i's and cross the t's.

Geometry Node editor

The **Geometry Node** editor is like the Shader Editor; they both use a node-based workflow, and using it, you can create complex systems. If you have already dabbled with the Shader Editor, you will find the node layout and connections in the **Geometry Node** editor intuitive. You will see input-output connections that let you control various parameters, from shaders to geometry. However, the main difference between the **Geometry Node** editor and the Shader Editor lies in what they control. The Shader Editor agenda is about defining surface properties such as color, texture, and how materials look. The **Geometry Node** editor is there to give you the power to manipulate the actual structure of models.

Here is a short list of steps on how to access the **Geometry Node** editor:

1. Open Blender and select the object you wish to apply geometry nodes to.

2. At the top of the screen, you will see a drop-down menu currently set to something such as **3D Viewport** or **Timeline**. Click on it and select **Geometry Node Editor** to switch to that editor, as shown in *Figure 2.4*.

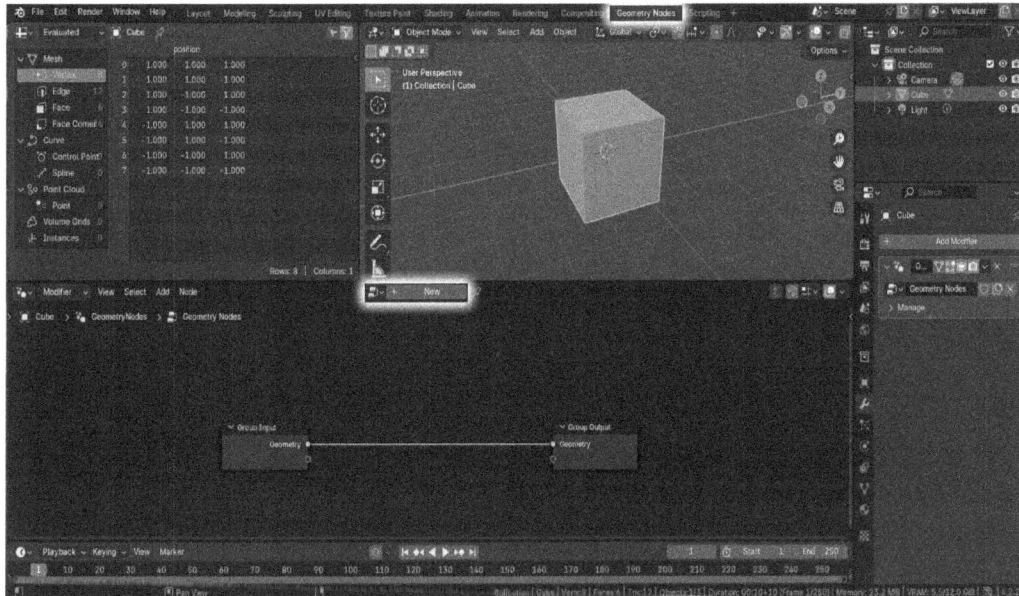

Figure 2.4: Switching to the Geometry Node editor in Blender

3. With your object selected, in the **Geometry Node** editor, you will find a button labeled **New**. Clicking this button creates a new node tree for your object.

4. Apply the geometry node to your object from within the **Modifier** menu, like in *Figure 2.4*.

Now, let's briefly take a look at some elements that we can see in *Figure 2.4*.

Sockets, Group Input, and Group Output

The connections on each node tree are made through points known as **sockets**. By dragging from one socket to another, you allow the flow of data from one operation to the next, which lets you build complex chains of operations. These sockets are color-coded to indicate the type of data they handle, such as green for **Geometry Data** or purple for **Vector Data**.

At the core of your node tree, you will find two special nodes:

- The **Group Input** node is the starting point of your geometry's journey through the node tree. It is the initial state before any operations are applied. You can also set up parameter controls here, allowing you to expose certain inputs to the modifier panel for easy customization.

- The **Group Output** node is the opposite; it showcases the outcome after your geometry has been through the series of transformations dictated by your node tree. You can also set up controls here so you can easily tweak certain settings right from the **Modifier** panel.

When you first start with geometry nodes, you will see a basic setup with **Group Input** and **Group Output** already connected. By default, it just shows the original object you created in **Object Mode**, without any changes. But here is the cool part: we are going to look at how we can add controls to the **Group Input** node so we can tweak our setup from outside the **Node Editor** in a couple of pages (i.e., in the *Customizing geometry nodes with Group Input* section). It makes things way easier to work with!

With this understanding of different aspects of the **Geometry Node** editor, from how sockets connect to pass data to the roles of the **Group Input** and **Group Output** nodes, I am happy to announce that you are ready to dive into a hands-on example. In the next exercise, you will see how these nodes work together by transforming a simple shape into something entirely new, such as a smooth Ico Sphere.

Practical exercise

Let us move on to an example. We will change a simple shape into a sphere using a few connected nodes:

1. In the 3D Viewport, select the object you want to transform (e.g., a cube or a plane).

2. Change your workspace to the **Geometry Node** editor. Then, with your object still selected, click **New** to create a new node tree.

3. Press *Shift + A* in the **Geometry Node** editor to open the **Add** menu, go to **Mesh Primitives**, and select **Ico Sphere**. This generates an **Ico Sphere** mesh, as shown in *Figure 2.5*.

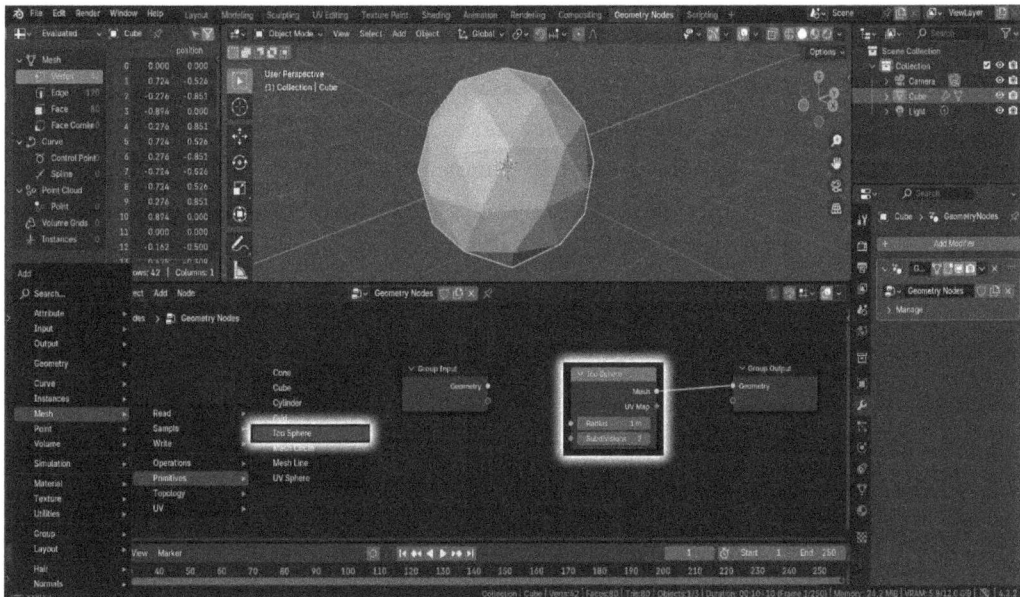

Figure 2.5: Example Ico Sphere mesh in Blender

4. You will see three nodes in your workspace now: the **Group Input**, **Group Output**, and **Ico Sphere** nodes. Connect the **Mesh** socket (mesh information in geometry nodes is color-coded in green) of the **Ico Sphere** node to the geometry socket of the **Group Output** node (also green: the same color coding rules apply), like in *Figure 2.5*. This tells Blender to replace your original object's geometry with the **Ico Sphere**.

5. Select the **Ico Sphere** node in your **Geometry Nodes** setup. You can adjust **Subdivisions** and **Radius** directly on the node itself. Increase the **Subdivisions** value to make your sphere smoother, or adjust **Radius** to make the sphere bigger.

6. By default, you only have two types of controls for the sphere. Additional nodes will give you more control. For example, the **Transform Geometry** node can be used to offset the sphere's position and rotate the object.

You have done it! You created your first geometry node setup, transforming your selected object into a sphere. Now, I want to take it a step further. I will show you how to make your setup even easier to use by adding **Group Inputs**. These let you control things such as size, shape, or other settings without needing to mess around with all the nodes again. It is like adding handy sliders and buttons to keep things simple.

Customizing geometry nodes with Group Inputs

Group Inputs are like a magic wand that lets you tweak your procedural models without needing to mess around in the complex node editor. They are super handy, especially if you are not too deep into all the technical stuff. By exposing certain parameters of your node setup as **Group Inputs**, you can create sliders and input fields that appear in the **Geometry Nodes Modifier** tab when applied to an object. This means you can adjust key aspects of your procedural models, such as size, density, or color, without diving back into the node editor.

To set up a group input and understand how it works, let us go through a practical example:

1. Start with a basic plane in Blender that you want to turn into a lively landscape. Apply a **Geometry Nodes** modifier to this plane.

2. Within your **Geometry Nodes** setup, use *Shift + A* and search for the **Distribute Points on Faces** node. Drag this node directly onto the connection line between **Group Input** and **Group Output**; this will automatically insert the node into the chain, replacing the original plane output with points.

3. To get our plane mesh back, we need to connect the original information of our geometry (i.e., the original shape or object we started with, so in this case, a plane) to the created points.

4. Add a **Join Geometry** node. Connect the **Points** output of the **Distribute Points on Faces** node to one input of **Join Geometry** and connect the **Geometry** output from the **Group Input** node to the other input. This way, both the original plane and the scattered points will be included in the output.

5. Now connect the output socket on the right side of the **Join Geometry** node to the first socket of the **Group Output** node. This makes sure that the combined result—your original plane and the scattered points, will appear in the final output of the **Geometry Nodes** modifier.

Now that you know how to use **Group Inputs** to customize your geometry node setups, let us move on to the next step: enhancing the scattered points with the **Instance on Points** node. This is important because it lets you turn scattered points into actual objects, such as trees in a forest or mushrooms on a fairy-tale field. Without it, you would have a bunch of floating dots—great for abstract art shows, but not for realistic video game environments!

Enhancing points with the Instance on Points node

To make better use of **Points**, you can add **Instance on Points** by dragging it onto the connection line between **Distribute Points on Faces** and **Join Geometry**. This will automatically insert it into the node chain:

1. On the **Instance on Points** node, click and drag from the **Instance** input socket (the small circle). Drop the connection into an empty space in the **Geometry Node** editor. From the pop-up menu, select **Collection Info**. Blender will automatically create and connect this new node, so you can feed in objects from a collection (e.g., a set of trees, rocks, or props) to be randomly spawned on your points.

2. To add a new parameter to your geometry node setup, simply drag out from an empty white socket on the **Group Input** node and connect it to the white **Collection** input socket on the **Collection Info** node. This will automatically create a new exposed **Collection** input in the modifier, allowing you to select a collection from the main interface.

> **Note**
>
> You can rename sockets by pressing *N* while on your **Geometry Graph**, which will open a side menu. There, click on **Select Group** and double-click on the parameter named **Socket** that we just created.

3. We can now create a new collection and add items to it. To visualize varieties, go to the modeling tab, create a cone, cube, and sphere within your 3D Viewport using *Shift + A* and then select **Add Mesh**. Select the objects and press *M*, then click **Create New Collection** and name your collection Items.

4. Now, we can go back to the **Geometry Node** tab. Select the plane with the geometry node. Within its **Modifier** tab, you will see a **Collection** parameter. Select the **Items** collection we just created onto it. Now, you will see objects spawning on the plane.

5. To make sure each object spawns individually, we are going to check **Pick Instance** within **Instance on Points**. We will also enable **Separate Children** to make sure each instance is treated as an individual item for placement. Afterward, check **Reset Children**, to make sure that their transformations are reset before being used.

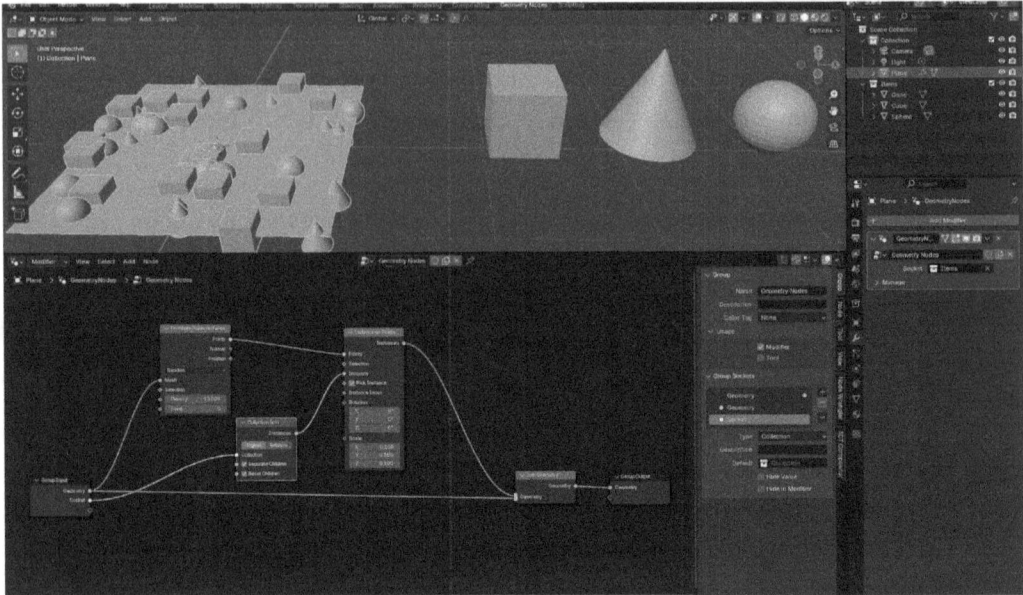

Figure 2.6: Geometry node example with Group Inputs

Now that you have learned how to use **Group Inputs** to create a dense forest, it is time to expand your skills and apply them to a more complex project. In the next section, we will work on a practical example: creating a customizable forest landscape.

Practical example: Creating a customizable forest landscape

In this example, I invite you to create a landscape with me. We will make use of a system as we did in the previous example. However, this time we will take a more practical approach. Looking at this differently will help us speed up the workflow for creating a forest in Blender.

We will use **Group Input** nodes to create sliders for elevation and vegetation density, as shown in *Figure 2.7*. So, follow these instructions:

1. Add a plane to your scene and apply a **Geometry Nodes** modifier to it. Select the geometry node we created in the previous practical example by clicking the icon to the left of geo-node naming.

2. Connect the **Density** input of the **Distribute Points on Faces** node to the **Group Input** node. By default, it will create a new parameter on your modifier named **Density**.

3. To control the scaling of objects, first create a **Random Value** node and connect it to the **Scale** input of the **Instance on Points** node. By connecting a **Float** value (gray) to a **Vector** input (purple), you will control the *X*, *Y*, and *Z* scale uniformly as a single entity. To fine-tune this scaling, attach the **Min** and **Max** values of the random scale to the empty sockets in the **Group Input** node.

4. Like in *step 3*, you can use a **Random Value** node for rotation. However, if you plug in a **Float** value directly, it will affect all rotation axes equally. To control each axis individually, switch the **Random Value** node from **Float** to **Vector** mode using the dropdown at the top of the node. Now, to make sure the objects only rotate on the *Z* axis, set the **X** and **Y** values to *0*, and adjust the **Z** value to range between *0* and *1*.

5. Now that the setup is in place, you can easily replace the default objects with custom tree meshes. For example, you can create your own low-poly trees and add them to the scene. To do this, simply add your custom tree mesh to the collection you are working with, and Blender will automatically instance the custom trees in place of the default objects.

Note

The position of objects spawned on a surface relies on their origin point. If you need to adjust the spawn height or position of an object, go into **Edit Mode**, select all vertices, and use *G + Z* to move the object up or down along the *Z* axis. This will change the origin point without affecting the object's geometry.

6. With your inputs set up, select your plane and go to the **Geometry Nodes Modifier** tab. You will see sliders for **Density** and **Min/Max** values. Adjusting these sliders will change your vegetation density without needing to open the node editor, like in *Figure 2.7*—all thanks to geometry nodes!

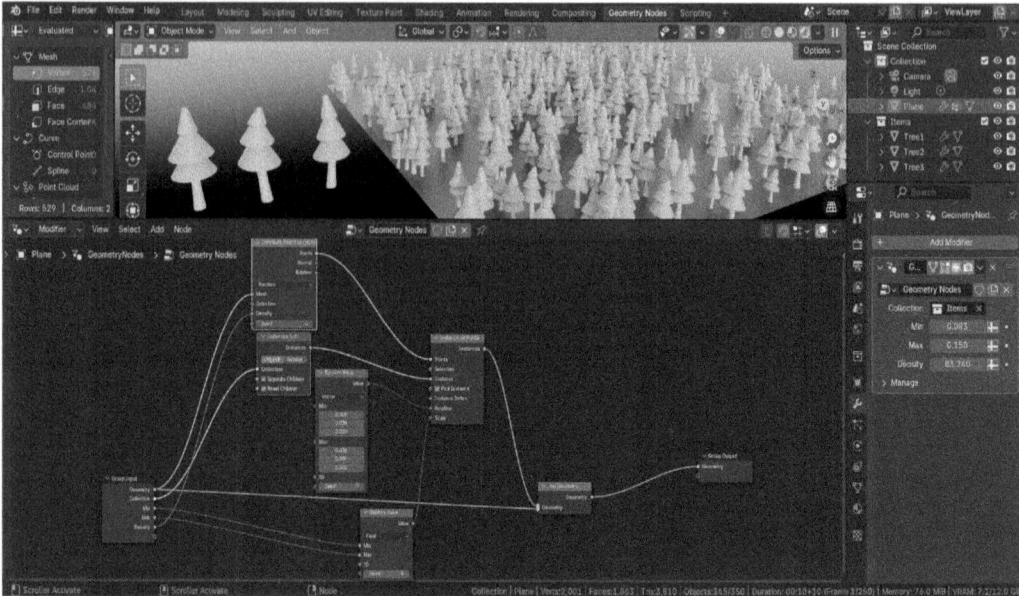

Figure 2.7: Customizable landscape geometry node example with group inputs

The benefits of interactive controls

Group Inputs help you make 3D models easier and with a lot of flexibility. Here are some of the key benefits:

- **Simplification of complex setups: Group Inputs** simplify complex setups so that even people who are new to using nodes can handle them without getting lost.

- **Efficiency**: In jobs where you need to make changes fast, such as in advertising, **Group Inputs** are a lifesaver. If a client wants to see a few different versions of an animation, you can quickly adjust settings right from the main Blender screen without having to open up and mess with the node setups each time.

- **Enhanced animation capabilities**: With **Group Inputs**, animators can make elements in their scenes change over time. For example, you can make trees change colors with the seasons just by moving sliders.

- **Greater control in 3D modeling**: By learning how to use **Group Inputs**, you will have a lot more control in your 3D modeling. One minute, you are adjusting the slider to sprinkle light snow across your mountains, and the next, you are summoning a summer storm.

Having a solid grasp of **Group Inputs** sets the stage for diving deeper into the more technical aspects of Blender's geometry nodes.

In the next section, we will talk about essential nodes such as the **Transform** node, mesh primitives, and the **Point Distribute** node.

Exploring fundamental geometry nodes

You will come across a bunch of different geometry nodes, each designed to help you with specific parts of the modeling process, such as making shapes or arranging objects. In this section, we will cover some of the nodes that you will use a lot. I will show you how to adjust their settings and take you through a step-by-step project to create a simple pattern.

Configuring node properties

Each node comes with a set of properties that you can adjust to achieve specific effects. *Table 2.1* shows how to configure the properties of the previously mentioned nodes:

Node	Function	Configuration Method	Example Use
Transform node	The **Transform** geometry node is super handy because it lets you move, rotate, and scale your objects. It is exactly what you need to get everything positioned just right in your scene.	Select the **Transform** node in your node setup. You will see parameters for **Location**, **Rotation**, and **Scale**. *Note*: **Rotation** values are displayed in radians, but you can switch to degrees by typing in the degree symbol after the number (e.g., 45°).	Imagine you are creating a digital model of a living room. You could use the **Transform** node to adjust the position of a sofa, rotate a coffee table to align with the room's layout, and scale a lamp to fit next to a reading chair.

Node	Function	Configuration Method	Example Use
Mesh primitives (e.g., Ico Sphere)	Mesh primitives create simple shapes such as cubes, spheres, and planes.	After adding an **Ico Sphere** node, you can adjust its **Radius** value to change the size of the sphere. Use **Subdivisions** to control the level of detail. *Note*: Increasing **Subdivisions** makes the sphere smoother but can increase how much power your computer needs to generate it.	For example, if you are modeling a simple piece of fruit such as an apple, you might start with a sphere. To do that, go to **Mesh | Primitives | UV Sphere**. You can then adjust its size and shape slightly to get a dimpled apple.
Mesh operations (e.g., Boolean)	Mesh operations such as the **Boolean** node let you combine or cut these shapes to make more complex objects.	Add a **Boolean** node and set its operation (**Union, Difference**, or **Intersect**). Connect geometry inputs for the two objects involved in the operation.	Combine a cube and a cylinder to create a detailed pillar or cut windows into a wall by subtracting one shape from another.
Point Distribute node	Scatter points evenly across a surface. It is a great node choice for instancing objects or creating patterns.	With the **Point Distribute** node selected, you can adjust the **Density** parameter to control how many points are scattered across your geometry's surface. Higher density values will give you more points and more instances of objects if you use it for scattering.	The **Point Distribute** node is great for spreading things out evenly over a surface, such as placing stars in the night sky.

Node	Function	Configuration Method	Example Use
Curve nodes	Curve nodes help you work with smooth paths or edges.	Use nodes such as **Curve to Mesh** to turn a drawn curve into a 3D shape. Combine it with **Profile Curve** nodes to control the cross-sectional shape of the curve.	**Curve** nodes are perfect for making things such as roads and river paths that need smooth, curved lines, as in *Figure 2.9*. Using nodes such as **Curve to Mesh**, you can turn a simple drawn curve into a 3D shape, which is great for adding details to your models or landscapes.

Table 2.1: Configuration methods for geometry nodes based on node type

By learning how to use these fundamental nodes, you will be able to handle a wide variety of modeling tasks in Blender. Let us dive into how to configure different node properties and see how they can be used in practical projects. In *Figure 2.8*, you will see **Curve** nodes in action; in this example, we used them to make a river path.

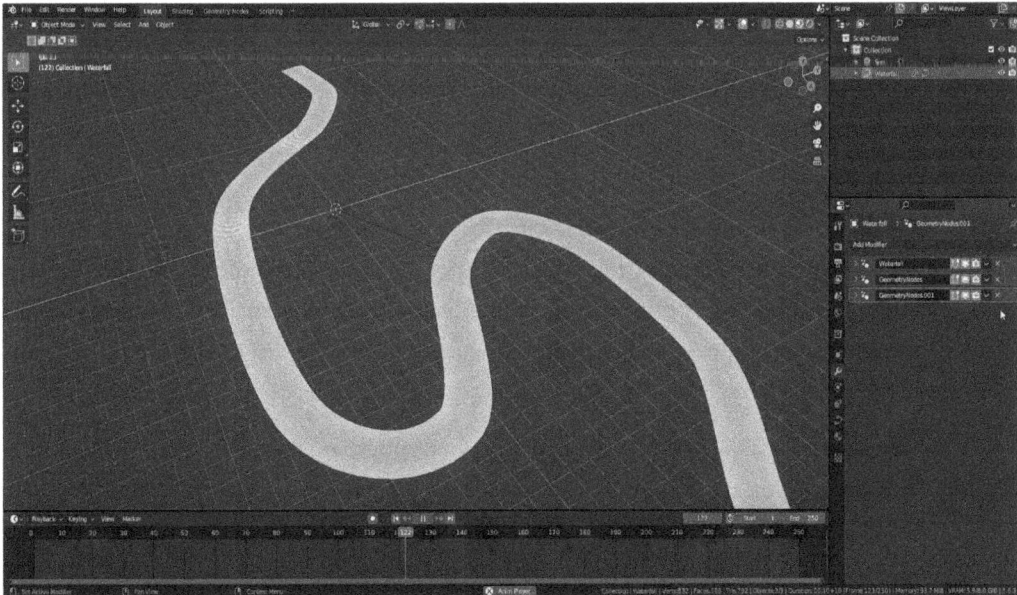

Figure 2.8: Curved water in Blender 4 Stylized Waterfall Geometry Node by 3D Tudor

Practical tools in Blender's geometry nodes

Some geometry nodes are the basic tools you will use all the time, but others are more specialized. In this section, we will talk about practical tips and nodes that are great for certain situations. These might not be the first nodes you use, but they can help you solve tricky problems or add extra details when you need them.

The **Set Position** node lets you set the exact position of points in your shape. This might sound confusing at first, but it is great for making detailed adjustments or deformations. For example, let us say you are modeling a creature with a flexible tail. You could use the **Set Position** node to create subtle or dramatic bends in the tail, positioning each vertex exactly where needed to achieve the desired curvature.

Now, to add more detail to your shapes, the **Subdivision Surface** node is your go-to tool. The **Subdivision Surface** node breaks down the surfaces of your mesh into smaller parts, making everything look smoother and more intricate. Picture this: you are working on modeling an intricate piece of jewellery, such as a brooch, in 3D, but it looks blocky. You have started with a simple flat plate as your base geometry. By applying the **Subdivision Surface** node, you can transform this base into a more curved and aesthetically pleasing form.

For merging or cutting shapes together, the **Mesh Boolean** node is your best bet. It runs complex operations that combine or subtract shapes from one another, making intricate designs that would be tough to make by hand. The best example for using the **Mesh Boolean** node I can think of is on a complex mechanical part that needs to fit precisely with other components. I mentioned this before, but you could use the **Mesh Boolean** node to merge several basic shapes or cut out parts where they adjoin to other parts.

To place objects across surfaces, such as trees in a forest or buildings in a city, you start with the **Instance on Points** node by connecting it to a setup. This node lets you choose which object, such as a tile or building, will appear at each point. By adjusting the density of a mesh, you can control how many objects appear and how they are spread across the surface. Blender's **Instance on Points** node is used to replace each point with an actual 3D object or collection of objects.

Now that you understand the power of these nodes, let us put them to use in a practical example project. This will help you see how these concepts come together in a real-world application.

Hands-on project: Creating procedural bricks

Now that we have covered some of the basics, let us dive into a hands-on project to see how these concepts come together. Yes, you can use Blender's geometry nodes to create a brick pattern.

Before you begin, select a default cube or any primitive object, and create a new **Geometry Nodes** modifier on it. This will serve as the base for your procedural setup. *Figure 2.10* shows you the finished setup if you follow along with this example.

Here is a basic list of steps:

1. First, set the base grid. Use a **Grid** node to lay out your bricks in a repeating pattern. Add a **Grid** node by pressing *Shift + A*, then going to **Mesh** and then **Grid**. Set its size to match the overall dimensions of your brick layout.

    > **Note**
    >
    > The **Grid** node defines a grid of points in the X and Y axes, and the number of points can be controlled by adjusting the **Vertices X** and **Vertices Y** parameters. These values will define how many rows and columns of bricks you will get.

2. Then, set **Vertices X** to the number of bricks in a row and **Vertices Y** to control the number of rows in your pattern. For example, a value of 6 for **Vertices X** and 13 for **Vertices Y** will create 6 bricks per row and 13 rows.

3. Now, we want to start adding bricks using a box primitive. Start by creating a basic shape for a single brick using a mesh primitive node, such as a cube, by pressing *Shift + A*, then selecting **Mesh** and then **Cube**. You can adjust the dimensions of the cube to match the proportions of a brick (e.g., **X:** 1m, **Y:** 0.3m, **Z:** 0.1m).

4. Now, we need to use **Instance on Points**; or, in other words, we need to instance these bricks at each point on the grid so that they spawn duplicates of the object on different points:

    a. Add an **Instance on Points** node (press *Shift + A* and go to **Geometry** and then **Instance on Points**).

    b. Connect the **Grid** node to the **Points** input and the **Cube** node to the **Instance** input. This will create a repeating grid of bricks, positioned exactly on the grid points.

5. To make the setup flexible and allow for easy adjustments, we will expose the grid pa-
    rameters (e.g., **Size, Vertices**) to **Group Input**. This way, you can control the grid settings
    directly from the modifier panel:

    a. Click on the sockets next to the **Size X, Size Y, Vertices X**, and **Vertices Y** parameters
        of the **Grid** node, and drag them to the **Group Input** node.

    b. Then, in the **Geometry Nodes** modifier panel, you can adjust the number of bricks
        and their size without going back into the node setup.

    Now that the grid settings are easy to adjust, let us work on making the bricks look smooth-
    er and more polished.

6. Add a **Subdivision Surface** node after the cube. This node helps in softening the sharp
    edges of the box, improving the way your brick pattern looks. However, before adding
    subdivision, make sure your cube has enough geometry to support the shape; otherwise,
    it may smooth into a disk-like form. You can add extra edge loops or use a more detailed
    primitive to prevent this. Afterward, set the **Subdivision** level to what you need, such as
    2 on **Level**, to add some softness to the brick edges without overly complicating the mesh.

    > Note
    >
    > At the time of writing this chapter, geometry nodes do not yet include a **Bevel** option,
    > so we are using **Subdivision** to soften edges here. To visualize the before-and-after
    > effect, select the **Subdivision Surface** node and press *M* (the mute toggle) to turn
    > its effect on or off in the 3D Viewport.

7. Add the **Set Shade Smooth** node after the **Subdivision Surface** node and double-check
    that the **Shade Smooth** box is checked. This is a quality check for rendering.

At this point, you will have a basic, uniform grid of bricks, as in *Figure 2.9*.

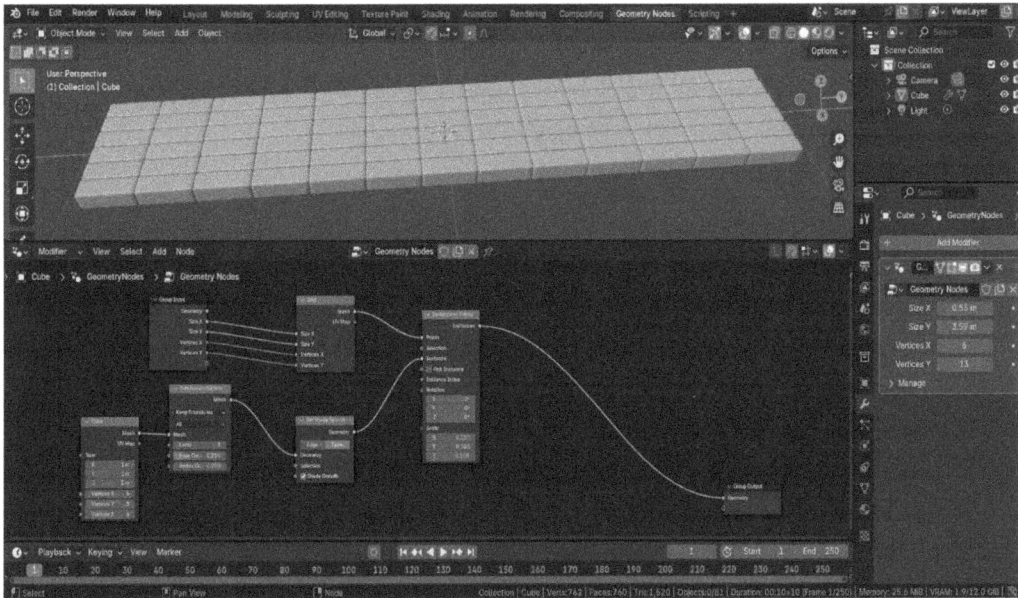

Figure 2.9: Brick layout using Blender 4 Brick Wall Geometry Node by 3D Tudor

Now, we will look at how to offset every second row of bricks to create the staggered brick pattern that is typical in brick walls.

8. Make sure you have your **Grid** node set up to control the grid layout for the bricks. At this point, your **Instance on Points** node is already connected and it is instancing bricks on the grid points.

9. Add an **Index** node by pressing *Shift + A* and going to **Input** and then **Index**. This node gives you a unique number for each point in the grid. Each vertex is assigned a unique ID. The next step is to determine which row each point belongs to.

10. To do this, add a **Math** node and set it to **Divide**. Then, plug **Index** into the first input of the **Math** node. In the second input, plug in **Vertices Y** from **Group Input**. This step figures out which row each point in the grid belongs to, but the numbers will have decimals for points in the same row. Do not worry, though, this formula adjusts automatically if you change how many bricks are stacked along the *Y* axis, so it always stays accurate.

Note

This division will give you the row number, but it will have decimal values for points within the same row. Put simply, whenever we change the brick count on the *Y* axis, the formula will adapt, keeping row values accurate.

11. If you are looking to refine this more, use the **Floored Modulo** operation. **Floored Modulo** combines Blender's **Floor** and **Modulo** maths operations into one. The **Floor** operation simply removes the decimal points, while **Modulo** will give us a return value of either 1 or 0 based on the second value. For the purpose of this example, set the second value to 2. This will give us a value of 1 on every second row. Connect the output of the previous **Math** node (i.e., the division result) to the input of this **Floor Modulo** node.

12. Now that we have isolated every second row using Blender's **Floored Modulo**, let us set up a way to identify these rows to adjust them further. Add a **Compare** node by pressing *Shift + A*, going to **Utilities**, and then selecting **Compare**. Set the comparison to **Equal**. Plug the result from the **Modulo** node into the first input of the **Compare** node. Set the second input to 1 to select every second row.

13. With that, we can move them to create that staggered brick pattern. Add a **Set Position** node by pressing *Shift + A* and going to **Geometry** and then **Set Position**. Then, drag the **Set Position** node onto the link between the **Grid** node and the **Instance on Points** node to insert it into the node flow.

14. To make sure only the selected rows are adjusted, connect the output of the **Compare** node to the **Selection** input of the **Set Position** node. This will ensure that only the selected rows are affected.

15. You can now **Offset** *X* value in **Set Position** node to offset the bricks. Alternatively, add a **Vector Math** node by pressing *Shift + A* and going to **Vector** and then **Vector Math**. Set it to **Add**. Use this to control how much you want to move the selected rows. For example, set the **X** value to 0.5 to move the selected rows horizontally.

You should now have every other row of bricks offset horizontally, creating the staggered brick wall effect, as in *Figure 2.10*.

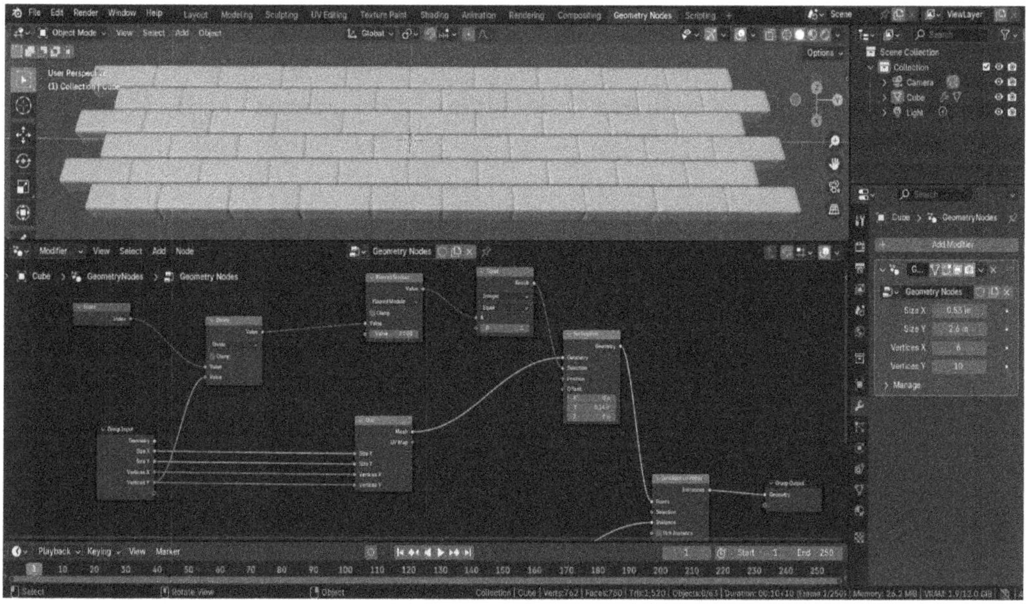

Figure 2.10: Final result of following a hands-on project – creating procedural bricks

Tip

You can control the rotation, location, and overall scale of your instanced objects by manipulating your **Object Mode** setup. Adjusting transformations, such as moving, scaling, or rotating the object, will not directly affect the geometry nodes per se. The reason for this is that these transformations are applied after the node calculations have been completed. This will help you fine-tune the placement and orientation of your objects without affecting the underlying geometry or node network.

Generating bricks in this way uses procedural modeling to create complex structures from simple, reusable components. Doing it this way will give you control over making easy adjustments to the wall's size, color, and texture without manually tweaking individual bricks.

If you are curious to explore this further, try muting and unmuting different nodes in your setup to see how each one changes the result; this is a simple way to understand individual node effects and experiment with more advanced workflows.

You have gotten the hang of the basic tools in Blender's geometry nodes for changing shapes and arranging objects. This means you are ready to dive deeper. This next section covers advanced nodes, as well as sharing some tips on how to keep your node networks organized by working on a creative project.

Enhancing your node networks

As you become more comfortable with the basics of Blender's geometry nodes, we will look at advanced features to unlock more shiny (and precious!) features in Blender.

Instances are major players in efficient modeling and animation workflows. An instance is like a copy of an object that stays linked to the original. If you make changes to the original (such as its shape or material), all the instances update automatically. This makes instances super-efficient because they do not take up as much memory or slow down your file like regular duplicates would.

Nodes such as **Instance on Points** and **Geometry to Instance** allow you to duplicate geometry without using too much memory. This happens because each instance references the original geometry rather than duplicating it. This is super useful for creating complex structures such as forests, crowds, or modular assets.

However, an important drawback, or at least a point of consideration, is that instances exist as a lightweight reference and not as actual geometry. If you need to manipulate the individual elements as editable meshes or export them as a unified object, you need to use the **Realize Instances** node. This node converts all instances into actual geometry.

Blender's **Realize Instances** node would also work great in an underwater environment for vegetation on a coral reef, as in *Figure 2.11*.

Figure 2.11: Underwater environment using Blender 4 Coral Reef Geometry Node by 3D Tudor

Apart from controlling movements and positions, Blender's geometry nodes offer powerful tools for managing and manipulating data within your models. **Attribute** nodes handle data associated with the points, edges, or faces of your geometry (e.g., position or custom data). For example, by using an **Attribute Fill** node, you could assign random colors to different parts of a mesh, which would be perfect for adding visual diversity if you are working on leaves on a tree, or a vine, as in *Figure 2.12*.

Figure 2.12: Color variation in Blender 4 Ivy Foliage Geometry Node by 3D Tudor

To effectively manage these powerful tools, organizing and optimizing your node networks is crucial. Organizing and optimizing your node networks not only makes them easier to understand and modify but can also improve performance. Here are some best practices:

- **Grouping nodes**: For complex setups, group related nodes into custom nodes (right-click and choose **Make Group**). You could also create custom node groups (select nodes and press *Ctrl + G*).

  Once grouped, you can use *Tab* to enter and exit your group node. You can ungroup it by right-clicking on the created **NodeGroup** and selecting **Ungroup** (*Ctrl + Alt + G*).

  Tip

  Sometimes the naming of group sockets can be confusing. You can rename them by entering the group and using the **Group** panel (located in the side tab, and accessed by pressing *N*) to rename them, like with any other parameter on a geometry node.

- **Framing and commenting**: Name your nodes and frames in a way that makes sense. This will be a blessing for your future self and for others who may work with your files.

  To add a frame, use *Ctrl + J* and make sure there are nodes selected. This will create a frame around them. You can then select the frame and press *F2* to comment on a section. To remove it from a frame, use the **Unparent** shortcut by pressing *Alt + P*.

- **Optimizing performance**: Be mindful of how much computer power nodes use. For example, do not use **Viewer** nodes too often because your 3D Viewport can be slow to update. To help, the number ending in **ms** above individual geometry nodes shows the execution time in milliseconds, indicating how long the node takes to process, as in *Figure 2.13*.

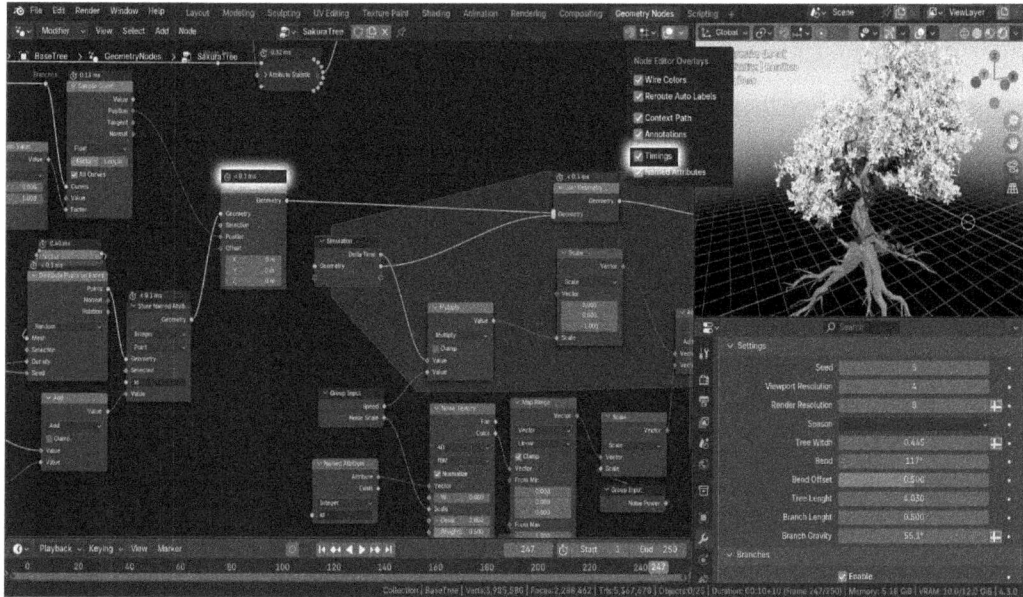

Figure 2.13: Time in ms for geometry node execution

It is usually displayed on more complex nodes that have a significant impact on performance. You might not see the **ms** display with simpler nodes because their processing time is too quick to be relevant.

> Note
>
> Nodes that do not show timing data are usually doing quick and light stuff, such as moving data around or changing a small value. They are so fast that it's not really meaningful to measure their timing. If you want to see how long each node takes to process, go to **Geometry Node Overlay** and turn on **Timings**. This will show a little time estimate above each node, so you can see how much work your computer is doing.

Creative challenge: Designing a cityscape

Now, let us tackle another project. This project challenges you to combine various nodes and techniques learned throughout this chapter. You will design a procedural cityscape:

1. **Plan your city layout**: Think about the layout of your city. Will it have a grid pattern or will it be more organic? What types of buildings will you see there?

2. **Create building variants:** Model a few different types of buildings for your city. These could be simple blocky structures or skyscrapers. Think about how much your computer can handle and how big you need your project to be.

3. **Distribute buildings using geometry nodes:** Use a plane as the base for your city. Apply a geometry node setup that uses the **Point Distribute** node to scatter your building instances across the plane. Use the **Vector Math** node to vary the rotation of buildings for a more natural look.

4. **Add roads and parks:** Use **Boolean** nodes to keep some areas free from building distribution for your roads and parks. You can also use **Attribute** nodes to change the color or material of different areas. This can be a technique for you to visually distinguish between building zones and green spaces.

5. **Experiment with lighting and atmosphere:** Once your basic cityscape is in place, experiment with different lighting setups and atmospheric effects to make your scene look lived in. You can also use geometry nodes to create streetlights, cars, and other details to add depth to your city.

This challenge is meant to get you thinking creatively and applying what you have learned in this chapter. The steps are not super detailed because the idea is for you to experiment and figure things out using the geometry node techniques we have covered so far. Do not worry about getting everything perfect. This is about exploring and trying new things. If you get stuck, you can always go back to earlier sections for guidance. Have fun designing your cityscape!

Summary

In this chapter, we took a close look at one of the coolest features in Blender, geometry nodes. They are awesome because they help you build complex effects and models step by step by connecting different blocks, called nodes. This chapter showed how using geometry nodes can save a lot of time, especially if you are generating models that usually take a long time to model the old-fashioned way. Despite their advantages, geometry nodes can be a bit complicated for beginners, and if the setup gets too complex, it could slow things down.

The chapter talked you through the main parts needed, such as the **Geometry Node** editor and the node tree, and the basic building blocks or nodes that change the model's shape. There were also practical examples and step-by-step guides on how to create different types of models, such as meadows or customizable landscapes. We also talked about the technical stuff that helps geometry nodes work smoothly, such as optimizing node networks and managing computational performance. By the end of the chapter, you came away with an understanding of the basics of geometry nodes.

Moving forward, in the next chapter, we will shift our focus to texture painting in Blender. There, you will learn how to effectively add and adjust textures directly onto your models as you work on them.

Further reading

- Just getting started with geometry nodes? *Blender 4 Geometry Nodes for Beginners* (https://3dtudor.gumroad.com/l/Blender_4_Geometry_Nodes_for_Beginners) is perfect for you. It is packed with easy-to-follow setups and examples to help you get a solid grip on the basics.

- If you are looking to enhance your workflow and creativity with Blender's geometry nodes, actual and pre-built geometry node setups can guide you through basic and advanced techniques. *Blender 4 Jungle Terrain Geometry Node* (https://3dtudor.gumroad.com/l/Blender4_Jungle_Terrain_Geometry_Node) shows you how to generate dense, realistic foliage and terrain with a few clicks.

- For customizable procedural setups, *Blender 4 Procedural Stairs Geometry Node* (https://3dtudor.gumroad.com/l/stairsgeonode) is your practical solution for creating scalable architectural elements such as stairs. It is like magic—just set it up and boom, perfectly customizable stairs for your project. Do you need extra help? Check out the accompanying course—*Blender Geometry Nodes – Procedural Bridge Generator* (https://3dtudor.gumroad.com/l/Blender_Geo_Nodes Beginners_Procedural_Bridge_Generator).

- If you are designing natural environments, *Blender 4 Grass & Flowers (Meadow) Procedural Geometry Node* (https://3dtudor.gumroad.com/l/Blender_4_Grass_Flowers_Procedural_Geometry_Node) allows you to quickly populate your scene with meadows, grass, and other vegetation. It's a total time-saver! Want to learn how? Check out *Blender Geometry Nodes for Beginners - Foliage Scatter* (https://3dtudor.gumroad.com/l/blender_geonodes_beginners_foliage_scatter).

- To explore dynamic simulations, *Blender 4 Coral Reef Geometry Node* (https://3dtudor.gumroad.com/l/blender4_coralreef_geometrynode) showcases how to use nodes such as the **Vector Math** node to mimic interactions such as wind or underwater currents.

- Building walls but tired of placing each brick manually? *Blender 4 Brick Wall Geometry Node* (https://3dtudor.gumroad.com/l/blender4brickwallgeonode) helps you generate realistic brick walls. Generate walls with adjustable size, color, and texture, and throw in randomization to make it look super realistic. We also have a step-by-step course about it: *Blender Basics Geometry Node Brick Walls Workshop* (https://3dtudor.gumroad.com/l/Blender_Basics_Geometry_Node_Brick_Walls_Workshop).

- Make your 3D foliage diverse and let it stand out with *Blender 4 Ivy Foliage Geometry Node* (https://3dtudor.gumroad.com/l/Blender_4_Ivy_Foliage_Geometry_Node). It lets you randomize colors and create natural-looking vines and leaves, so your environments look less "meh" and more "wow."

- Dreaming of creating a stunning stylized waterfall? *Blender 4 Stylized Waterfall Geometry Node* (https://3dtudor.gumroad.com/l/Blender_4_Stylized_Waterfall_Geometry_Node) is what you need. It is a ready-made setup that makes creating flowing, animated waterfalls super quick and pretty much automated.

Subscribe to Game Dev Assembly!

We are excited to introduce **Game Dev Assembly**, our brand-new newsletter dedicated to everything game development. Whether you're coding, designing, animating, or managing a studio, we've got insights, trends, and expert advice to help you create, innovate, and thrive. Sign up now and get exciting benefits.

https://packt.link/gamedev-newsletter

Join the 3D Tudor Channel Discord Server!

Join the 3D Tudor Channel Discord Server, a creative hub for learning Blender, Unreal Engine, Substance Painter, and 3D modeling, for discussions with the authors and other readers:

https://discord.gg/5EkjT36vUj

3

Unlocking Creativity with Blender Texture Painting

Texture painting is a key technique in 3D modeling, helping make your models look real and detailed by adding colors, patterns, and details directly onto a 3D model's surface. Instead of needing to create and map individual textures in 2D software, texture painting lets you paint directly onto the model. It adjusts textures in real time and you can see immediate results.

Texture painting is not just about adding colors. It is a toolset that adds depth, emotion, and context to your models in a way that lets you tell their story. I think of a detailed dragon with scales and scars when I think of the limits texture painting can push your textures to. Imagine each scale reflecting light uniquely, and the scars telling the story of its past battles.

For beginners, learning texture painting might seem tough, but it is very rewarding. This chapter will help you understand the basics and move on to more complex skills. By the end, you will be ready to use texture painting in your projects, using one of the ideas in this book or one of your own. Let us get started with understanding all there is to know about the texture painting process, common pitfalls, and tips to succeed.

So, in this chapter, we will cover the following topics:

- Defining texture painting
- Setting up materials and textures
- Your first texture painting project
- Exploring Blender's texture painting brushes

- Advanced texture painting techniques
- Finalizing and exporting your textures

Technical requirements

As for **Blender 4.5 LTS (Long-Term Support)**, the general requirements include a macOS 11.2 or newer (Apple Silicon supported natively) operating system, or a Linux (64-bit, glibc 2.28 or newer) operating system. Blender now requires a CPU with the SSE4.2 instruction set, at least 8 GB of RAM (32 GB recommended for heavy scenes), and a GPU supporting OpenGL 4.3 with a minimum of 2 GB of VRAM.

For a full list of technical requirements, please refer back to *Chapter 1* of this part.

Defining texture painting

In simple terms, texture painting means putting 2D images or textures onto the 3D surface of a model. These textures could be simple colors and gradients or complex patterns and detailed images that imitate real-world materials.

You know how in video games, characters and environments look insanely real? That's all thanks to texture painting. It is what a games artist designing games such as *League of Legends* (https://www.leagueoflegends.com/) uses to create detailed skins to make roleplay more immersive.

Now, there are loads of perks to using texture painting:

- For starters, you can tweak things on the 3D model in real time. This means you can adjust the colors until the shade you selected is just what you were looking for.
- Another benefit is adding intricate details directly onto the model without switching back and forth between different software. This streamlines the workflow and enhances creativity.
- I also find texture painting to be a more intuitive and artistic approach because it helps me get the final look of my model right away. You might tell me that is a good enough reason to **Texture Paint**, but this technique also saves a ton of time compared to the old-school way of doing textures separately.

Regardless, texture painting is not all smooth sailing. It can be pretty tough to get the hang of because it needs a good grip on both painting and 3D modeling skills. Plus, if you are working with high-res textures, you need some serious hardware to handle it, which can be a hurdle. Once you have painted your textures onto a model, changing them later can be a bit of a headache compared to other methods where you can tweak things more easily.

So, getting a good handle on texture painting can help you figure out how to best fit this technique into your workflow.

The texture painting workspace

Blender's interface includes specialist tabs for different parts of your workflow, including texture painting. To access the texture painting workspace, at the top of the Blender window, click on the **Texture Paint** tab to switch to the texture painting workspace.

The **Texture Paint** workspace is divided into several areas:

- The 3D Viewport is where you will see your model and apply textures directly
- On the left, the Tool Shelf provides access to painting tools and settings
- The **Properties** panel on the right allows you to manage materials, textures, and other relevant properties (see *Figure 3.1*)

Figure 3.1: A first look at Blender's Texture Paint workspace

Depending on your project needs, you might want to customize your **Texture Paint** workspace. You can adjust the layout by dragging the borders between areas or by opening new panels for specific functions, such as the UV Editor or the Image Editor for managing texture images.

Note

You might want to customize your **Texture Paint** workspace if you need more control over texture placement and editing. This is because having these tools readily accessible can significantly streamline your workflow, especially if you are working with complex textures and UV maps.

Preparing your model for texture painting

Before you get knuckle-deep into texture painting, you need to prepare your model to get the best results. When you are working in Blender, first make sure your model is scaled properly in the scene. If things are out of proportion, it can mess up how the textures look and resolve.

To fix any scale issues, just hit *Ctrl + A* and choose **Scale** while you are in **Object Mode**, as we have done on the right side of *Figure 3.2*. This will apply your scaling changes.

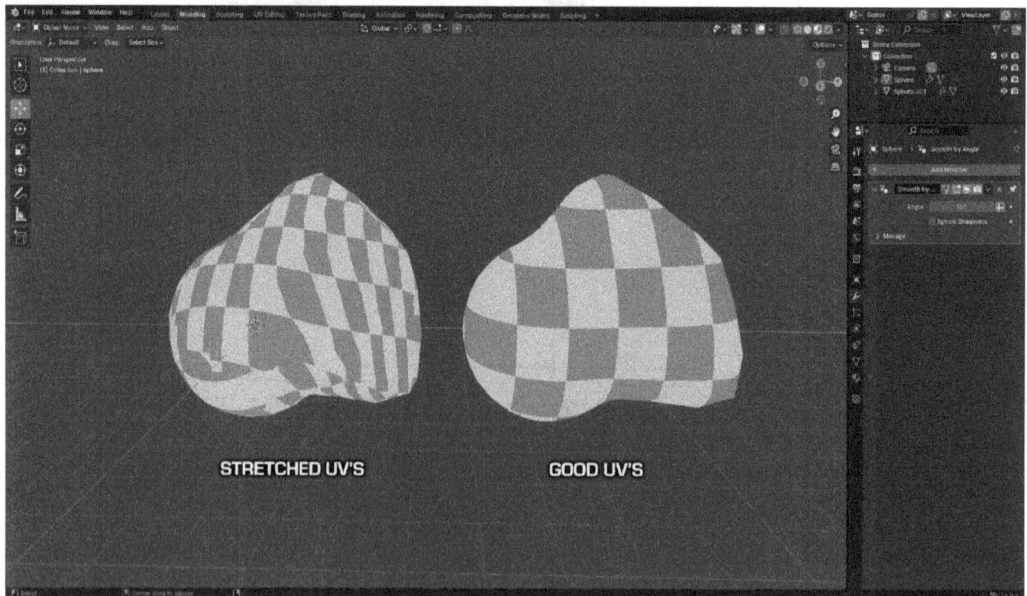

Figure 3.2: Before (left) and after (right) applying scaling changes for texture painting

Before you start texture painting, you should also apply any modifiers that change your model's shape:

- Modifiers such as **Subdivision Surface** can affect your geometry. If you do not apply them first, your textures might not match up with your final model. For example, you are working on a troll with rugged features, such as a bumpy skin texture and a tangled beard. If you try to texture paint this model without applying any modifiers, the skin might look unnaturally smooth and the beard might lack depth. If you apply the **Subdivision Surface** modifier first, the bumps on the skin become more pronounced and realistic, and the beard appears fuller and more textured.

- Another modifier that can be tricky is the **Boolean** modifier because it can create non-manifold edges and unexpected results in texturing, as in *Figure 3.3*.

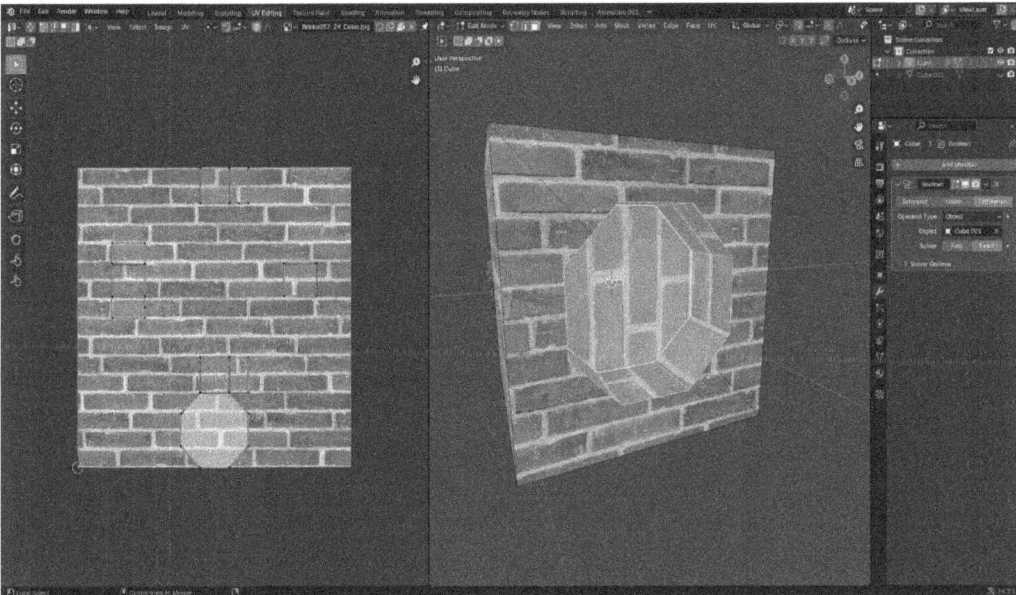

Figure 3.3: A visual representation of Boolean modifier inconsistencies in texturing

- Finally, unwrap your model. Unwrapping a model means turning the 3D surface into a 2D layout that you can paint on. To do this, mark the seams on your model where you want the cuts to be. Then, press *U* in **Edit Mode** to unwrap the model and create a UV map, as in *Figure 3.4*.

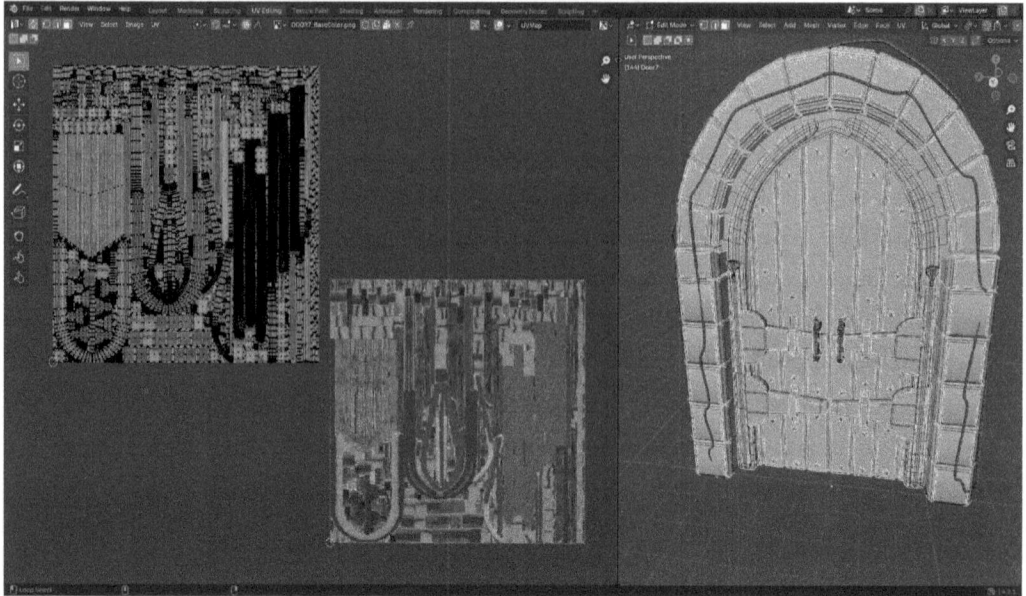

Figure 3.4: Example UV map of a medieval door in Blender 20 Massive Fantasy Doors Asset Pack by 3D Tudor

If you do not UV unwrap your model before using **Texture Paint**, you will end up with distorted textures. This could impact the realism and aesthetics of your model. By doing these steps first, you can focus on the creative part, whether you are going for a realistic look or something more stylized. The troubleshooting distractions can also slow down your workflow, and none of us wants that.

In the next section, we will dive into setting up materials and textures, which is crucial before you start painting. You will learn about creating and assigning materials to your model and preparing texture slots in Blender.

Setting up materials and textures

A crucial step before you start texture painting is making sure that your model is properly prepared with the right materials and textures. Here is a detailed walk-through guide on how to set up materials and texture slots in Blender:

1. In **Object Mode**, select the model you want to texture paint. Let us imagine it as a flower, as in *Figure 3.5*.

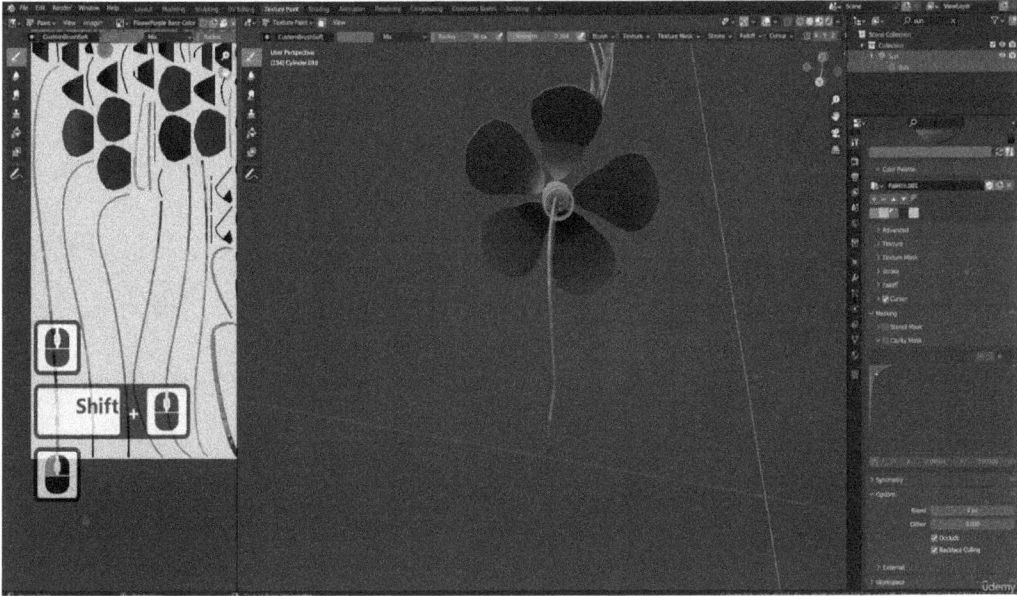

Figure 3.5: Texture painting a flower in Blender to Unreal Engine 3D Plants and Vegetation by 3D Tudor

2. Go to the **Properties** panel on the right side of the Blender interface and click on the **Material Properties** tab, which is represented by a red sphere icon.

3. If your model does not already have a material, click the **New** button to create one. This material acts as a container for your textures and defines how they will look in different light and environmental conditions. Note that your model might already have a material assigned to it if it was imported from another project or template, or if it has been used in previous work.

4. Give your material a name that matches its purpose or the type of texture you will be painting.

   When you have finished assigning a material to your model, the next step is to create a texture slot specifically for the texture you will be painting.

5. In the **Material Properties** tab, you will find a section labeled **Surface**. Click on the dot next to **Base Color** to open the texture menu, as shown in *Figure 3.6*.

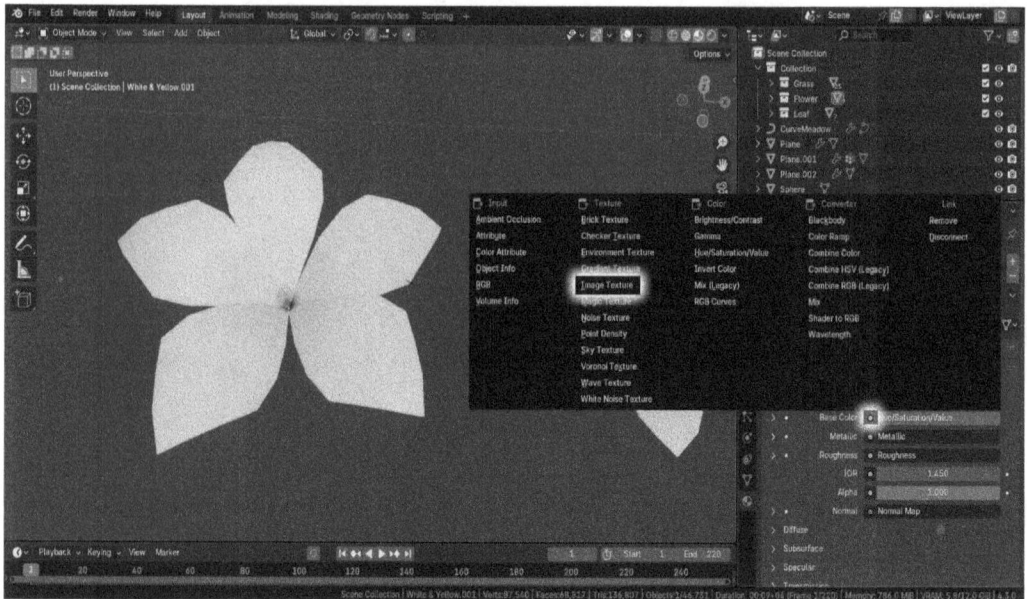

Figure 3.6: Surface Base Color menu options in Blender

6. Choose **Image Texture** from the list of options. This will create a new texture slot linked to the base color of your material.

7. For texture painting, you need an image to paint on. Click **New** to create a new image. A dialog box will appear, where we need to configure the image setting, like so:

    *   **Name**: Give your image a descriptive name, such as DiffuseMap or CharacterSkin.

    *   **Width** and **Height**: Common resolutions include **2048x2048** or **4096x4096** pixels for high-detail work.

    Note

    With a higher-resolution image, your treant might have more detailed textures, and the variations in bark texture and leaf arrangements can be depicted with much greater precision. For example, each leaf could be distinctly textured, and the bark could have deep, realistic grooves and knots that add to the character's rugged appearance. However, it is worth noting that a higher resolution increases memory usage.

- **Color:** You can set a base color for your image. This color will be visible wherever you have not painted yet, as you can see in *Figure 3.7*.

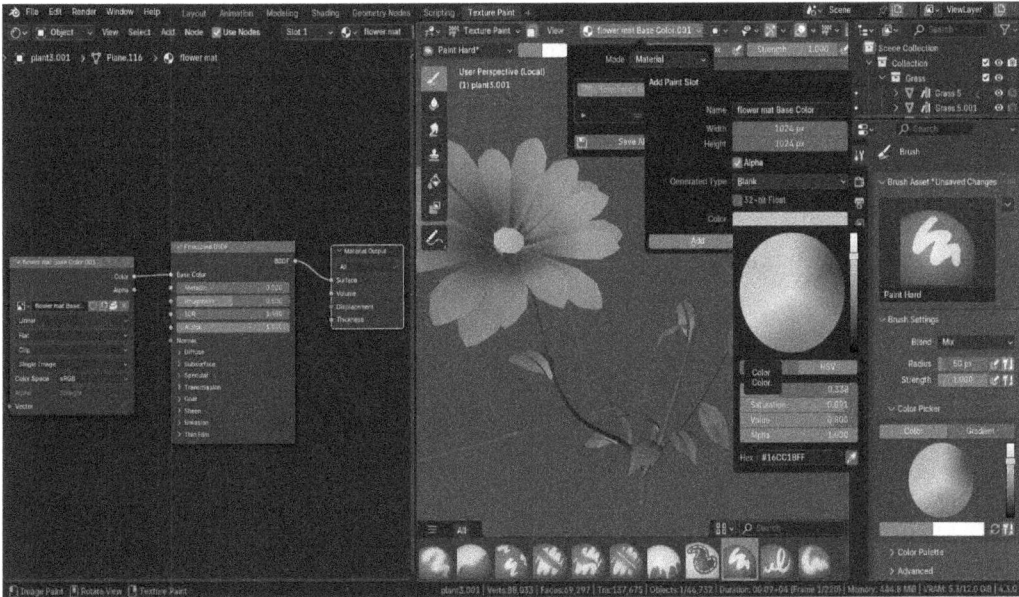

Figure 3.7: Image base color process

8. Before starting to paint, save your new image externally. While in **Texture Paint** mode, you can do this by clicking on the material slot dropdown located at the top middle of your 3D Viewport, then selecting **Save All Images**. This extra step will make sure that your texture painting progress will not be lost.

By carefully setting up your materials and texture slots, you create a solid foundation for you to texture paint on. Now that you have prepared your model with all the necessary settings, you are ready to start your first texture painting project.

Your first texture painting project

Starting your first texture painting project in Blender is an exciting step where you can bring your 3D models to life with colors and details. From setting up your material and texture slots to navigating Blender's **Texture Paint** workspace, you will learn how to prepare your model and your workspace.

And just for a bit of fun, remember that like any art, texture painting can come with its challenges. I once heard of an artist who spent hours painting detailed textures on a model, only to realize they were painting on the wrong layer. None of the work was saved on the actual model! It was a tough lesson in checking your settings, but it sure made for a memorable step in their learning curve.

Creating a new texture

To create a new texture, do the following:

1. Make sure your model is ready for painting by following the preparatory steps we talked about before, including material and texture slot setup.

2. Switch to the **Texture Paint** workspace.

3. In **Texture Paint** mode, you need an image to paint on. If you have not already created an image in the material setup, you can do that now in the **UV** panel or the **Image Editor** panel. Click **New** to create a new image, name it, and specify its resolution.

4. Make sure the newly created image is selected in the texture slot you prepared in your material. This links your painting directly to the model's surface.

In the next section, we will explore these basic painting tools, providing you with the knowledge to apply colors, patterns, and details to your model.

Basic painting tools

Blender's **Texture Paint** mode gives you access to many tools and settings designed to help you start painting your 3D models. First of all, we will talk about the **Brush** tool, then move on to **Color Selection** and then **Stroke Method**.

Brush tool

The **Brush** tool will become your best friend for texture painting. It comes with a variety of brush types available on the tool shelf, letting you create different effects such as soft shading for subtle transitions or sharp lines for defining edges and details.

For example, in a sword model, you might see someone using a sharp brush to highlight metallic edges and soft shading to create depth in the blade. The **Fallof** value used in *Figure 3.8* would give you a sharp brush.

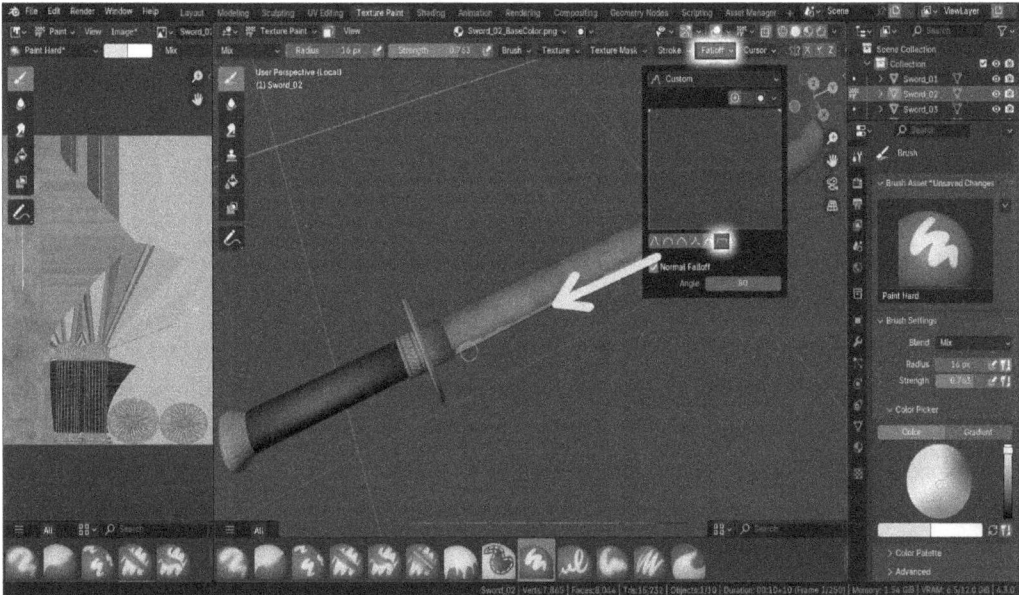

Figure 3.8: Adding a blade edge to a sword by painting it in a brighter color using a sharp fallow brush

You can adjust the **Brush** size to change how much area you cover with each stroke. The strength of the brush also determines the opacity of the paint. If you are working on a model of a forest scene, by increasing the strength of your brush, you can intensify the greens and browns, making the trees and earth look lush and richly colored. By decreasing the strength, you can paint shadows beneath the trees that appear more translucent to capture the light through the leaves. Experiment with these settings to create different painting effects. The sky is your limit!

Color selection

Color selection uses the **color picker** to help you select any color (as shown in *Figure 3.8*). You can also do some more fine-tuning by adjusting the saturation and value of the color.

Think of a project where you are painting a character to be in a scene set at sunset. You might start with a flat, somewhat dull initial skin tone. By using lighter tones and increasing the saturation, you can transform this to capture the warm, radiant hues of sunlit skin.

Stroke Method

Last but not least, the **Stroke Method** option in Blender gives you control over how the brush applies the paint. Here are a couple of options and how you might use them:

- Choices such as **Space** let you make continuous strokes, which are great for filling large areas or smooth gradients.

- **Dots** creates a dotted effect, which is ideal in projects where you are creating texture on animal fur or adding stipple effects to landscapes.

- **Stroke Method** can be incredibly useful when you want to add unique textures or intricate patterns to your model. The best example I can give you is leafy camouflage, where using varied stroke methods creates a realistic blend of natural textures, as you can see on the ground of the camping scene in *Figure 3.9*.

Figure 3.9: Blender 3 Unreal Engine 5 Complete Guide Stylized Camping Trip Gone Wrong by 3D Tudor

Now that we have explored the basics of Blender's painting tools, such as the **Brush** tool, **Color Selection**, and **Stroke Method,** it is time to put them into action. Let us try a simple exercise to see how these tools come together to create textures and patterns on your 3D models.

Painting basic shapes and patterns

Now, let us put these tools to use in a simple exercise:

1. Make sure your model is visible in the 3D Viewport and that your newly created image is selected for painting.

2. Choose the standard **Brush** tool from the Tool Shelf on the left side of the **Texture Paint** workspace (or from the brush palette at the bottom of the 3D Viewport in newer versions) and select a vibrant color to start with.

> Tip
>
> Adjust the brush size to a medium setting for better control.

3. In the active tool and workspace settings on the right-hand toolbar, under **Texture Properties**, create a new texture or select **Open** from the settings.

4. Find a custom brush alpha file, which you can download online.

> Note
>
> An alpha is a grayscale image, where white areas are completely opaque and black areas are fully transparent. In an alpha, shades of gray are used to indicate which areas of the image have partial transparency. Make sure the mask does not touch the edges of the texture because this can cause unwanted artifacts such as visible lines or clipping when rendered. You can search for brushes or alphas on the *Artstation* marketplace and find some free brushes there (https://www.artstation.com/marketplace).

5. In the **Brush Settings** panel, scroll down to find the **Texture Mask** section. Here, you can add your alpha texture. Under the **Image** section, click **Open** and pick the alpha image you want (e.g., a grayscale image where white defines the brush shape and black represents transparency).

6. Adjust the **Strength** slider under **Brush Settings** to control the opacity of your brush. You should now have something like in *Figure 3.10*.

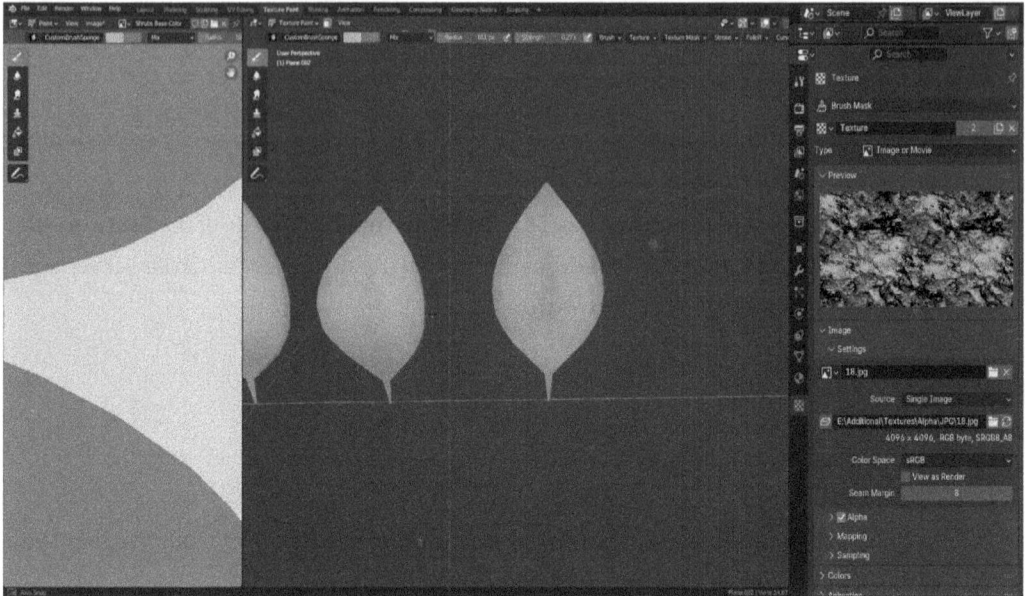

Figure 3.10: Controlling brush settings in Blender to Unreal Engine 3D Plants and Vegetation, Lesson 7, Time: 13:00 by 3D Tudor

7. To further refine the brush's interaction, use the options in the **Stroke** section to modify how the brush behaves while painting.

8. Regularly save your progress by saving the image you are painting on. Go to the Image Editor, select your image, and click **Image** | **Save As**.

Blender's texture painting brushes are powerful. Each brush is tailored for specific tasks, whether you are laying down smooth gradients, creating textured hair effects, or replicating intricate patterns across your model's surface. In the next section, we will go over more interactive activities. These exercises will help you understand each brush's capabilities and how to manipulate it to get what you want, a bit like training a cat to do tricks: unpredictable but rewarding when it works!

Exploring Blender's texture painting brushes

Blender's texture painting toolkit is equipped with many brushes, each designed to focus on and cater to different aspects of the texture painting process. From adding base colors to sculpting intricate details, understanding what each brush does is important if you want to make a name for yourself in this field. Let's take a look at some of them:

- The **standard brush (paint hard)** is used for general painting but is versatile enough to be able to do many things. It is great if you are looking to define the basic shapes and forms of a model. For example, if you are working on a basic character model, the standard brush can help you paint the general proportions and major muscle groups before you start using other specialized brushes.

- The **clone brush** is your go-to tool for duplicating textures or colors from one part of a model to another. Blender's clone brush will save you a lot of time when you need to cover a large area with a consistent texture without visible seams. For example, let us say you are texturing a landscape. You can use the clone brush to extend a grassy texture across uneven terrain. It is super handy for making large areas look seamless (see *Figure 3.11*).

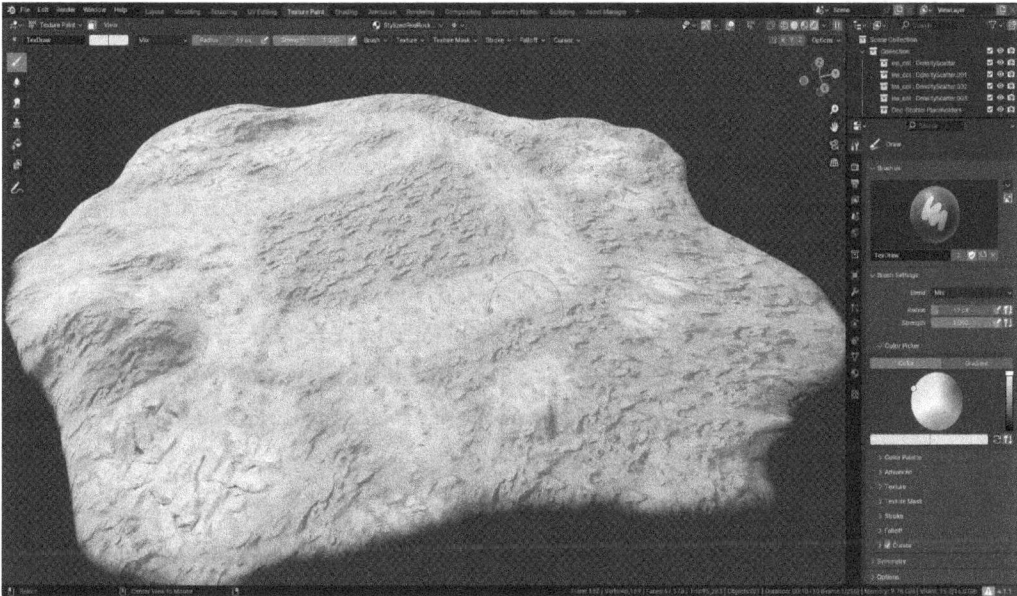

Figure 3.11: Uniform multi-level landscape

- Compared to the clone brush, the **fill brush** is all about covering big spaces quickly with a single color or material. This brush is ideal for quickly changing the color of large areas. If you are working on an architectural model, you can use the fill brush to paint walls or large surfaces so that the whole area has a consistent base color before you add more detailed textures.

- The **mask brush** is different from both of the previous brushes because it is there to help you protect specific areas of your model from being altered by other sculpting or painting actions. The best thing I can compare the mask brush to is masking tape: you use it to protect different parts of your wall, such as a skirting board or a window frame, from the paint you are applying to the rest of the wall. For example, if you are adding details to the face of a character model, using the mask brush can make sure that the rest of the head is free from accidental modifications.

- The smear brush is used to smudge or blend colors and textures directly on the model's surface (it reminds me of children's finger painting!). The smear brush is excellent for projects such as creating a gradient effect on a creature's skin or blending the colors on a sunset sky background in a scene. While the smear brush is great for blending and smoothing out colors and textures on your model, creating a natural, cohesive look, the draw brush gives you just the right amount of control to add specific, fine details such as wrinkles or textures.

- The **draw brush** is the go-to for freehand sculpting and texturing. It gives you the power to add fine details, such as wrinkles, scars, or engravings, to parts of your model. The draw brush lets you make strokes that can mimic engraving on a character's armor, for example. Going back to the other brush we just discussed, you would use the smear brush to soften and blend your work, and the draw brush to carefully apply the defining touches. The soften brush is the last of this trio since it is there to refine the details you created with the draw brush.

- In a few words, the soften brush (paint soft) is used to smooth out harsh edges and blend strokes naturally. This is why it is your best tool for achieving realistic textures and shapes. When you are sculpting facial features, it is a good idea to use the soften brush after more aggressive sculpting to smooth the transitions between the nose and cheeks to make them integrate into the face better.

Something else we should mention is that in Blender, you are not just stuck with the standard brushes that come out of the box. You can tweak them to fit exactly what you need. You can change things such as the texture, shape, and how the brush behaves when you use it. This means you can create custom brushes that do exactly what you want, making your projects stand out. It is like having the freedom to mix your paint colors or shape your sculpting tools in a traditional art studio. You can get super creative and detailed in your texture painting. We will not focus on ways to customize your brushes in this chapter, but a good place to start would be *Blender Secrets - Texture Painting with Custom Brushes* (https://www.youtube.com/watch?v=uz03aeKQzYc).

By understanding the unique properties and best uses of each brush, you can use them to improve your texture painting workflow. As you get the hang of using Blender's texture painting brushes to bring some serious life and detail to your 3D models, why not take things up a notch? Next up, we will be diving into some advanced texture painting techniques that will help you nail those professional and intricate textures. This stuff is crucial if you want to make your work stand out.

Advanced texture painting techniques

Ready to take your texture painting to the next level with Blender? This section is all about giving you the tools and know-how to shine in your projects. We will explore four powerful methods: utilizing layer management for non-destructive editing, using stencils for detailed work, incorporating images and decals, and applying cavity masking to add layers of detail, from weathered stone walls with cracks and dirt to shiny, polished metal surfaces.

Utilizing layer management

Layer management is like when the **Icecrown Citadel** (**ICC**) update landed in *World of Warcraft*. It is a game-changer! It lets you juggle different aspects of your texture painting without messing everything up. You can create and organize layers for each part of your texture, such as the base color, details, and highlights. Working with layers also means that you can tweak and experiment without ruining your base layers. It is like Blender has given you an undo button that does not wipe out everything.

> Note
>
> This is only accessible through the **UCUPaint** add-on. You can download and set up UCUPaint directly through Blender's **Get Extensions** feature inside the programme itself. To do this, go to **Edit | Preferences | Add-ons**, then click on the **Get Extensions** button. Search for UCUPaint and simply download and enable the add-on in your Blender preferences.

Within the **Texture Paint** mode, you can create new layers for different parts of your texture, such as base color, details, and highlights, as in *Figure 3.12*.

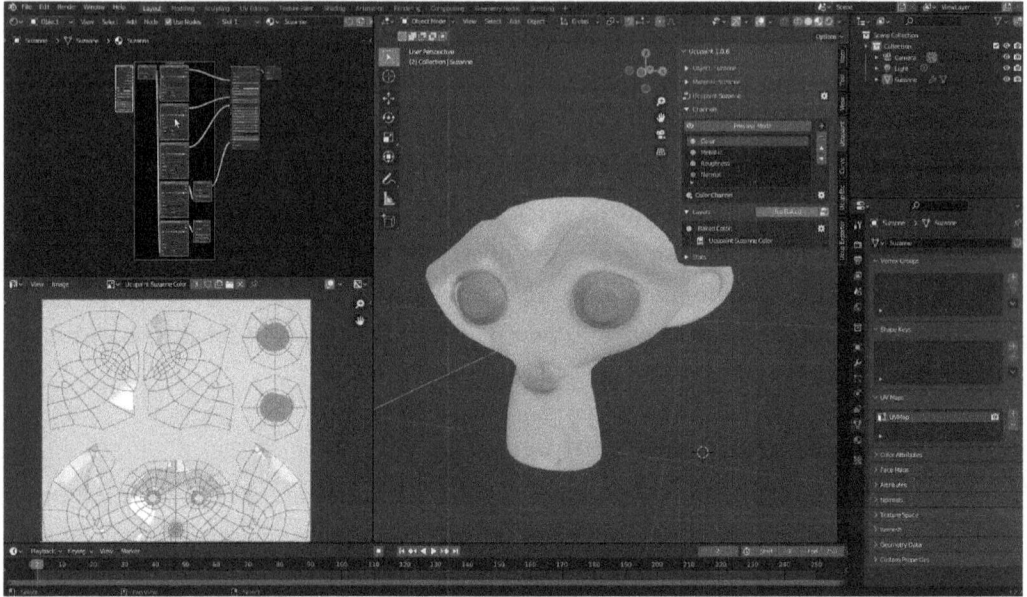

Figure 3.12: Using layers in texture painting – a visual example with Suzanne

You can make changes, try out different effects, or correct mistakes on one layer without altering the underlying layers, which is called non-destructive editing.

Each layer can have its blending mode and opacity adjusted, like layers in 2D image editing software. Blending modes determine how the layer interacts with the layers beneath it, letting you add effects such as shading, lighting, or color adjustments. Also, adjusting the opacity of a layer can help blend it seamlessly with the rest of the texture.

Using stencils for detailed work

Stencils are your secret weapon for adding details, patterns, logos, or things such as tattoos without a hitch. You can create stencils from any image or image file and use them to apply directly to your models.

To do that, import the image into Blender and set it as a stencil in the **Texture Paint** mode. With the stencil set, you can paint through it onto your model. The stencil confines the paint to its design, meaning it will not affect how the rest of your texture looks.

Blender then gives you the tools to move, scale, and rotate stencils directly in the 3D Viewport, meaning that you can choose exactly where to place them. Once you have set a texture for your stencil, activating it on the screen gives you intuitive control options to position and adjust it with ease:

1. *Right-click* to move the stencil around your workspace, ensuring precise placement.

2. Holding *Shift + right-clicking* scales the stencil, allowing you to adjust its size quickly, while *Ctrl + right-click* rotates it, giving you full control over its orientation, as in *Figure 3.13*.

Figure 3.13: Texture painting stencil in Blender 3 Unreal Engine 5 Vintage Music Hall Game Design by 3D Tudor

Incorporating images and decals

In Blender, you can import external images as planes or directly into the **Texture Paint** mode as brushes or stencils. By setting an image as a brush texture, you can paint with the image, applying it directly to your model's texture. This method is ideal for adding specific details or textures that would be difficult to paint by hand.

Decals are different because they are images applied on top of your base texture to add details such as labels, signs, or wear and tear. You can import decals as planes, position them on your model, and then bake them into your texture. Essentially, using stencils is like brushing in color information directly onto the texture, while decals are a separate plane mesh with transparency. They can potentially give the same outcome, so if you want, you can totally merge the two approaches!

Once your images or decals are applied, you can use blending modes, opacity adjustments, and layer masks to integrate them into your texture. You might need to blend edges, adjust colors, or apply filters to make sure your decals match your overall texture. Blender 4 also includes an alternative to this stencil setup that can be very cool.

Cavity masking

Cavity masking is a handy trick in texture painting that lets you focus on the dips or raised parts of a surface. It is great for adding details such as dirt, scratches, or highlights. It looks at the little crevices and edges of your model and applies the mask just to those spots. This makes it super easy to add realistic details that really show off the surface of your model.

With cavity masking, you can easily add dirt in the grooves, scratches along the edges, or even subtle highlights that make your model look like it is from real life. Let us break down how to set it up and use it to level up your texture painting game:

1. To easily preview cavities on your model, you can use the **Viewport Shading** settings. Open the **Viewport Shading** dropdown (the small sphere icon) at the top of the 3D Viewport.

2. Scroll down and enable **Cavity** to reveal the **Ridge** and **Valley** sliders, which let you adjust how much the cavity effect highlights edges and recesses in your model, as in *Figure 3.14*.

Figure 3.14: Adjusting the Ridge and Valley sliders in cavity masking in Blender to Unreal Engine 3D Plants and Vegetation by 3D Tudor

3. This makes it easier to visualize the details of your models and where textures will be applied more intensely.

4. In **Texture Paint** mode, you can make cavity masking specifically target these recessed or elevated areas when you are painting.

5. Go to the **Masking** panel located in the center, enable **Cavity Mask**, and adjust its intensity using the **Curve** settings. You can switch from **Edge Masking** to **Cavity Masking** by flipping the curve horizontally, as seen in the **3D Viewport** preview image. This lets you control how textures are applied to various depths, as shown in the highlighted settings in *Figure 3.15*.

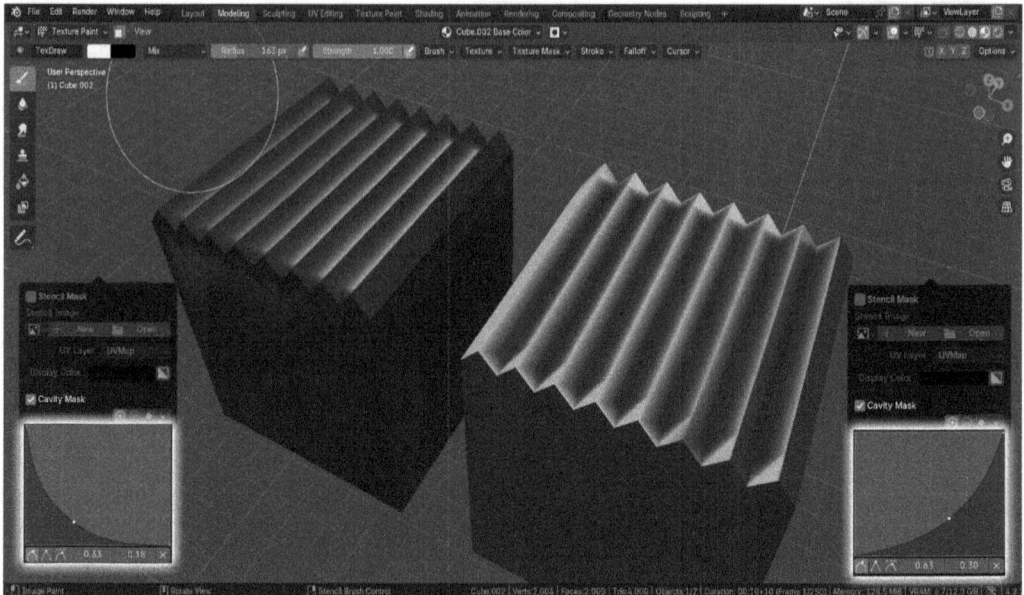

Figure 3.15: Adjusting the curve settings in Cavity Mask

6. This setup makes texture detailing better, which would be great for adding realistic effects such as dirt or wear on crevices and edges.

7. To refine the intensity of your cavity mask, use **Curve Graph**, which uses **X** and **Y** values that correspond to the mask.

8. Clicking on the **Curve** icon opens a graph that allows you to control how strongly the mask affects different depths on the model. Adjusting the **Curve** values will enhance or reduce the mask's impact on specific areas, whether they are elevated or recessed.

Now, to finish up this chapter, let's look at how to finalize and export the textures you created.

Finalizing and exporting your textures

As part of the final steps in texture painting, you need to refine your textures to get that professional finish we all look for. You also need to know how to export them for use in other projects or software. This is important because it will help you make sure that your hard work translates well across different platforms and applications.

Polishing your textures

To achieve a professional look for your textures, you need to have a keen eye for detail:

- Review your textures in different lighting conditions in Blender. Different lighting setups can reveal areas that may need more detail, highlight color inconsistencies, or show where additional smoothing is required. By rotating lights or changing the environment, you can see how your textures respond and ensure they look good in various scenarios. Look for areas that may need more detail, color adjustments, or smoothing.

- Make sure that your textures are consistent across the model, especially if you have worked on different parts separately. Pay attention to color saturation, brightness, and detail levels.

- Consider adding fine details that can make your texture look more realistic, such as wear and tear, subtle imperfections, or additional patterns, as you can see in *Figure 3.16*. These small touches can make a significant difference to the overall quality of your work.

Figure 3.16: Fine texture details in Blender 3 Unreal Engine 5 Complete Guide Stylized Skyrim Style Dungeon Environment Tutorial by 3D Tudor

- Use the soften and sharpen brushes to polish your textures further. Soften areas that require smooth transitions and sharpen details that should stand out.

Exporting textures

Exporting your textures properly is key to making sure the texture quality you see on screen remains the same and is compatible with other software. To do that, follow the next steps:

1. Make sure all your texture layers are finished and visible.

Tip

If you have used multiple layers or masks, consider merging them as needed while keeping a separate saved file with the layers intact for future edits.

2. Go to the UV Editor or Image Editor, depending on what you are doing.

3. Select the texture you want to export, then click on **Image | Save As**.

4. Choose an appropriate file format based on your needs. The .png image file format is a common choice for its balance of quality and file size, but you can use .tiff for higher-quality needs.

5. Adjust the **Export** settings, such as the file format's compression level and color depth, as shown in *Figure 3.17*.

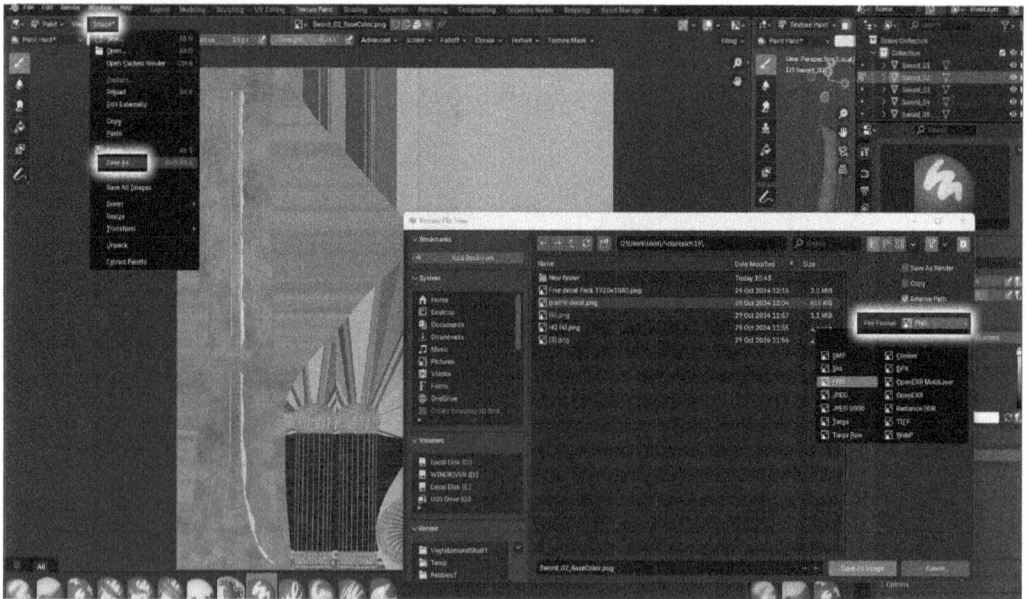

Figure 3.17: Texture export settings in Blender

Tip

Choose settings that match the quality you need and do not get too tempted to unnecessarily inflate the file size.

6. If your project involves multiple textures (e.g., **Diffuse**, **Normal**, **Specular Maps**), organize and name them. Organizing these well will also make things easier for you when you are importing and applying your textures in other projects or software.

7. Click the **Save** or **Export** button to finish the process.

Properly exporting your textures makes sure they keep the quality you want and are ready for use in other projects or software applications.

Summary

So, we traipsed through the vast landscape of texture painting in Blender, and boy, what a ride it has been! I would call it an adventure, and that sounds like something Bilbo Baggins would say! The Shire is what I think of when I picture the process of texture painting in my mind. It is colorful and perfectly reflects the power that Blender gives you.

This chapter has covered a lot of ground. Texture painting is not just slapping colors on a surface; it is about adding depth, emotion, and context to what you have made. Think about a robotic arm textured to perfection with each scratch and scuff telling a story of battles won. You are now armed with brushes, knowledge of texture painting, and a whole arsenal of skills.

But here is the thing: your journey does not stop here. You should not forget about our trusty companions on this adventure: the Blender community (`https://www.blender.org/community/`). They will be like your virtual tribe, always ready to lend a hand, share insights, and cheer you on. Tutorials, forums, online courses—you name it, they have it.

In the next chapter, we will tackle something similar. We will learn about the mysteries of vertex painting and more advanced techniques. What exactly is vertex painting? Well, it is a technique where we apply color directly to the vertices of a mesh. Unlike texture painting, which involves painting onto a 2D texture that is then applied to the model's surface, vertex painting changes the color of each vertex. So, let's get to it!

Further reading

- If you are looking for a step-by-step tutorial on texture painting and setting up materials, check out *Blender to Unreal Engine 3D Plants and Vegetation* (`https://www.udemy.com/course/blender-to-unreal-engine-3d-plants-and-vegetation/?referralCode=EC9D04E18B7749F5CE4D`). It covers everything from creating texture slots and using alpha brushes to adding stencils and cavity masking for extra details.

- If you want to understand UV unwrapping from the ground up, the official *Blender Manual* (`https://docs.blender.org/manual/en/latest/modeling/meshes/editing/uv.html`) on UV editing is a solid place to start. It explains how to mark seams, unwrap your model, and create a clean UV map so you can paint textures easily.

- If you need example models to practice unwrapping and texture painting, the *Blender Fantasy Doors Asset Pack* (`https://3dtudor.gumroad.com/l/blender_fantasy_doors_asset_pack`) is perfect. It includes detailed models with clean UV maps to help you see how it is done.

- If you want more practice working with materials and textures, the *Blender Fantasy Lamps & Lamp Posts Asset Pack* (`https://3dtudor.gumroad.com/l/Blender_Fantasy_Lamp_Asset_Pack`) has great example models. You can experiment with setting up materials, adjusting the base color, and texture painting.

- If you are curious about stencils and texture masking, the *Blender & Unreal Engine 5: Vintage Music Hall Game Design* pack (`https://3dtudor.gumroad.com/l/3dtudor_blender_unreal_engine_5_vintage_music_hall_game_design`) is a great choice. You can use the example models to practice adding patterns, logos, or wear and tear details.

Subscribe to Game Dev Assembly!

We are excited to introduce **Game Dev Assembly**, our brand-new newsletter dedicated to everything game development. Whether you're coding, designing, animating, or managing a studio, we've got insights, trends, and expert advice to help you create, innovate, and thrive. Sign up now and get exciting benefits.

`https://packt.link/gamedev-newsletter`

Get This Book's PDF Version and Exclusive Extras

UNLOCK NOW

Scan the QR code (or go to packtpub.com/unlock). Search for this book by name, confirm the edition, and then follow the steps on the page.

Note: Keep your invoice handy. Purchases made directly from Packt don't require one.

4

Releasing Colorful Creativity with Vertex Painting in Blender

Welcome to vertex painting in Blender! Instead of just slapping on textures, here you are coloring the individual vertices of your mesh. In my eyes, vertex painting is like finger painting but for grown-up digital artists, and trust me, it is just as fun.

As we talked about back in *Chapter 15* in *Part 1* of this book, traditional texture mapping involves applying 2D images (textures) to the surface of a 3D model. This process typically requires creating UV maps, which can sometimes feel like you are trying to unlock a door with a key that does not quite fit. It involves carefully aligning the texture to the model, which can be time-consuming and complex.

Vertex painting is a tool that keeps everything in one spot so you're not juggling a million tabs, and it's actually easy to use. It helps you finish stuff faster and collaborate with your team without getting lost in endless email threads. Plus, it gives you just enough data and insights to feel in control without burying you in spreadsheets. It's like having a personal assistant that's always on top of things.

This chapter will cover a comprehensive range of topics, starting with an introduction to vertex painting and its benefits, followed by step-by-step instructions on setting up your mesh for vertex painting in Blender. We will use practical applications with real-world examples from different fields, such as game development and animation. Finally, we will address common issues, provide troubleshooting tips, and share best practices for optimizing your vertex-painted models.

 The cherry on top of the cake is that you can even bake **Ambient Occlusion** effects using vertex colors. Vertex painting in Blender is basically coloring straight onto the geometry itself, no textures, no UV maps, just raw paint slapped onto the vertices. Because those colors are stored per vertex, how much detail you get is entirely down to mesh density. On a low-poly mesh, you will end up with big chunky strokes, while a denser mesh lets you blend softer gradients and add a bit more finesse. It is brilliant for quick, lightweight texturing, blocking out ideas, or giving things a stylized touch. Just do not mistake it for a full swap-in for texture painting: think of it more as a handy shortcut than the entire paint studio.

So, in this chapter, we will cover the following topics:

- Understanding vertex painting
- Getting started with vertex painting
- Advanced vertex painting techniques
- Practical applications of vertex painting
- Enhancing your models with vertex painting

Technical requirements

As for **Blender 4.5 LTS (Long-Term Support)**, the general requirements include a macOS 11.2 or newer (Apple Silicon supported natively) operating system, or a Linux (64-bit, glibc 2.28 or newer) operating system. Blender now requires a CPU with the SSE4.2 instruction set, at least 8 GB of RAM (32 GB recommended for heavy scenes), and a GPU supporting OpenGL 4.3 with a minimum of 2 GB of VRAM.

For a full list of technical requirements, please refer back to *Chapter 1* of this part.

Understanding vertex painting

Vertex painting is a neat way to add color directly to the vertices of your 3D models. Imagine it as a form of digital finger painting, simple, expressive, and incredibly fun. With vertex painting, each vertex holds color info, and Blender smoothly blends these colors across the model's surface.

Here are a few reasons why vertex painting stands out:

- **Low-poly art:** For stylized, low-poly models, vertex painting lets you apply a simplified color scheme without the need for detailed textures. This can save time and maintain the aesthetic appeal of your art. At the same time, it also helps with efficiency because it reduces the need for large texture files and simplifies the rendering process.

- **Dynamic visual effects**: In game development, vertex painting can be used to create VFX such as fiery explosions, magical auras, or eerie lights. By manually tweaking vertex colors, you can achieve just the right intensity and effect.

- **Blending textures on large surfaces**: For large objects such as terrains or gigantic structures/creatures, vertex painting helps you blend repetitive textures seamlessly. Adjusting vertex colors means that you can create smooth transitions between different textures (e.g., grass, dirt, or rocks) without needing detailed UV mapping. This will help you avoid tiling artifacts and give your terrain a more natural, varied look.

Now that we have seen how vertex painting can help you, let us step into the actual workflow. The following subsections will guide you through the technical steps of entering **Vertex Paint** mode and applying colors directly to your mesh.

Vertex Paint mode

Getting started with vertex painting is easy:

1. First, make sure you are in **Object Mode** and select the mesh you want to paint.

2. Go to the mode selection menu at the top of the Blender workspace and choose **Vertex Paint** mode.

   The **3D Viewport** is your canvas now, and you can paint directly on your model, as shown in *Figure 4.1*.

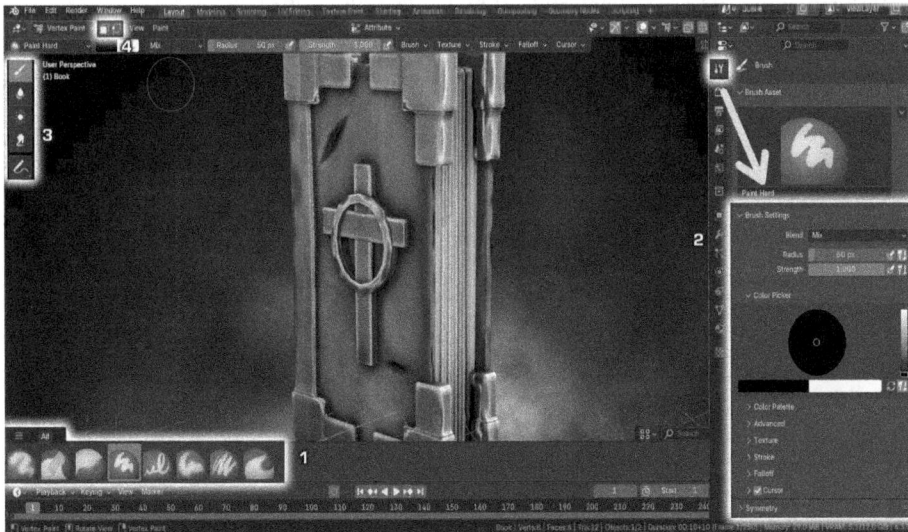

Figure 4.1: Vertex Paint mode in Blender using a book from Blender 20 Massive Stylized Fantasy Books Asset Pack by 3D Tudor

Figure 4.1 shows the following options:

- At the bottom, you will see a toolbar with different brushes and tools (highlight **1**), and on the right, the **Properties** panel lets you adjust brush settings and painting options (highlight **2**). Vertex painting is all about making the painting process smooth and intuitive.

> Tip
>
> If you do not see the vertex paint being applied, make sure you are in **Solid Material Preview** mode. Check that in **Viewport Shading**, the **Color Shading** option is set to the attribute in the shading options.

- The left-hand toolbar has several tools for painting, including **Draw**, **Blur**, **Average**, and **Smear** (highlight **3**).
- In the top-left corner, you will find **Select** options that allow you to mask parts of your model by vertex or face. Once one of these options is enabled, the **Select** bar appears next to it. You can then use tools such as **Box Select** (press *B*) or **Circle Select** (press *C*) for quick masking (highlight **4**).

Vertex colors

Vertex colors do more than just make your model look good. They can have a big impact on your mesh. First of all, they are great for **stylization**, an art style where you intentionally exaggerate or simplify how things look to create a whimsical feel, instead of trying to make it look realistic, like in *Figure 4.2*.

Figure 4.2: Stylized wizard's tower in Blender 4 Modeling and Geometry Node Workshop by
3D Tudor

Unlike normal colors, which are typically applied through textures or materials that cover the entire model, vertex colors are embedded directly into the vertices of the mesh. In game development or any stylized project, you can use vertex colors to give your model a distinctive look without getting into complicated texturing.

Using vertex colors does way more than just giving your models a cool, stylized vibe. For example, think of a massive forest scene in a game. You can color each tree's leaves at the vertex level instead of loading big texture files, which keeps everything running smoothly. If you want glowing runes on a sword or chipped paint on a robot's armor, you can quickly tweak the color on the fly without dealing with a bunch of separate textures. And when you want to really nail the lighting, such as by adding a soft glow around a magic orb, you can paint highlights right into the vertices so the whole thing looks extra polished and cinematic.

Starting to vertex paint in Blender is such an exciting step. It is like adding your splash of color to your 3D models. The best part? You get to color directly on your mesh, making the whole process straightforward and super effective. Let us prep your mesh for vertex painting.

Preparing your mesh

First things first, you have got to get your mesh ready. Think of it like preparing a canvas before you paint. Optimizing your mesh is key to making sure your colors look smooth and detailed:

1. Start by optimizing the geometry. The more vertices you have in the areas you want to paint, the smoother your color transitions will be. It is all about having enough points to work with, like in *Figure 4.3*.

2. Here, we are using **Paint** and then **Dirty Vertex Colors**. This generates a dirtmap gradient based on the cavity. *Figure 4.3* shows the effect that it has on a mesh based on its topology.

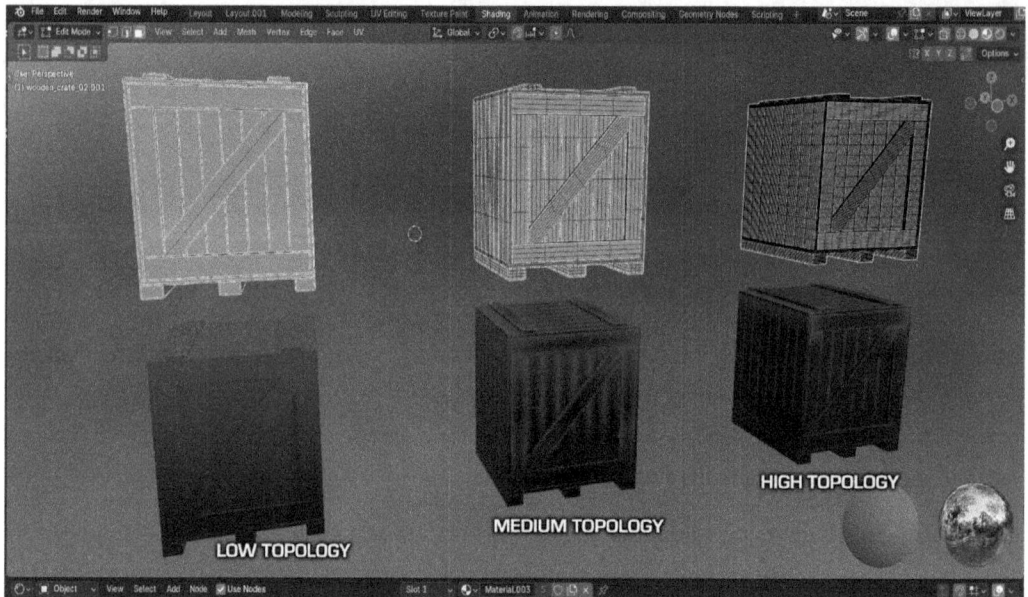

Figure 4.3: Density of mesh effects on Vertex Paint detail

3. Next, clean up your mesh. Get rid of any non-manifold edges or double vertices, like what you can see in *Figure 4.4*.

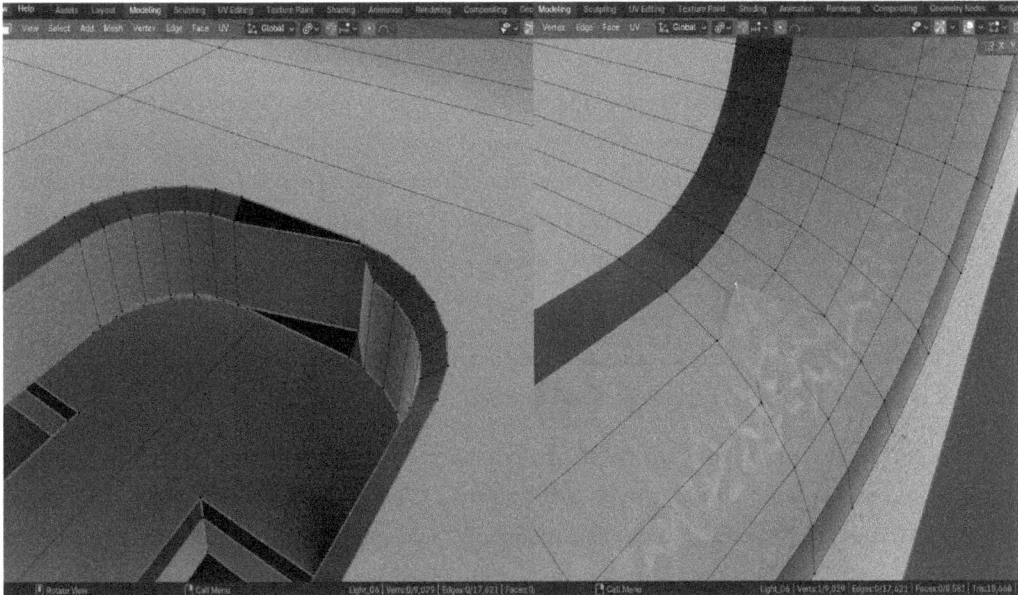

Figure 4.4: Non-manifold edges (left) and double vertices (right) examples

Blender's **Clean Up** tools are perfect for this, helping you fix any issues and giving you a clean slate to paint on. To access these tools in Blender, go to **Edit Mode** and select the mesh you want to clean up. Then, go to the **Mesh** menu, find the **Clean Up** submenu, and you will see several options, the most prominent ones being the following:

- **Merge by Distance** is useful for removing double vertices by merging them if they are within a specified distance from each other.

- **Delete Loose** can help remove edges or vertices that are not properly connected to the mesh.

- **Fill Holes** can automatically fill in small holes in your mesh, making sure there are no gaps that can disrupt your painting process.

- **Decimate Geometry** reduces the number of vertices and faces in a mesh, simplifying the geometry while preserving the overall shape.

> Tip
>
> When you are working on something that needs a lot of detail, try adding subdivisions. In Edit Mode, select a face, right-click, and choose Subdivide. If you are using Subdivision through a modifier, you need to make sure it gets applied; otherwise, the vertices will not be made use of, and Subdivision Modifier will simply blur the setup.

4. Last but not least, do not forget to apply scale and rotation. Just hop into **Object Mode**, hit *Ctrl + A*, and apply the scale and rotation.

This is super important to avoid any weird brush behavior, you want to make your brush behave in a consistent and predictable way as you are painting. When a mesh has been scaled or rotated in **Object Mode**, these transformations can affect how tools and brushes interact with the surface. By applying scale and rotation, you reset these transformations and make sure that the mesh's geometry is accurately represented.

Basic vertex painting techniques

To set up **Vertex Paint** in a material shader in Blender, switch to **Shader Editor** and add a **Color Attribute** node. Then, connect the output of the **Color Attribute** node's **Color** socket to **Base Color** of your material's **Principled BSDF** or other shader. This means that **Vertex Paint** will influence the material.

Now comes the fun part—adding color! To get started, in **Vertex Paint** mode, pick a color from the color picker, like in *Figure 4.5*.

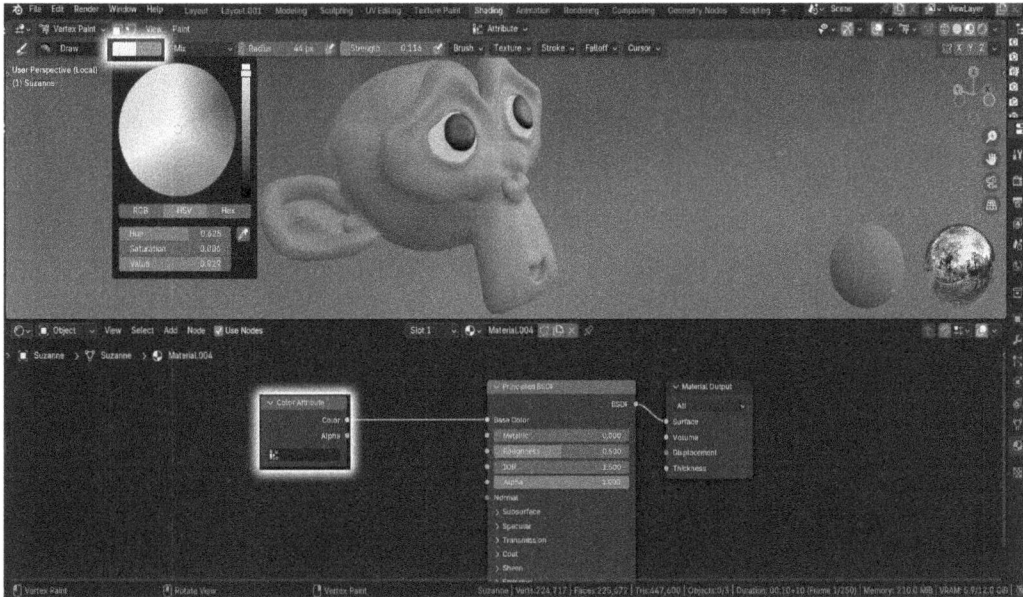

Figure 4.5: Picking a color from Blender's color picker

This will be your starting color. Now, begin painting by clicking and dragging your brush across the mesh. The vertices under your brush will take on the color you have selected, and you will see your model start to come to life.

Tip

If you do not see any color while painting in **Vertex Paint** mode, double-check that the name in your **Color Attribute** node matches the name of your vertex color data. By default, it is set to **Attribute**. Also, if you have never entered **Vertex Paint** mode for a mesh before, it will not have any vertex paint data created by default, so make sure to enter **Vertex Paint** mode at least once to generate it.

Here are some basic techniques to help you get the most out of vertex painting. All these options can be found at the top left of your screen, except for **Symmetry** painting:

- **Brush Size and Strength**: The **Brush** tool is your main way of applying color in **Vertex Paint** mode. Getting comfortable with its settings is key to creating awesome effects.

  Adjust the brush **Size** and **Strength** settings to control how much color is applied and how it spreads across the vertices. Use a larger brush for broad areas and a smaller one for precise details. The **Strength** setting determines the opacity of the color, which can help with blending and layering colors. Higher strength means bolder colors, while lower strength allows for softer blending.

- **Blending colors**: Practice blending colors by gradually changing the color as you paint. Start with a base color, then pick a slightly different color and paint over the edges. This creates smooth transitions and gradients, which are useful for adding depth and realism.

- **Using the blur brush**: The **Blur** brush can help soften the transitions between colors. After applying your base colors, use the **Blur** brush to smooth out harsh lines and create a more natural look.

- **Layering colors**: Build up layers of color to create more complex and interesting effects. Start with a base color, then add additional colors on top by switching to blending mode. By default, this is set to **Mix**, but you can change it to **Screen** to create highlights or to **Multiply** to create shadows. Finally, using **Overlay** is great for adding more detail and texture to your model, and it is very similar to using the **Strength** option.

- **Symmetry painting**: If your model is symmetrical, enable **Symmetry** painting (located at the top right of these options) to apply color to both sides of the model at the same time.

Another great way to get the hang of it is to practice with simple shapes or patterns. Try painting some stripes or dots. This will help you understand how colors blend between vertices and how to achieve the effects you want.

You could also explore other techniques beyond the basics, and if you are unsure how to use them, look up tutorials or guides online for step-by-step instructions.

- **Gradient painting**: Use the **Gradient** tool to create transitions of color over larger areas of your model. This is particularly useful for backgrounds or large surfaces where you want a seamless color shift.

- **Using masks**: Create vertex groups to mask off areas of your model. This allows you to paint specific parts without affecting the rest, giving you more control over detailed sections.

- **Texture stencils**: Use the **Texture** tab to apply detailed patterns and textures directly onto your mesh.

By mastering these additional techniques, you will be able to add even more depth and personality to your models, making your vertex painting skills truly stand out. As you get into vertex painting, think about how these two groups of techniques can bring out your models' personalities. The **Brush** tool will be your first choice when it comes to texturing. Whether you are adding subtle shadows to a character's face or creating eye-catching patterns on an object, vertex painting has you covered. As you become more comfortable with the basics, you can start exploring more advanced techniques.

Vertex painting project examples

Here are a couple of fun project ideas to get you started:

- Add glowing accents or extra details to a PBR textured sign, like in *Figure 4.6*.

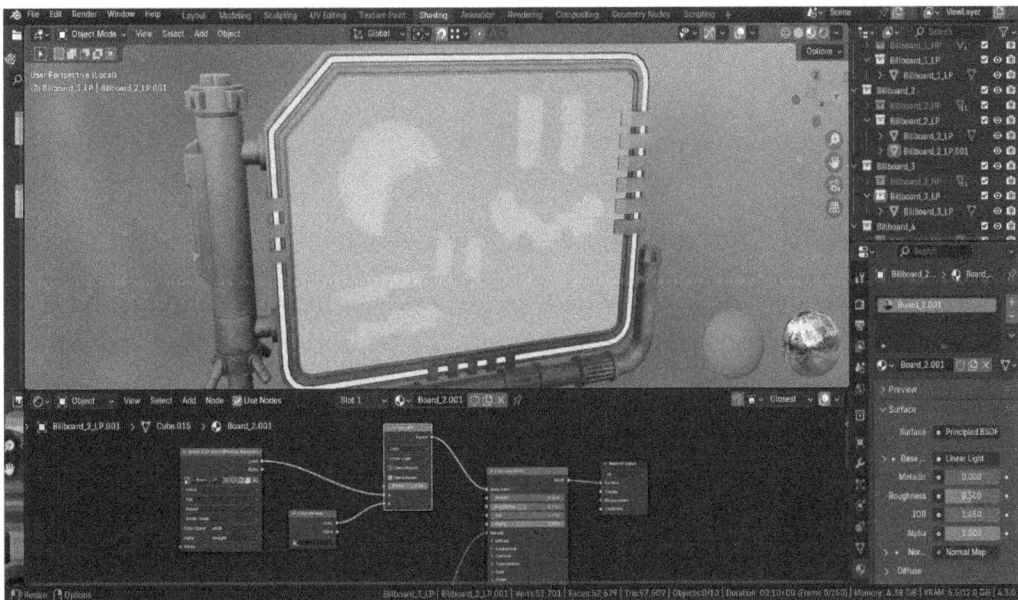

Figure 4.6: PBR textured sign example

- You can try using vertex painting along with a **Color Mix** node on your main color. This lets you experiment and change things up without messing up the original design. It is non-destructive, so you can explore different looks and keep the main design safe!

- Model some fantasy props such as magical stones, enchanted trees, or whimsical houses. Use blending modes to create interesting effects such as glowing edges or mystical patterns. Paint them with bright, bold colors to give them a magical feel, like the stylized well in *Figure 4.7.*

Figure 4.7: Medieval well in Stylized Environments with Blender 4 Geometry Nodes by 3D Tudor

Apply vertex colors to these models. For a tree, you could paint different shades of green on the leaves and various browns on the trunk. This helps in creating vibrant and cohesive scenes without needing detailed textures.

Get creative and have fun experimenting with vertex painting in Blender! It is a great way to add personality and style to your models.

Exploring advanced vertex painting techniques

If you are ready to take your vertex painting skills to the next level, you have come to the right place because we are about to explore advanced techniques. We are talking about **Shader Editor**, smooth color transitions and gradients, using vertex colors for soft selection editing, and applying dynamic effects in real-time applications such as games.

Shader Editor

Vertex colors can be your best friend for shading effects and blending materials. Imagine having a character where you want to blend the skin into the clothing seamlessly. By using vertex colors in **Shader Editor**, you can mix different materials based on the painted vertex colors, making the transition look natural without juggling a bunch of textures. You can also use vertex colors to add environmental effects such as mud or rust. Just paint the vertices where you want the effect, and let the shader handle the rest, making your model look more realistic, like in *Figure 4.8*.

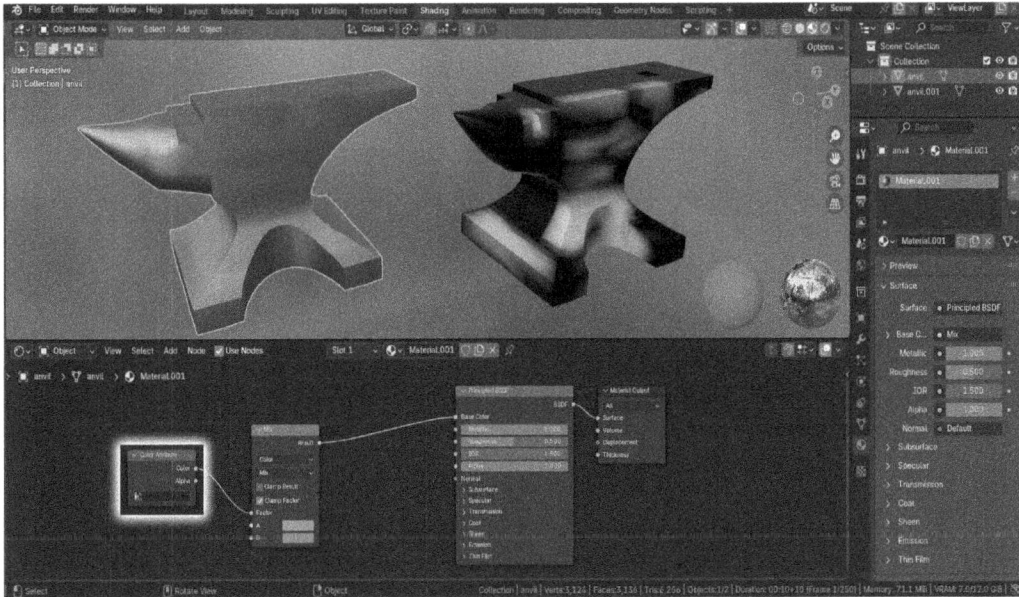

Figure 4.8: Rust effect achieved with vertex painting on an anvil

For efficient vertex painting, here are some tips to keep in mind. Think of it like traditional digital painting. Even though Blender does not support layers directly in vertex painting, you can create multiple vertex color sets and blend them in **Shader Editor**, mimicking a layered approach. Custom brushes are another big help. Adjust the settings of your brushes, such as **Strength** and **Falloff**, to suit the task, and save these custom settings for future projects. Keep a consistent color palette across your project to ensure a uniform look, especially when working with a team. Blender's palette tool can save and reuse specific colors, making this much easier. Do not forget about mirroring. For symmetrical models, using Blender's mirroring options lets you paint both sides at once, saving time and helping you make sure everything is symmetrical.

Color blending, gradients, and weights

You should try creating smooth color transitions and gradients with vertex painting:

1. Start by painting your base color on the area you want to work on.

2. Then, gradually introduce new colors by painting over the edges of the previous color with a slightly different shade.

3. Using a low-strength brush setting helps to gently blend the new color into the existing one, creating a nice gradient effect like in *Figure 4.9*. Here, we have used **Strength** of **0.300**.

Figure 4.9: Color blending and gradients in Blender

Another technique is weighted vertex painting, where you control the intensity of color application with the pressure of your brush strokes. To try out weighted texture painting, do the following:

1. Adjust your brush pressure sensitivity (provided that you have a graphic drawing tablet). In the **Brush** settings, enable pressure sensitivity if you have a pressure-sensitive tablet.

2. Begin with lighter strokes for a base layer of color.

3. Gradually increase the pressure to add darker shades and more intense colors. This allows for a smooth gradient effect, but you can only follow these steps if you have a graphic drawing tablet.

4. Experiment with different brush blending modes such as **Mix**, **Darken**, and **Lighten** to achieve unique gradients and control how the colors merge on your mesh.

> Note
>
> You can skip steps 1 and 3 if you do not have a graphic drawing tablet. It is also worth mentioning that vertex painting resolution is tied directly to vertex count. A low-poly mesh will only allow for broad, blocky swathes of color, while a dense mesh gives you the freedom to add subtle gradients and precise detail exactly where you want them. In short: more vertices = more paint control.

Sharp coloring

If you have ever noticed your vertex colors looking a bit blurred, especially at the boundaries between different parts of your model, it is because of higher mesh density.

Even with dense topology, vertex painting cannot produce perfectly sharp edges between colors. Transitions will always be somewhat blended. To achieve a crisp separation, the mesh itself must be physically split at the color boundary you choose. So, vertex painting shines when you want something quick and stylized, or when you are knocking out a prototype and need color fast without fussing over UVs.

For example, imagine a character's arm ending where a sleeve begins. Splitting at that boundary forces a crisp color change. At the same time, you avoid that unwanted blending you get when all the faces are connected.

Here is a simple workflow to make those transitions pop:

1. Select your object and press *Tab* to switch from **Object Mode** to **Edit Mode**.
2. Press *3* on your keyboard to enter **Face Select** mode. Pick the faces where you want sharper color boundaries.
3. Press *Y* to split those faces from the rest of the mesh. This effectively creates a hard edge, giving you a separate "island" where you can control color transitions with precision.
4. Hover your mouse over the newly separated faces. Press *L* to select all connected faces on that island.
5. Press *Tab* again to switch back to **Object Mode**.
6. With the object still selected, choose **Vertex Paint** from the **Mode** dropdown at the top left of the **3D Viewport**.

7. In **Vertex Paint** mode, click **Face Selection Masking** (cube icon) at the top of your **3D Viewport**. This confines your painting to whichever faces (or islands) you select.

8. Pick your color and paint on the selected island. Notice how the transition stays sharp where you split the mesh, like in *Figure 4.10*.

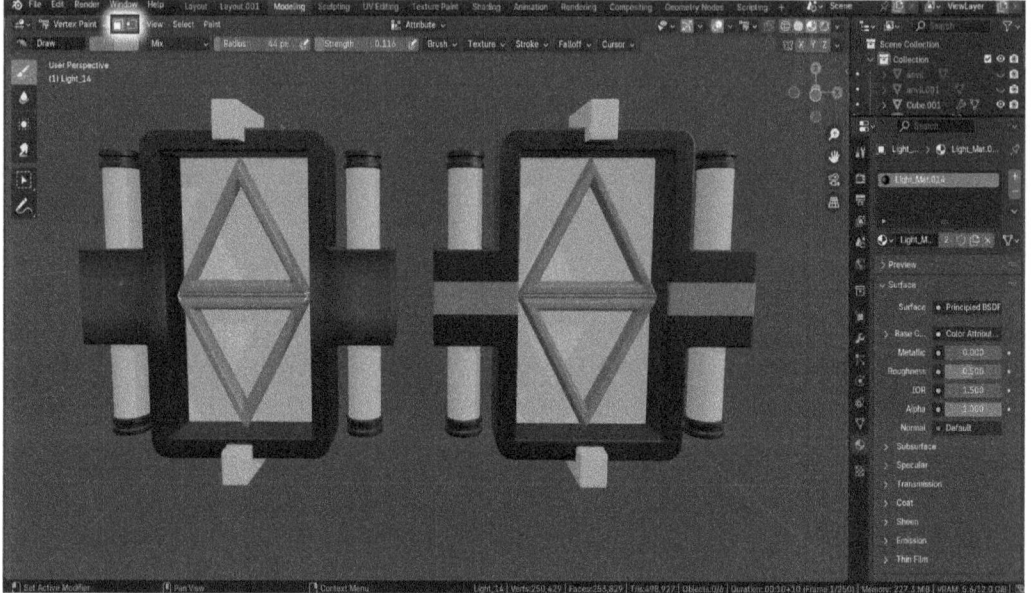

Figure 4.10: Split mesh into multiple pieces before (left) and after (right) following steps 1-8

That is all there is to it! Splitting up your mesh like this gives you greater control over where your colors blend, so you can say goodbye to muddy edges and hello to crisp, clean color boundaries. Have fun painting!

Using vertex painting for material blending (especially on large terrain)

Sure, weight painting is often the go-to for physics or VFX, but there is another vertex painting trick we have not explored yet: material blending using vertex colors. This method is fantastic for large-scale objects, think terrains, cliffs, or any environment piece that needs smooth transitions between different materials (such as grass, dirt, or rock). The cherry on the cake is that it helps keep things light and efficient, without juggling tons of texture maps.

Ready to give it a go? Here's how:

1. Start by modeling or sculpting your terrain (using **Sculpt** mode if needed).

2. Once your terrain's shape looks good, switch to **Vertex Paint** mode from the dropdown at the top left of your **3D Viewport.**

3. Pick a color for each material you want to blend. You can do that using an **RGB** (i.e., **Red, Green, Blue**) pallet, where each color can act as an individual alpha mask. You could pick maybe green for grass, brown for dirt, gray for rock, and so on.

4. Paint these colors using **RGB** (as highlighted in *Figure 4.11*), where you want each material to appear. These will act as masks later on. For example, set **Blue** to 1 and all other colors to 0. This will allow you to treat it as a shader mask.

5. Open **Shader Editor**, create a new material, and add a **BSDF Shader** for each material (e.g., grass, dirt, rock).

6. Drop in a **Mix Shader** node to blend between two of the shaders.

7. The **Factor (fac)** input will determine how the colors are mixed. Here is where we can use **Vertex Paint** as a mask.

8. Add an **Attribute** node and type in the name of your vertex color layer (usually **Attribute** by default). Then, create a separate **Color** node to break the color into three separate masks of **RGB.**

9. Connect the **Separate Color Blue** node output to the **Fac** input of the **Mix Shader** node. Your vertex colors are now blue, and they control where each material appears, like in *Figure 4.11*!

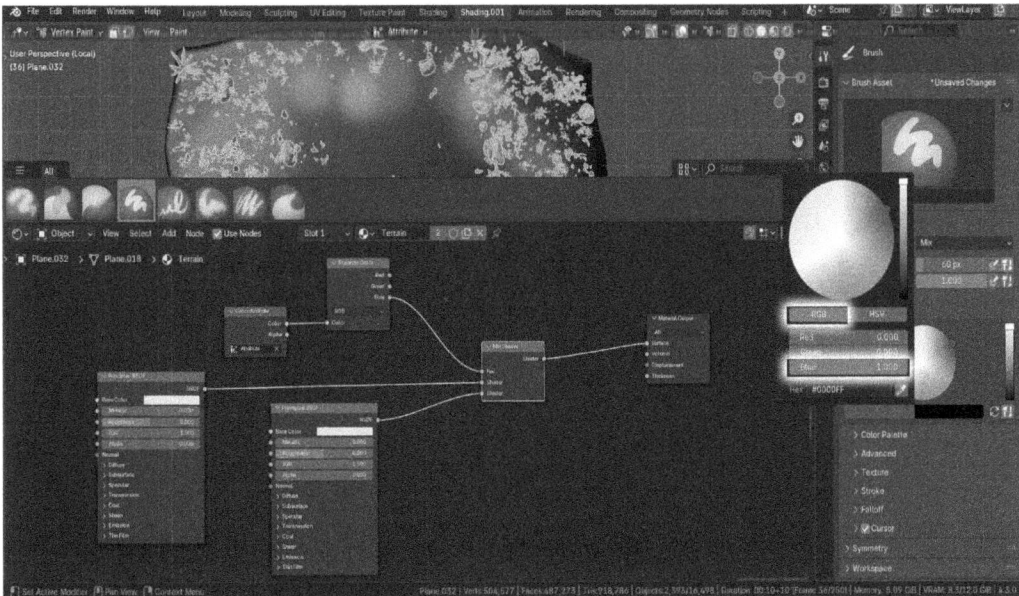

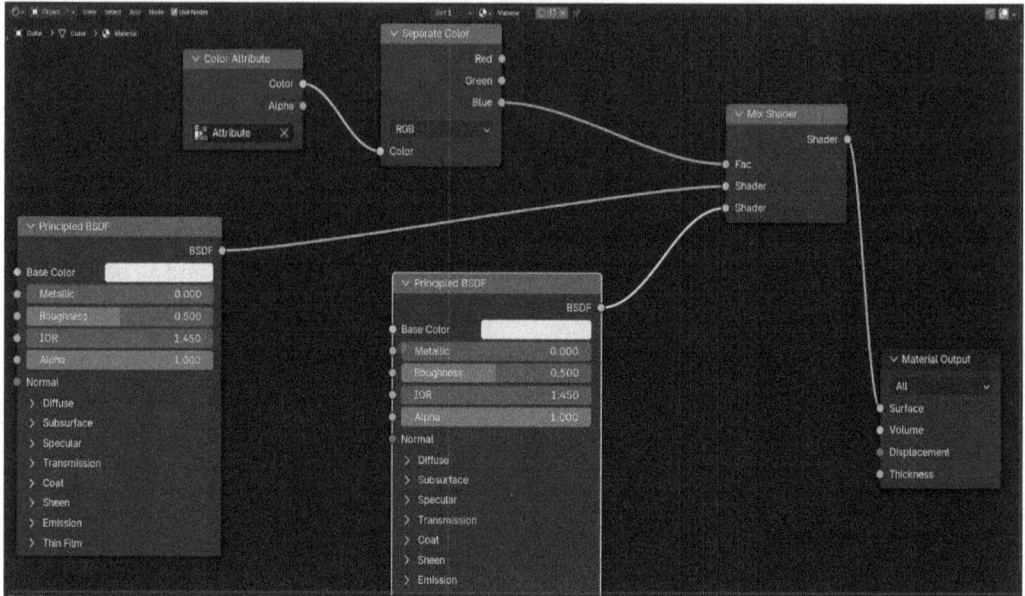

Figure 4.11: Using vertex painting for material blending steps 1-9

10. If you have more than two materials, keep adding **Mix Shader** nodes. Use different channels (or paint different vertex color layers) to control each blend.

11. Finally, fine-tune everything by tweaking your vertex painting and shader settings. The more precisely you paint, the cleaner your material transitions will be.

That is all there is to it! In *Figure 4.12*, you can see the result of following these steps: the method of blending multiple principled shaders with PBR textures.

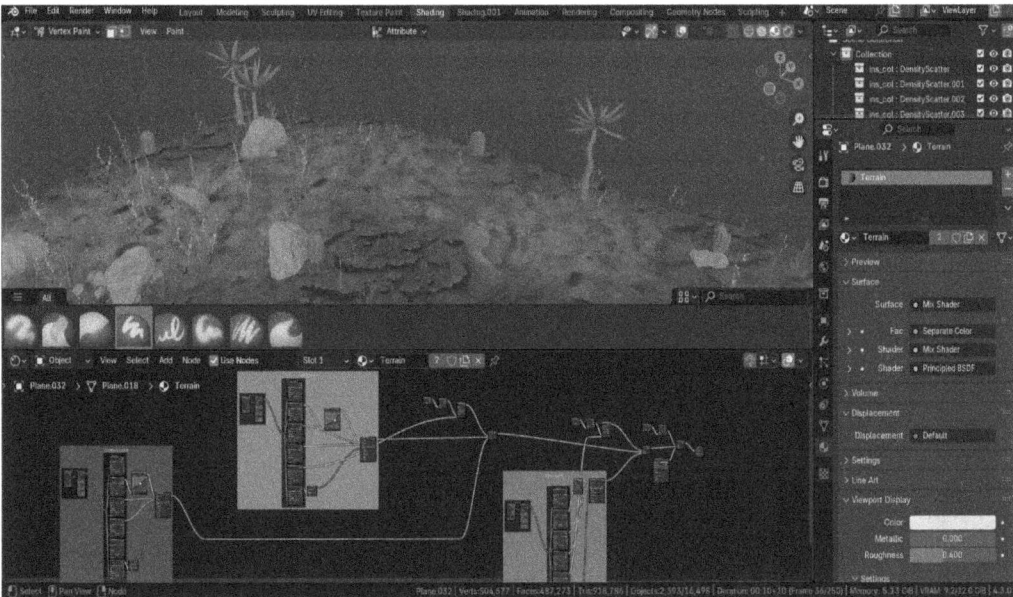

Figure 4.12: Using vertex painting for material blending – the final result

By harnessing vertex colors in this way, you will have a lightweight, versatile tool for blending materials across large assets or terrains, no heavy texture painting needed. Give it a try and see how much easier it makes your environment work!

In the next section, we will explore the practical applications of vertex painting in various scenarios. From enhancing low-poly art by simulating **Ambient Occlusion** to creating detailed textures without relying on heavy texture files, we will dive into how vertex painting can add depth and realism to your projects, while making them quicker to make.

Practical applications of vertex painting

Vertex painting in Blender is a specialized and versatile technique for various technical scenarios where you create detailed textures and shade directly on the model. Put simply, you might want to do that if you need to enhance the visual depth and realism of your model without relying on heavy textures. Let us dive into some of these practical applications.

Low-poly art

Low-poly art is known for being minimal and simple, and it benefits immensely from vertex painting. This style often skips detailed textures in favor of flat colors and subtle gradients. Vertex painting works great with this style because it lets you add bright colors or soft shading right onto the points of your low-poly models. This way, you make them look better without needing complicated textures. Like this, you boost their visual appeal without needing complex textures.

As if that were not enough, vertex painting also cuts down on the need for **UV mapping** and texture creation. For example, if you were making a low-poly art version of a mushroom, you could use vertex painting to add different shades of green and brown to the cap and stem, improving your mushroom's appearance with smooth gradients and highlights, like in *Figure 4.13*.

Figure 4.13: "Blender 20 x stylized mushrooms Massive Pack Blender 3 in ZBrush and Substance Painter" by 3D Tudor

It is simple; remember how we talked about vertex colors pulling double duty as masks? Here is where that really pays off. Instead of repainting masks in every bit of software you touch, you can bake your vertex colors into an ID map and send that straight into *Substance Painter* (see *Chapter 3* in *Part 2*), *Mari*, *Unreal*, or even **Cycles**. Export it as an FBX, and Blender kindly carries those colors across as a color ID map. Suddenly, you are not spending hours re-masking every metal plate or leather strap, you have already done the hard part in Blender. *Figure 4.13* shows how this little trick can save you a mountain of time (and keep you from wanting to launch your stylus across the room).

Here is how you do it:

1. Go into **Vertex Paint** mode and color different areas of your model. Each color basically marks where you will want different materials in *Substance Painter*: metal, plastic, or fabric.

2. Once you are done painting, make sure to save the vertex colors when you export (usually as FBX or OBJ).

> Note
>
> In Blender 4.0+, the export option label may differ depending on the format, for example, in FBX it appears as **Vertex Colors**, while in OBJ it may simply be listed as **Colors**. Be sure to enable this so your **Vertex Paint** data is included in the exported file.

3. Bring that model into *Substance Painter*. Bake your mesh maps to turn the vertex colors into an ID map that *Substance Painter* recognizes.

4. Now you can apply materials or textures just to those colored parts by creating a mask linked to the ID map. This means you do not have to manually mask every little section, which is a huge timesaver, especially for complex models.

Note

When using vertex painting for real-time projects (such as *Unity* or *Unreal*), keep in mind that too much vertex color detail on dense meshes can slow rendering. Use it wisely, especially on large environments. About exporting: vertex color data is preserved in most common formats (FBX, GLTF), but always check your engine's import settings to ensure the colors display correctly. Finally, if you see artifacts (such as blotchy shading), double-check your normals and make sure the mesh has enough vertex density to carry smooth color gradients.

To wrap it up, this workflow keeps your texturing process organized and cuts down on repetitive tasks. For example, if you are painting a sci-fi helmet with metal, rubber, and glass parts, a quick vertex color setup will let you jump straight into targeted material application in *Substance Painter* without tedious masking. It is a simple trick that can save you a ton of time!

Ambient occlusion using vertex baking

Ambient occlusion adds depth and realism to 3D models by highlighting crevices where objects meet, adding a natural look. In a few words, ambient occlusion mimics the way light behaves in the real world, boosting the overall visual quality of your work.

Vertex painting offers a manual approach to ambient occlusion, saving you the hassle of texture baking. If you carefully paint darker colors in areas that naturally receive less light, such as under arms, between fingers, or at the base of objects, you can simulate ambient occlusion directly on your model.

Doing it this way, you will have a lot of control over the shading, letting you make subtle adjustments more easily. On the other hand, if you are working on real-time applications where traditional ambient occlusion textures might be too resource-intensive, you can use vertex colors to simulate these effects as an efficient alternative.

As a visual example, imagine a low-poly dungeon scene with pillars and stone walls, like in *Figure 4.14.*

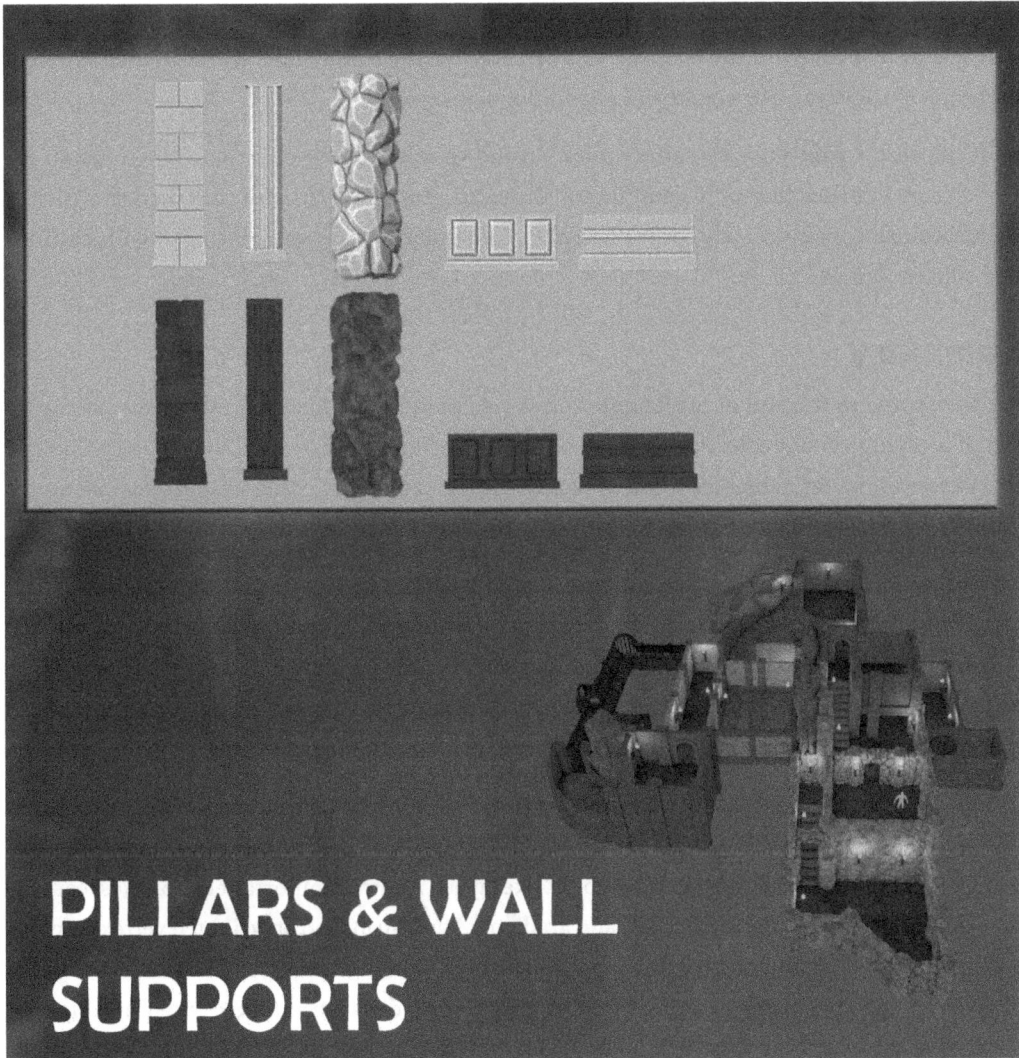

Figure 4.14: Dungeon scene pillars and walls in "Blender 3 to Unreal Engine 5 Dungeon Modular Kitbash" by 3D Tudor

In low-poly art, you can use vertex painting to simulate depth as if you had used **Ambient Occlusion**. This connection is important because low-poly art often requires efficient techniques to maintain performance while achieving a polished look. Vertex painting will allow you to add shadows and depth to the crevices between the stones and the bases of the pillars, enhancing the overall realism of the scene. This technique simulates ambient occlusion, which naturally occurs where light is less likely to reach, such as in the cracks and corners of the dungeon. By manually painting darker colors in these areas, you can achieve the same effect as traditional ambient occlusion without the extra overhead of additional textures.

All in all, vertex painting's versatility goes beyond simple color application. Whether you are working on a stylized low-poly game, manually enhancing the realism of your models with **Ambient Occlusion**, or intricately controlling physics simulations, vertex painting provides a direct and efficient way.

Summary

We have come to the end of our chapter on vertex painting in Blender. Starting from the basics of applying vibrant colors directly to your mesh, we moved through to mastering advanced techniques for material blending and dynamic effects. Remember when we talked about vertex painting being like finger painting for grown-up digital artists? It is just as fun as it sounds.

Instead of wrestling with UV maps and textures, vertex painting lets you dive right into the mesh, coloring individual vertices. It is direct and intuitive, and can give your work a hands-on, organic feel. For projects such as low-poly art, it can give your models a stylish, simplified color scheme without the hassle of creating detailed textures. And if you are into game development, vertex painting is perfect for creating VFX such as fiery explosions or magical auras.

One of the coolest things we covered is how you can bake **Ambient Occlusion** effects using vertex colors. We also talked about some handy tips for making vertex painting easier. For example, you can create multiple sets of vertex colors to act like layers. Another important lesson was learning how to create smooth color transitions and gradients. We also looked at weighted vertex painting, where you control the intensity of color application and brush stroke pressure, and at the end of the chapter, we experimented with different brush blending modes such as **Mix**, **Darken**, and **Lighten**.

Forgetting about the technical stuff, vertex painting is really exciting because each project is an opportunity to experiment, refine your skills, and discover new applications. Let trial and error become part of the process.

Speaking of bringing your creations to life, get ready for a not-so-nervous jump into rendering in Blender. This is where your models truly come alive with realistic lighting, shadows, and textures. Let's take your 3D scenes from raw meshes to stunning images.

Further reading

- Curious about how vertex colors can take your stylized creations to new heights? Here are a few resources to inspire you:

- Want to see a whimsical wizard's tower in action? *Blender 4 Modeling and Geometry Node Workshop* (`https://www.udemy.com/course/blender-4-modeling/?referralCode=2E CBF4BA115166314468`) shows off a vibrant approach to Blender modeling, with a heavy focus on stylization and bold color choices. Perfect if you are going for that charming, fantasy-inspired look.

- Ever dreamed of painting magical wells or other fantasy props? *Stylized Environments with Blender 4 Geometry Nodes* (`https://www.udemy.com/course/stylized-3d-environments-with-blender-4-geometry-nodes/?referralCode=315F0878C0DB5CB5B5AA`) offers a hands-on guide for blending modes, glowing edges, and mystical patterns.

- If you are into creating low-poly mushrooms with smooth gradients and highlights, *Blender 20 x Stylized Mushrooms Massive Pack* (`https://3dtudor.gumroad.com/l/stylized-mushrooms-blender`) has you covered. It can help you understand how vertex painting can enhance subtle details.

- Want to keep things stylized yet performance-friendly? *Blender 3 to Unreal Engine 5 Dungeon Modular Kitbash* (`https://3dtudor.gumroad.com/l/ivmzy`) focuses on low-poly dungeon scenes, complete with pillars and stone walls. It demonstrates how vertex colors can mimic effects such as **Ambient Occlusion** without the overhead of large texture maps.

Subscribe to Game Dev Assembly!

We are excited to introduce **Game Dev Assembly**, our brand-new newsletter dedicated to everything game development. Whether you're coding, designing, animating, or managing a studio, we've got insights, trends, and expert advice to help you create, innovate, and thrive. Sign up now and get exciting benefits.

`https://packt.link/gamedev-newsletter`

Join the 3D Tudor Channel Discord Server!

Join the 3D Tudor Channel Discord Server, a creative hub for learning Blender, Unreal Engine, Substance Painter, and 3D modeling, for discussions with the authors and other readers:

https://discord.gg/5EkjT36vUj

5

Introducing Blender's Rendering Engines: A Comprehensive Exploration

I am not embarrassed to tell you that I was excited about starting this chapter. Diving into Blender's rendering engines is like starting the final level of a game where you get to meet the final boss. We will go over Blender's main engines: **Cycles**, **EEVEE**, and **Workbench**.

First up is **Cycles**. Even though it is on the old side as far as Blender updates go, it still goes strong. Cycles is known for creating super-realistic images because it uses a physically based, unbiased path-tracing algorithm. It is great at simulating real-world lighting and materials.

Then there is **EEVEE**, which takes a different approach. It focuses on speed and real-time rendering. EEVEE is perfect for when you need quick previews and fast changes, such as in animation and visual effects projects. It gives you fast, approximate previews of your scenes. Even though EEVEE is focused on speed, it still produces impressive results with features such as screen-space reflections, **Ambient Occlusion (AO)**, and volumetric lighting.

Last but not least, we have the **Workbench** renderer. It is often overlooked, but it is super handy for specific tasks. Blender's Workbench renderer is all about speed and simplicity. This makes it ideal for modeling, layout, and technical visualization.

By getting to know the strengths and weaknesses of Cycles, EEVEE, and the Workbench renderer, you will be able to make smart choices. This chapter will help you confidently navigate Blender's rendering options and do more with what you can already do. I will be there with you from setting up your first render to fine-tuning the final output.

So, in this chapter, we will cover the following topics:

- Understanding Blender's render engines
- Mastering Cycles: A comprehensive guide
- Mastering EEVEE: A comprehensive guide
- Exploring the Workbench renderer

Technical requirements

As for **Blender 4.5 LTS (Long-Term Support)**, the general requirements include a macOS 11.2 or newer (Apple Silicon supported natively) operating system, or a Linux (64-bit, glibc 2.28 or newer) operating system. Blender now requires a CPU with the SSE4.2 instruction set, at least 8 GB of RAM (32 GB recommended for heavy scenes), and a GPU supporting OpenGL 4.3 with a minimum of 2 GB of VRAM.

For a full list of technical requirements, please refer back to *Chapter 1* of this part.

Understanding Blender's render engines

Blender is an amazing tool for working in 3D space. As you read in this chapter's introduction, it comes with three different rendering engines. Knowing the ins and outs of Cycles, EEVEE, and the Workbench renderer will really help you get the most out of your projects. Let us break them down and see what makes each one special.

Cycles versus EEVEE versus Workbench

Cycles is Blender's ray-tracing render engine, and it is all about realism and detail. When you are using ray tracing, you can imagine that each pixel sends out a little ray of light into the scene, and that ray travels until it hits something, such as a wall or a tree. Then, depending on what it hits, the ray might bounce off, change direction, or even split into more rays. Eventually, these rays gather information about the color and brightness of the pixels they hit, helping to create the final image you see on your screen.

> **Note**
>
> Cycles simulates how light interacts with objects in a very accurate way, which makes it perfect for projects that need to look super realistic. Think architectural visualizations, product design, and detailed character renders. Cycles is great at generating rich detail, accurate shadows, and complex lighting effects, such as caustics and **Global Illumination (GI)**. The downside? It takes longer to render, especially for scenes with lots of light and material complexity.

EEVEE is Blender's real-time render engine, which means it is designed to be fast while still looking good. It uses a different method than Cycles, which makes rendering quicker, called **rasterization** (converting 3D models into a 2D image by approximating how surfaces and textures are displayed). This is great for animation and interactive projects where you need to see changes quickly. EEVEE supports many advanced lighting and shading features found in Cycles, such as reflections, AO, and volumetrics, but with some approximations.

Workbench is the simplest of the three and is focused on speed and ease of use. It is not about advanced lighting or shading. Blender's Workbench is focused on functionality with a clear and customizable viewport for tasks such as modeling, texturing, and layout. It offers various shading modes, such as **Flat**, **Studio**, and **Matcap**, which are very useful for technical visualization and quick previews. In a few words, I would say that Workbench is your go-to during the early stages of creation or for projects that do not need complex lighting and materials.

Choosing the right engine for your project

Picking the right rendering engine is key to getting your project done efficiently and with the quality you need. Here is what you should think about:

- **Project requirements**: Look at what your project needs in terms of how visually accurate you need to be:

  - If you need photorealism, go with Cycles
  - If you need speed and interactivity, EEVEE is great
  - Workbench is perfect for quick previews and technical visualizations

- **Render time versus quality**: Think about the balance between how long it takes to render and the quality of the image:

    - Cycles gives the best quality but takes the longest.

    - EEVEE is a middle ground with faster render times and good quality.

    - Workbench is the fastest, ideal for real-time feedback during modeling and layout.

- **Hardware resources**: Consider what kind of hardware (especially graphics card) you have:

    - Cycles can use both **Central Processing Unit (CPU)** and **Graphics Processing Unit (GPU)** rendering, supporting **CUDA**, **OpenCL**, and **OptiX**, parallel computing platforms and APIs used for utilizing the power of GPUs, which makes it versatile for different setups.

    - EEVEE has real-time capabilities, which need a powerful GPU to run smoothly, for example.

    - Workbench is optimized for fast rendering of scenes in the 3D Viewport, requiring relatively low hardware resources compared to Cycles and EEVEE, making it better for quick previews and less powerful setups.

By understanding each rendering engine's strengths and limitations, you can choose the one that best fits your project's goals, your workflow, and your hardware. Now, let us look at Cycles in more detail.

Getting started with GPU rendering in Blender

As we talked about earlier in this chapter, Blender's rendering engines, Cycles and EEVEE, let you choose between rendering with the CPU or GPU. This guide will help you understand the benefits of GPU rendering and how to set up Blender to use your graphics card for faster and more efficient renders.

GPU rendering has several advantages over CPU rendering. A typical GPU can handle many tasks at once, making it perfect for rendering because it is a demanding process. Both Cycles and EEVEE benefit from GPU rendering, with Cycles seeing the biggest speed improvements because of its ray-tracing nature.

Note

There are times when CPU rendering is still useful, such as when your scene uses more memory than your GPU has, or when using features that are not fully optimized for the GPU. A CPU can handle data more flexibly, making it a good choice for scenes with lots of geometry or very high-resolution textures.

To set up Blender for GPU rendering, start by opening Blender and going to **Edit** and then **Preferences**. In the **System** tab, you will find options for **CUDA**, **OpenCL**, and **OptiX**, depending on what kind of graphics card you have:

- **CUDA** is used for NVIDIA graphics cards and provides stable and fast rendering with good support for various features.

- **OpenCL** is designed for AMD graphics cards, but while support has improved, some features might not be as optimized as with CUDA.

- **OptiX**, also for NVIDIA cards, uses RTX technology for even faster ray-tracing performance, which is especially beneficial in Cycles for scenes with complex lighting and reflections.

All in all, managing **Video RAM (VRAM)** usage is crucial. High-resolution textures and complex models can quickly use up VRAM, so it is a good idea to use lower-resolution textures for background objects and simplify your models where possible. Blender's **Simplify** option can also help reduce VRAM usage without damaging your visual quality too much.

Tip

If you are rendering animations, consider rendering smaller batches of frames instead of the entire sequence at once. This can help manage VRAM usage and make it easier to restart or troubleshoot if something goes wrong.

GPU rendering can be demanding on your hardware, so use software to monitor your GPU temperature and make sure your system is well cooled to prevent overheating, which can reduce performance or damage your hardware.

For example, imagine you are working on a detailed scene of a medieval village. With GPU rendering, you can quickly see the effects of changes in lighting as you adjust the torches lining the cobblestone streets or the flickering candles inside a grand hall. By leveraging the power of your GPU, you can bring these medieval scenes to life with greater speed and detail.

While CPU rendering still has its place, especially for memory-intensive scenes, setting up Blender for GPU rendering is the way to go. Update your graphics drivers, manage VRAM usage effectively, and monitor your hardware to prevent overheating.

Mastering Cycles: A comprehensive guide

Cycles is renowned for its ability to produce stunningly realistic renders, thanks to Blender's physically based ray tracing engine. This section sets the stage for an in-depth exploration of all Cycles render properties, helping you understand how to optimize your workflow and achieve high-quality results. I will talk you through practical tips that can help you get there, whether you are a beginner looking to understand the basics or an advanced user looking to fine-tune your render settings. We will talk about sampling, adaptive sampling, **Noise Threshold**, and light paths. For each of those, you will learn how your settings can influence render quality and performance.

Sampling in Cycles: Enhancing image quality and efficiency

Sampling determines the clarity and quality of your final rendered image. This involves calculating the path of light rays and their interaction with surfaces. Generally, the more samples you use, the more accurate and less noisy your image will be. But there is a catch: more **samples** also mean longer render times, so you have to find the right balance between image quality and efficiency.

Render **samples** determine the number of light path calculations for the final render, and you can easily adjust them with a slider, as shown in *Figure 5.1*.

Figure 5.1: Cycles samples slider in Blender

Higher sample counts reduce noise, resulting in cleaner images, but they also increase render times. The optimal sample rate really depends on how complex your scene is and how much detail you want.

On the other hand, viewport samples control the sample count for the viewport's rendered preview. By keeping viewport samples lower, you can speed up interactive previews without affecting the final render quality.

This lets you have a smoother workflow when setting up scenes and tweaking materials. For example, for a bubbling cauldron with steam and liquid effects, using lower viewport samples will let you quickly adjust the bubbles, steam, and lighting without long wait times. Viewport samples will ensure you can rapidly see changes and make necessary tweaks to achieve the perfect look and feel for your bubbling cauldron scene.

Adaptive sampling is another cool feature in Cycles that helps optimize render times without sacrificing image quality. It adjusts the number of samples based on the complexity of different areas within your scene, as *Figure 5.2* shows.

Figure 5.2: Viewport samples in Blender in Blender 4: The Modular and Kitbash Environment Guide by 3D Tudor

Areas with little to no noise can get away with fewer samples, while more complex areas with intricate lighting and materials need more sampling attention.

When you render in Cycles, noise is just part of the deal. Ray tracing is all about bouncing light around realistically, and with complex lighting, you are bound to get some grain. Cranking up sample counts will eventually clean it up, but at the cost of time (and probably your sanity). That is where the denoiser steps in: it smooths out the noise and gives you a cleaner image without needing to push samples into the thousands.

This smart way of using computer power makes rendering faster, especially for scenes with different levels of detail. **Noise Threshold** helps define how much noise is acceptable. A lower threshold means less noise but might lead to longer render times since Cycles will keep sampling until it hits the specified noise level across the image.

My advice is to start with lower counts and gradually increase until you hit an acceptable noise level for your project. **Noise Threshold** lets Cycles focus its efforts where needed. This will let you have lower overall sample rates. For 3D Viewport previews, use lower **samples** to keep the 3D Viewport responsive and fast while you work, and save higher sample rates for final renders or critical checks. Try cranking up the noise threshold first to get your initial renders out quickly, just like in *Figure 5.3*, where the bottles on the right have more noise because their fancy, semi-transparent shader bounces extra rays. Then, once you are happy with the overall look, dial the **Noise Threshold** value back down. That way, you will even out the noise levels (more like the bottles on the left) but still keep that cool transparency effect.

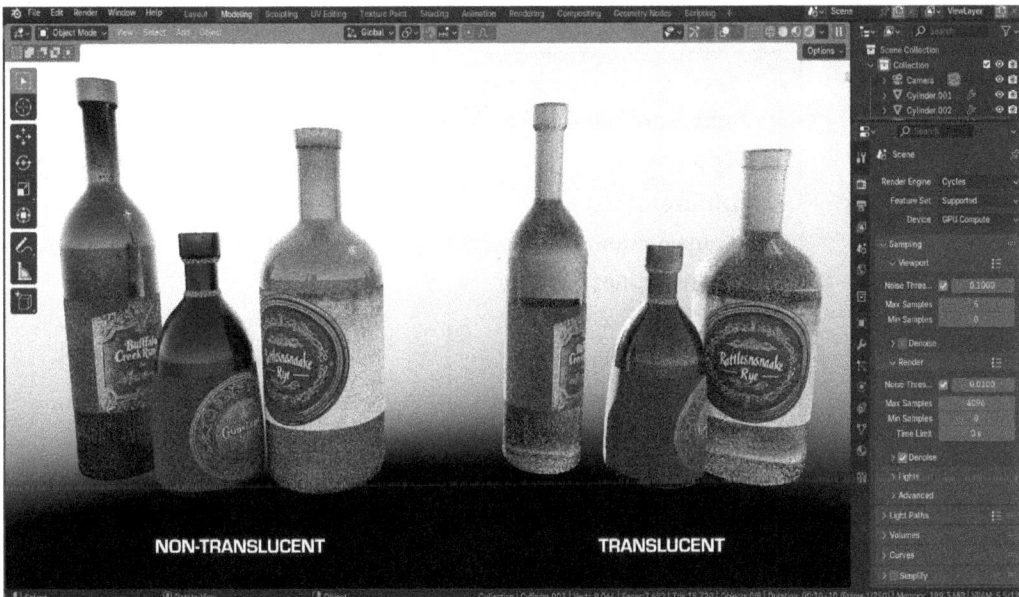

Figure 5.3: Noise Threshold manipulation in Cycles rendering

The sample count is the same on both sides of the image (note: higher adaptive sample counts will increase your sample on each render). Both sides have identical setups, but one uses translucency and the other does not. The side with translucency will always produce more noise in the render.

This way, you get a good balance of quality and efficiency in your work.

Light paths in Cycles: Controlling ray-tracing precision

Light paths are a critical component in Cycles, dictating how light interacts with objects in a scene. By adjusting the light path settings, you can significantly influence render times and the visual outcome of your projects. These settings control how complex Blender's light calculations will be, including reflections, refractions, and the simulation of real-world lighting phenomena such as caustics.

In *Table 5.1*, you will be able to compare the functions of some of the most common light path settings in Blender:

Light Path Setting	Function	Better For
Max Bounces	• **Total:** Sets the maximum number of bounces for all light types. • **Diffuse, Glossy, Transmission, Volume:** These settings allow for fine-tuning of specific light types, controlling how many times a light ray of a particular type can bounce. • **Diffuse:** Controls how many times diffuse light (scattered light) bounces. • **Glossy:** Controls bounces for shiny surfaces. • **Transmission:** Manages bounces for transparent materials such as glass. • **Volume:** Affects how light interacts within volumes, such as fog or smoke.	• **Total:** Reducing this value can decrease render times at the cost of less accurate lighting and shadow details. • **Diffuse, Glossy, Transmission, Volume:** Lowering the number of bounces for **Glossy** and **Transmission** rays, for example, can speed up renders in scenes where accurate reflections and refractions are less critical. • **Diffuse:** Reducing this can be useful in scenes where subtle light scattering is less important. • **Glossy:** Lowering this value can speed up renders in scenes where detailed reflections are not crucial. • **Transmission:** Reducing this can help in scenes where accurate light passing through objects is less critical. • **Volume:** Lowering this can speed up renders in scenes where volumetric lighting is minimal or not the focus.

Light Path Setting	Function	Better For
Clamping	• **Clamping:** Limits the intensity of light to prevent overly bright spots.	Can be useful for reducing noise in scenes with small light sources or strong reflections. Setting these values too low might lead to a loss of contrast and detail.
Caustics	• **Caustics:** Controls whether Cycles simulates caustics (i.e., complex light patterns created when light bounces off reflective materials or passes through refractive materials).	While turning **Caustics** off can speed up rendering, enabling it adds realism to scenes with glass, water, and similar materials.
Filter Glossy	• **Filter Glossy:** Softens sharp reflections and refractions to reduce noise.	**Filter Glossy** is especially useful in scenes with many glossy surfaces. Adjusting this setting can help achieve a balance between render speed and how visually accurate something looks.
Fast GI Approximation	• **Fast GI Approximation:** Offers a way to approximate GI effects quickly.	**Fast GI Approximation** can greatly reduce render times by simplifying the calculation of indirect light bounces. You will enjoy using it in scenes where an exact simulation of GI is not necessary, but some level of indirect lighting is needed to make it realistic.

Table 5.1: Light path settings

Practical application of light paths

If you want to optimize your renders in Cycles, you need to understand how to adjust the light path settings. By carefully configuring all the settings in *Table 5.1*, you can balance render quality and speed.

Let's imagine you are working on a reflective glass sculpture in a sunny outdoor environment. For this project, you would set the following:

- **Total Bounces**: Set **Total Bounces** to 4 to keep the render time manageable. This means that each light ray can bounce up to four times before stopping. More bounces result in more realistic lighting but increase render times:
    - **Before**: With **Total Bounces** set to 12 (default), the render time is long but produces highly detailed reflections and shadows.
    - **After**: With **Total Bounces** reduced to 4, render time is shorter with slightly less detailed reflections and shadows, but still visually acceptable.

- **Glossy Bounces**: Set **Glossy Bounces** to 2 to ensure decent reflections without excessive calculation. **Glossy Bounces** controls how many times light can reflect off shiny surfaces:
    - **Before**: **Glossy Bounces** set to 4; detailed reflections but longer render times.
    - **After**: **Glossy Bounces** reduced to 2; adequate reflections with faster render times.

- **Direct Clamping**: Use **Direct Clamping** at 3 to limit the intensity of direct light sources. This helps reduce overly bright spots and noise in your scene:
    - **Before**: With **Direct Clamping** off, bright spots and noise are more pronounced.
    - **After**: With **Direct Clamping** at 3, bright spots are controlled and noise is reduced.

- **Indirect Clamping**: Set **Indirect Clamping** to 10 to manage the intensity of indirect light (i.e., light that has bounced off surfaces):
    - **Before**: **Indirect Clamping** off; more noise and brighter indirect lighting.
    - **After**: **Indirect Clamping** at 10; balanced indirect lighting with reduced noise.

- **Caustics**: Enable **Refractive Caustics** to capture the beautiful light patterns through the glass:
    - **Before**: **Caustics** off; no light patterns through glass, looks less realistic.
    - **After**: **Caustics** enabled; beautiful light patterns through glass, enhanced realism.

- **Filter Glossy**: Set to 0.3 to soften sharp reflections and reduce noise. This setting helps smooth out harsh reflections, making the scene look more natural:
    - **Before**: **Filter Glossy** set to 0; sharp reflections with more noise.
    - **After**: **Filter Glossy** set to 0.3; smoother reflections with less noise.

- **Fast GI Approximation**: Enable this to approximate GI. **Fast GI Approximation** will speed up the render while maintaining a realistic look:

    - **Before**: **Fast GI Approximation** off; longer render times with accurate GI.

    - **After**: **Fast GI Approximation** on; faster render times with slightly less accurate but acceptable GI.

By tweaking these performance settings, you can balance render quality and speed across a wide range of materials. In *Figure 5.4*, you can see a saloon environment that mixes wood, glass, metal, and fabric, all benefiting from faster GI without an excessive hit to render times. Whether it is reflective bottles, rough timber, or cloth banners, **Fast GI Approximation** keeps the look believable while cutting down on noise and long waits.

Figure 5.4: Render settings comparison before (left) and after (right)

Volumes and curves in Cycles: Enhancing atmosphere and detail

Atmospheric detail is where Cycles truly shines. It can turn a dull and gray rain-soaked scenery into a dramatic medieval battlefield. Imagine knights slipping in the mud, their shiny armour glistening in the misty rain, while an overexcited squire struggles to keep a soggy war banner from falling apart. In the background, the dense fog slowly reveals a group of soaked peasants trying to rescue their stubborn sheep, who do not seem to care about the chaos around them. Now that is a scene worth rendering!

One of the ways that Blender's Cycles render engine can bring your scenes to life is with volumes and curves.

Volumes

Volume is fantastic for simulating things such as fog, smoke, fire, and other gaseous effects. By tweaking the **Volume** settings, you can control how light interacts with the particles in the air, creating anything from a subtle mist to thick, rolling smoke.

Higher volume sampling rates will give you finer detail and smoother gradients, though this will also increase render times. It is important to find the right balance between detail and performance.

> Note
>
> You will need to adjust the **Step Size** and **Max Steps** values to find the right balance between performance and quality. For simple effects such as fog, homogeneous volumes work great because they assume a uniform distribution of particles. But if your goal is to have more dynamic simulations, such as the smoke billowing from a castle's chimneys, heterogeneous volumes let you vary densities. This will capture the natural flow of smoke and fire.

Step Size and Max Steps

You will need to adjust the **Step Size** and **Max Steps** values to find the optimal balance between performance and quality.

Step Size determines the distance between each sample point within the volume. Smaller step sizes mean that you will get more accurate results but increase render times. **Max Steps**, on the other hand, will control the maximum number of steps the ray will take within the volume. Increasing **Max Steps** will make your work more detailed, but it also adds to the render time.

Homogeneous volumes

For simpler effects such as fog, homogeneous volumes are ideal. Using this option, your particles will follow a uniform distribution, making them easier to render. Particles with a uniform distribution are good for scenes where detail can be consistent throughout. For example, you might be working on a medieval European castle surrounded by a dense morning mist. By tweaking the volume settings, you can create a uniform mist that envelops the entire scene.

Heterogeneous volumes

For more dynamic simulations, such as smoke or fire, you should choose heterogeneous volumes. You can have varying densities within the volume, capturing the natural flow and movement of gases. The best place to use heterogeneous volumes is in a scene with smoke billowing from a castle's chimneys. Heterogeneous volumes will let you vary the smoke density, simulating the turbulence and movement of natural smoke.

Curves

Curves are all about rendering hair, fur, and other fibrous materials with stunning detail. Think of creating the coarse bristles of a broom in a medieval tavern. In Blender 4.x, curves got a bit of a makeover. You can now tell them what shape to take, whether that is a neat ribbon, a full 3D curve, or something in between. You also get more control over how smooth they look, with options for subdivisions and control vertices, plus handy viewport settings right there in the curve's properties panel. The **Curve** settings in Cycles let you fine-tune these details, adjusting thickness, shape, and shading to get just the right look. For example, you can mimic the natural taper of hair or fur by defining the thickness of the curves at their root, tip, and along their length.

Thickness

Thickness settings determine the width of the curves at different points:

- **Root Thickness**: Defines how thick the curve is at the base. For example, the coarse bristles of a broom in a medieval tavern can be rendered with a thicker root to mimic their sturdiness.

- **Tip Thickness**: Adjusts the thickness at the end of the curve. Tapering the tip to a finer point so that the fur is narrow on both sides but there is a bulge in the middle can simulate the natural taper of hair or fur.

- **Lengthwise Thickness**: Allows you to control the thickness variation along the entire length of the curve.

Subdivision levels

Subdivision levels affect the smoothness and flexibility of the curves:

- **Higher subdivision levels**: Increase the smoothness and allow for more natural movement and deformation, which is super important for animation. For example, animating an animal moving through the forest will look more natural with higher subdivision levels.

- **Lower subdivision levels**: Reduces the computational load, but you might end up with less smooth and flexible curves.

Shading curves

Curves can be shaded using both physically based materials and traditional textures:

- **Physically based materials** simulate realistic lighting and material properties, which is ideal for hyper-realistic scenes.

- **Traditional textures** can be used for more stylized or cartoonish looks.

So, picture this: a scene set in a medieval English village, with thick fog rolling in from the moors, softening the outlines of stone cottages and creating an eerie, mysterious atmosphere. A stable nearby shows off the fur of some horses and the straw caught in their manes. You will have rendered this with intricate detail thanks to curves.

Simplify, Motion Blur, and Film settings in Blender's Cycles

Blender's Cycles rendering engine has some fantastic features that can make your renders look more realistic at the same time as cutting out those unnecessary details. Three key features to focus on are **Simplify**, **Motion Blur**, and **Film**.

Simplify

First of all, **Simplify** is a powerful tool for managing the overall complexity of your scenes. This feature is great for cutting down rendering times without losing too much visual quality. You will find the **Simplify** settings under the **Render Properties** tab, as shown in *Figure 5.5*.

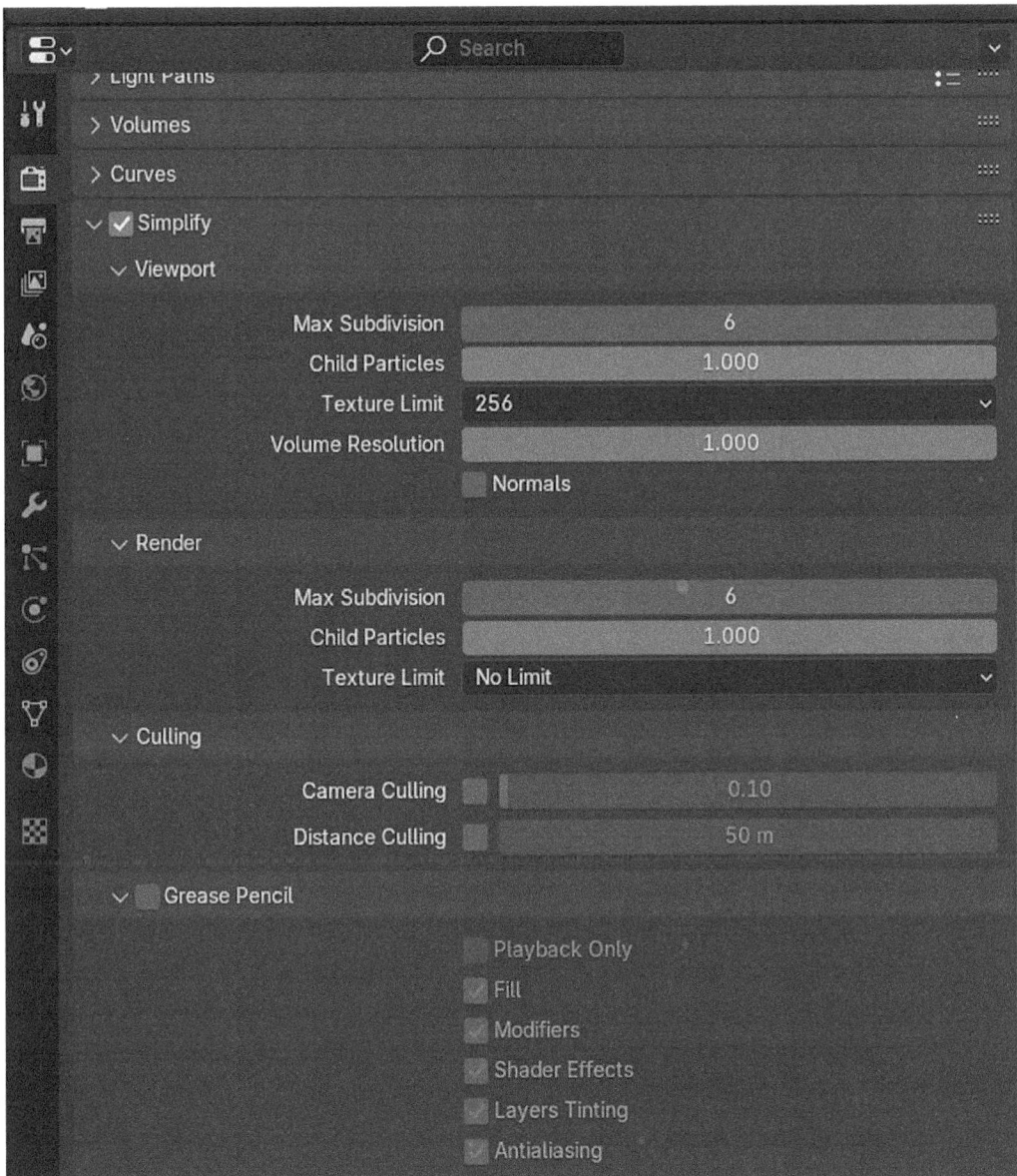

Figure 5.5: Simplify parameters

Simplify has options for optimizing your 3D Viewport and your render. These settings include limiting subdivision, particle amount, and texture (e.g., *Figure 5.6*), as well as volume resolution and **camera culling** (i.e., when objects start disappearing based on screen use percentage or distance).

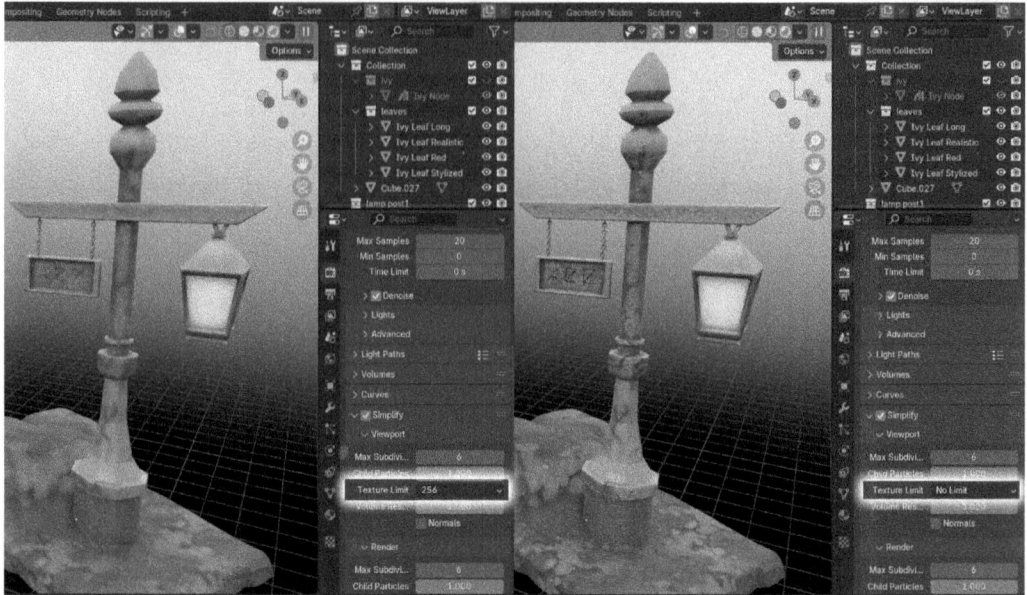

Figure 5.6: Texture Limit set (left) versus no limit (right)

Here is how some of these settings can help keep your workflow smooth and frustration-free:

- **Limiting particle amount (child particles)**: In scenes with complex particle systems, particularly with child particles, Blender allows you to control how many particles are calculated and displayed. The **Child Particles** option under **Simplify** reduces the number of particles in your 3D Viewport and during rendering. You might want to use it in scenes with grass, hair, or other complex particle-based effects. Reducing **Child Particles** speeds up the scene without affecting how your primary system looks.

- **Volume resolution**: For scenes involving volumetric effects such as fog, smoke, or fire, you can adjust the volume resolution. You can use it to control how detailed volumetrics are displayed and rendered. Reducing the volume resolution improves performance without drastically impacting the overall visual result. You should add that to your render checklist for animations or complex visual effects.

- **Camera Culling and Distance Culling**: Culling helps optimize scenes by limiting the rendering of objects based on how visible or far away they are from the camera. **Camera Culling** stops rendering objects that are outside the camera's field of view. **Distance Culling** goes a step further, so that objects beyond a specified distance from the camera are not rendered. While both settings will improve 3D Viewport and rendering performance, you might want to keep **Distance Culling** in mind if you are working on large environments where far-off objects do not contribute much to the final scene.

Also note that the **Max Subdivisions** option lets you limit how detailed your subdivision surfaces are. This reduces the geometric complexity and speeds up rendering. You want to play around with **Max Subdivisions** if you are working on, for example, a medieval castle scene, such as in *Figure 5.7*, with lots of intricate stonework, and you need to keep things running smoothly.

Figure 5.7: Medieval castle with intricate stonework in Building Medieval Worlds - Unreal Engine 5 Modular Kitbash by 3D Tudor

Similarly, setting **Max Texture Size** can lower the resolution of textures, drastically cutting down how much memory is used nd speeding up rendering times.

Reducing **Shadow Samples** can also speed up scenes with complex lighting, such as a torch-lit banquet hall, even though it might make shadows a bit noisier.

Motion blur

Motion Blur is all about adding a realistic blur effect to moving objects or cameras, making fast movements look smoother, just like in real life. This effect is especially important for animations.

The **Shutter** setting is in the **Render** panel, and it controls how long the motion blur effect lasts, simulating the exposure time of a camera. A higher **Shutter** value will increase the blur effect. The **Steps** setting determines how many steps are used to calculate the motion blur, affecting its smoothness. Higher values result in smoother motion blur but will take longer to render. This setting, as shown in *Figure 5.8*, is useful for scenes with fast action, such as a jousting tournament, where you want the movement to appear fluid and natural.

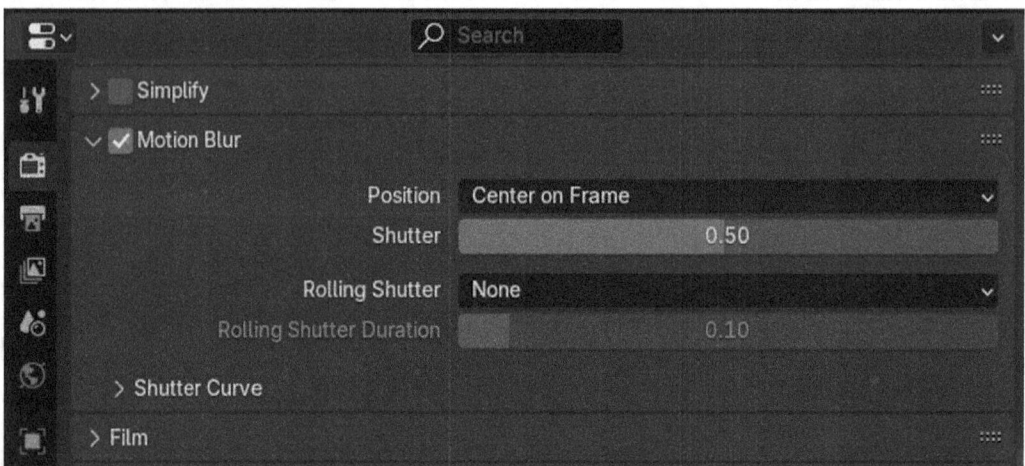

Figure 5.8: Motion Blur settings

> **Note**
>
> Rolling shutter effects, those subtle (and sometimes not-so-subtle) distortions you get when fast-moving objects are captured line by line, were already covered in *Chapter 16* in *Part 1* of this book, alongside motion blur. If you want a refresher or technical deep dive, Blender's documentation has you covered (https://docs.blender.org/manual/en/latest/render/camera/rolling_shutter.html).

Film

Film settings offer extra control over the final look of your renders. These settings include options for rendering with a transparent background, which is essential for compositing work. For example, if you need to overlay a rendered medieval tower onto different backgrounds, enabling the **Transparent** option will render the background as clear, using a programme such as Photoshop, as we have done in *Figure 5.9*.

Figure 5.9: Medieval tower with non-transparent background (left) versus transparent background (middle) versus other backgrounds (right) in Building Medieval Worlds - Unreal Engine 5 Modular Kitbash by 3D Tudor

The **Exposure** setting lets you adjust how bright or dark your image is, which can be crucial when rendering scenes with varied lighting, such as a dimly lit medieval dungeon or a bright, sunlit courtyard.

The **Gamma** setting controls the contrast and overall tonal balance of the image, helping you achieve the perfect look. This can be particularly useful in achieving the right mood for your scene, whether it is the dark and foreboding interior of a castle or the warm and inviting atmosphere of a medieval feast.

Enhancing performance and utilizing Bake in Blender's Cycles

Blender's Cycles rendering engine is famous for creating photorealistic renders, but this high quality often makes your computer struggle to get up that steep hill. To help with this, Blender has various **Performance** settings and **Bake** functionalities to optimize rendering times and efficiency, as you can see in *Figure 5.10*.

Figure 5.10: Performance settings (right) and Bake left) in Blender

Performance settings

The **Performance** settings are there to speed up render times without losing image quality. These settings allow you to control how Cycles uses your computer's resources during rendering. For example, the **Threads** setting determines how many CPU threads are used. You can let Blender automatically decide on the optimal number of threads based on your system, or you can set a custom number yourself. **Cycles** renders images in tiles, and the size of these tiles can impact performance.

> Tip
>
> For CPU rendering, smaller tiles (such as 32x32) are usually more efficient, while GPU rendering works better with larger tiles (such as 256x256).

The **Start Resolution** option controls the resolution at which rendering begins, and using a lower **Start Resolution** can speed up the initial process. You might want to do that if you quickly want to see what your scene will look like without switching to EEVEE.

Enabling the **Persistent Data** feature allows Cycles to keep certain data between renders, which reduces the time needed to recompute information. Trust me, you will be surprised how useful this is for animations or minor adjustments, so take note of that.

The importance of baking

Another useful feature in Cycles for improving performance and efficiency is **Bake**. **Bake** in Cycles lets you pre-calculate complex details such as lighting, shadows, and textures, and store them as textures, as shown in *Figure 5.10*. This can greatly reduce rendering times, especially for static scenes or objects, as in *Figure 5.11*, where we used different bake types to limit what details are kept.

Figure 5.11: Clean, artifact-free textures in Stylized Fantasy Sign Asset Pack for Blender & Game Design | 3D Asset Pack by 3D Tudor – Mesh (left) and UVs of albedo color textures with or without margin (right)

Mastering FreeStyle, Color Management, and Grease Pencil in Cycles

Even though these are not all the tools you have available in Cycles, FreeStyle, **Color Management**, and **Grease Pencil** stand out. Each of these tools is specialized, letting you add artistic touches or provide control over the final look of your render. Let us explore how these features can enhance your rendering projects.

FreeStyle

FreeStyle is a non-photorealistic rendering engine integrated into Blender that can give your renders a hand-drawn or illustrative look, as in *Figure 5.12*. It does that by applying lines and strokes to objects in the scene.

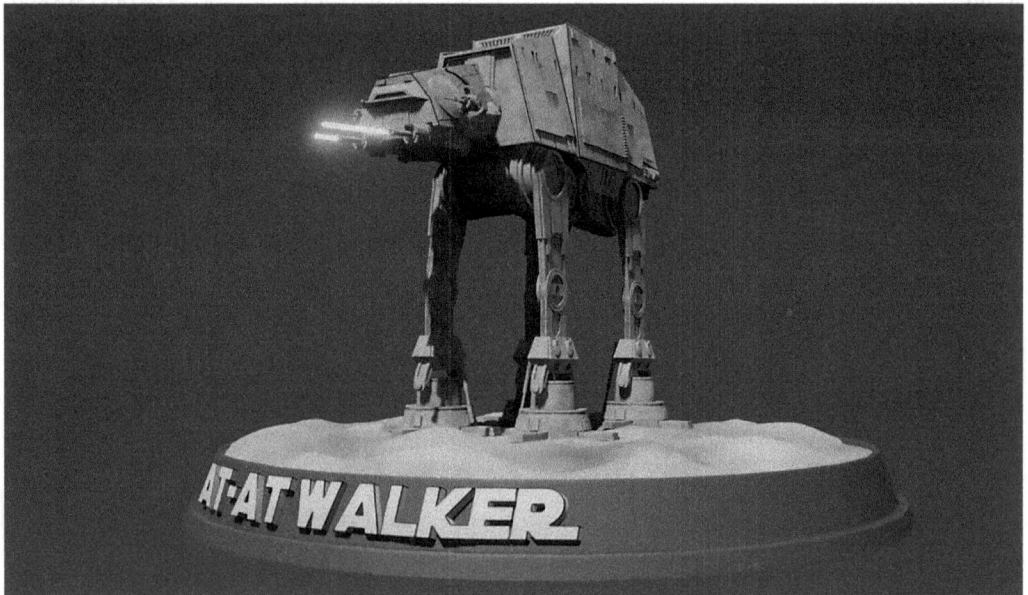

Figure 5.12: FreeStyle render in Star-Wars AT-AT Walker Model Blender 3 File & Unreal Engine 5 Project by 3D Tudor

You can create multiple line sets, each with its own rules for which edges to include or exclude. Within each line set, you can customize line styles, controlling aspects such as **Thickness**, **Color**, and **Opacity**. This allows you to achieve a wide range of effects, from ink sketches to technical drawings. For example, if you are rendering a medieval castle, you could use FreeStyle to highlight the contours of the stone walls and the intricate details of the battlements, giving it a unique, illustrated feel.

FreeStyle also gives you control over which edges it outlines through options such as **Crease**, **Material Boundary**, and **Edge Mark**, letting you emphasize contours, separations between materials, or manually marked edges.

> **Note**
>
> These lines can be rendered as a separate pass, making it easy to composite over the **Cycles** render or integrate with other elements in post-processing.

Color Management

Color Management in Blender is crucial for making sure the colors and brightness levels in your renders look as intended across different devices and output formats.

The **Display Device** setting adjusts the render preview according to the device you are using. This makes sure that the color is accurately represented on your specific monitor. The **View Transform** options, such as **Filmic, Standard**, and **Raw**, control the dynamic range and contrast of the image. For high-contrast scenes, **Filmic** is ideal as it offers a wider dynamic range.

Also, the **Look** setting provides tonal mapping presets that adjust the render's overall color and contrast. This means that you can make quick stylistic changes without changing the scene's lighting or materials.

The **Exposure** and **Gamma** sliders give you fine control over the render's brightness and contrast. For example, when you are rendering a medieval village at dusk, you want to have the warm glow of the lanterns contrast with the cool evening shadows.

> **Note**
>
> In Blender, the **Film** settings have an **Exposure** slider that controls how bright or dark your rendered image looks, kind of like adjusting exposure on a real camera. But here is the catch: if you change this setting, you have to re-render the whole image to see the difference because it affects how the scene is actually rendered.
>
> On the other hand, **Color Management** works more like a filter you apply *after* rendering. You can tweak the exposure and other color settings without re-rendering, making it a much faster and more flexible way to fine-tune your final image.

Grease Pencil

While **Grease Pencil** is primarily known as a tool for 2D animation and drawing directly in the 3D Viewport, like we spoke about in *Chapter 9* in *Part 1* of this book, it also plays a valuable role

> **Note**
>
> Even though **Grease Pencil** deserves a chapter of its own, this is not within the scope of this book. The current chapter takes a focused approach of discussing how to use Blender's **Grease Pencil** for rendering.

You can use **Grease Pencil** to add annotations or artistic guides directly onto 3D objects or scenes. I imagine this working really well during the planning stages of a project or when collaborating with others. You can also use **Grease Pencil** to draw over renders, adding artistic flourishes, highlights, or extra details. Imagine sketching decorative patterns on the walls of a medieval cathedral or adding detailed plans to a castle blueprint directly within Blender. What could be better than that?

As we wrap up our exploration of Cycles, it is clear that mastering this rendering engine will let you make stunningly realistic and unique images. By understanding and using its various settings and features, such as **Sampling**, **Volume**, **Curves**, **Performance**, and **Bake**, the right way, you can make your renders higher-quality and pump them out quicker. As we move to the next section, we will explore how rendering works in EEVEE.

Understanding EEVEE further through its key differences with Cycles

EEVEE is all about speed and real-time rendering, using rasterization to deliver fast results. If you are working on a medieval village scene and need to see changes quickly as you tweak the layout, EEVEE is your best friend. Its real-time capabilities are also great for animation playback and viewport shading (talked about in *Chapter 5* in *Part 1* of this book), giving you immediate visual feedback as you make adjustments.

When it comes to lighting and shadows, EEVEE uses simplified lighting models and screen-space reflections to quickly simulate complex lighting effects. However, you need to take a mental note that these approximations might not have the depth and accuracy you get from ray-traced renders in Cycles. Shadows in EEVEE are quick to render but may need some extra tweaking to look as soft and deep as real-world shadows. Cycles, on the other hand, uses GI to simulate light bouncing off surfaces. Shadows in Cycles are naturally softer and more accurate, with options to fine-tune their softness.

EEVEE supports most of Blender's material nodes, but some shader effects, such as subsurface scattering and volumetrics, are approximated rather than physically simulated. For example, a knight's armour might look slightly different in EEVEE compared to Cycles, a bit like the floor reflections coming from an emissive signpost in *Figure 5.13*.

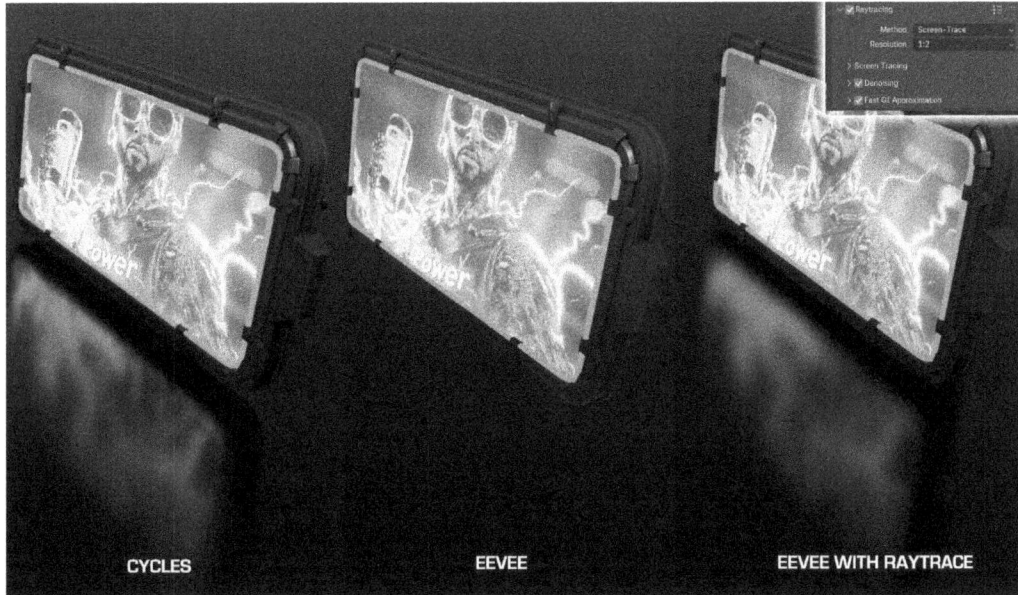

Figure 5.13: Cyberpunk billboards in Stylized Cyberpunk Billboard Pack for Blender & Game Design | 3D Asset Pack by 3D Tudor

EEVEE shines in scenarios that need real-time feedback, such as game development, previsualization, and stylized animations. Many artists use EEVEE for real-time previews and then switch to Cycles for the final render to combine how fast EEVEE is with how realistic scenes rendered in Cycles are. This hybrid approach leverages the strengths of both engines, and it is what I would personally recommend for most projects.

By exploring the differences between EEVEE and Cycles, you can strategically choose the engine that best suits your project's needs. Now you are ready to explore the unique features of EEVEE that will help you get the most out of this powerful real-time engine.

Mastering EEVEE: A comprehensive guide

EEVEE is Blender's real-time render engine, designed to let artists create high-quality visuals much faster than with Cycles. This section will introduce you to the main features of EEVEE and its benefits, setting the stage for a deep dive into its render properties. I will guide you through practical tips that can help you get there, whether you are a beginner looking to understand the basics or an advanced user aiming to fine-tune your render settings. We will cover key concepts such as AO, screen space reflections, volumetrics, and light probes. For each of these, you will learn how your settings can influence render quality and performance. Visual examples and practical scenarios will help you see the impact of different settings, ensuring you can apply this knowledge in your own work from the start.

Unique EEVEE properties

The **Render Properties** panel for EEVEE includes settings unique to its real-time rendering approach, as shown in *Figure 5.14*.

Figure 5.14: Render Properties panel for EEVEE

Blender 4.2 brings a cool update to EEVEE with **Screen Space Global Illumination (SSGI)**, which makes lighting look way more realistic by simulating how light bounces around.

Before, AO was its own setting, but now it's built into SSGI. That means you do not have to turn AO on separately. It just works automatically as part of the lighting system. This makes shadows and lighting look more natural without you having to mess with extra settings.

Adjusting bloom settings in EEVEE in Blender 4.2

Bloom effects in EEVEE mimic the way bright light sources create a glow in photography. Bloom is that soft glow you see around bright lights in photos, such as the cozy glow of torches in a medieval tavern. It makes your scene look more realistic and atmospheric.

> **Note**
>
> If you are using Blender 4.2 or later and wondering where the **Bloom** effect went, do not worry, it is not gone; it has just moved! In EEVEE Next, **Bloom** is now part of the Compositor, which means you set it up differently than before.

Here is a quick walk-through of how **Bloom** now works in EEVEE Next:

1. Give an object an emission material:

    1. In the **Modeling** tab, pick an object and go to the **Material** tab.

    2. Set its material to **Emission** and tweak the **Strength** and **Color** values. This becomes your glowing light source.

2. Switch over to the Compositor:

    1. Go to the **Compositor** tab.

    2. At the top, turn on **Use Nodes**. Now you can start using nodes in your scene.

3. Add a **Glare** node:

    1. From the **Add** menu, search for **Glare** and drop it between the default **Render Layers** and **Composite** nodes.

2. In the **Glare** node settings, change **Glare Type** to **Bloom**, as in *Figure 5.15*.

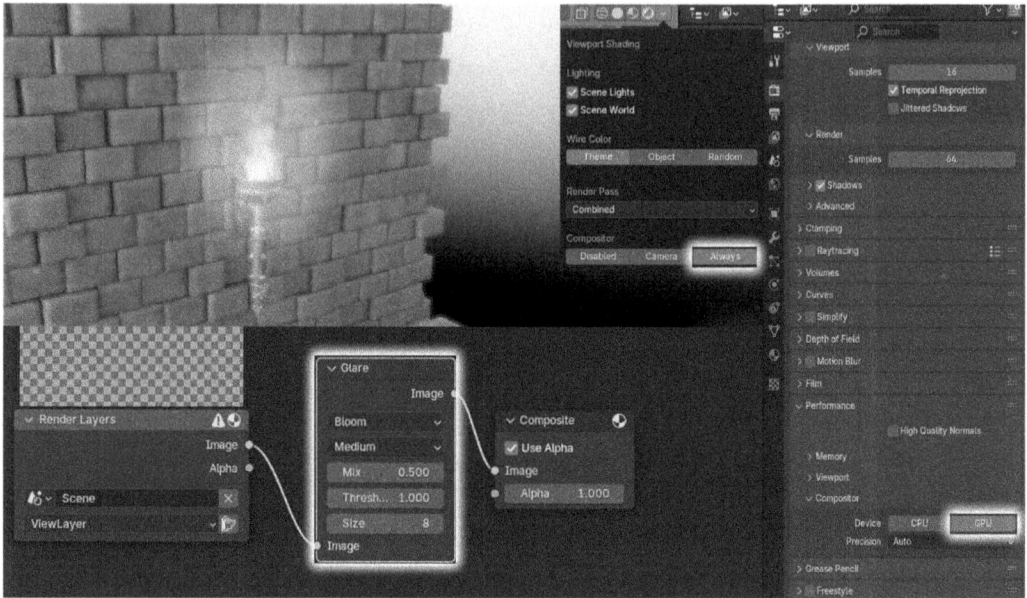

Figure 5.15: Setting up Bloom in Eevee Next Visual Options Preview in Blender
20 Massive Fantasy Torches Asset Pack by 3D Tudor

4. See the bloom in your 3D Viewport:

    1. Go back to the **Modeling** tab.

    2. Under **Viewport Shading** (i.e., the little dropdown for display settings), set **Compositor** to **Always**. You will see your bloom effect in real time on the object that has emission.

5. Tweaking the bloom:

    - **Size:** Makes the glow bigger or smaller. Lower size = subtler glow, higher size = larger halo.

    - **Mix:** Controls how strong or faint the bloom is. A high mix means a more obvious glow.

    - **Threshold:** Lets you decide how bright something has to be before it glows. If you lower it, even slightly bright objects will bloom.

6. Speeding up real-time preview:

    1. Head to **Render Properties**, then **Performance**, and finally, **Compositor**.

    2. Enable **GPU** for the Compositor.

This makes everything faster so you can preview your bloom smoothly, like in *Figure 5.16*.

Figure 5.16: Bloom (left) versus no bloom (right) using Blender 20 Massive Fantasy Torches Asset Pack by 3D Tudor

And that is it! Even though **Bloom** moved to the Compositor, you can still get that nice, warm glow for your scenes, perfect for a cozy tavern or any project that needs a touch of magic. Have fun experimenting!

Screen Space Reflections (SSR) and ray tracing in EEVEE Next (Blender 4.2)

In Blender 4.2, EEVEE Next also brings a whole new level of realism to reflections. By switching on ray tracing in EEVEE, you can tap into **Screen-Trace** technology, which gives you sharper, more detailed reflections, perfect for shiny objects such as armor, shields, or glossy environments. It is a great way to get near-real-time reflections without the heavy performance hit of full-on ray tracing.

Here is what's new in EEVEE Next reflections:

- **Screen-trace method:**

  - **How it works:** When you enable ray tracing in EEVEE, it uses the screen-trace method to calculate reflections by tracing rays within the camera's view.

  - **Pros and cons:** It is super-fast and great for real-time (such as games), but it cannot reflect objects that are not visible on your screen at the moment.

- **Improved GI:**

  - **More realistic lighting:** EEVEE Next has an upgraded GI approximation that makes indirect lighting look more natural.

  - **Better together:** Combine SSR with GI and you will get lifelike light bounces and reflections.

- **Tweaking ray-traced reflections:**

  - **Trace precision:** Turn it up for crisper reflections, but remember that higher precision might slow things down a bit.

  - **Thickness:** Adjust how deep rays go into objects. Finding the right balance helps keep your scene looking good without tanking performance.

  - **Clamp:** Tones down overly bright reflections so they do not wash out the rest of your scene, as in *Figure 5.17*.

Figure 5.17: Ray tracing with SSR (left) versus without SSR (right)

- **Real-time reflections with GI:**

  When you combine GI with ray-traced reflections, you can capture natural-looking lighting scenarios, such as the morning sun reflecting off a knight's armor in a medieval court-yard. The armor bounces light around the scene, adding a sense of depth and realism you wouldn't get otherwise.

- **Optimizing shadows:**

  EEVEE Next also enhances your shadows with the following options:

  - **Soft Shadows**
  - **Contact Shadows**
  - **High Bit Depth Shadows**

  Play with settings such as **Shadow Map Size**, **Softness**, and **Bias** to get smooth, natural shadows without bogging down your renders.

- **Quick tips for better performance:**

  - Tweak the screen-trace and GI settings until you find a good balance between speed and quality.
  - Enabling ray tracing will improve reflection quality, but you can always adjust the performance settings in Blender's render properties if things start to slow down.

EEVEE Next makes it easier than ever to combine screen-space ray tracing, screen-trace reflections, and GI for beautifully realistic lighting and reflections. With these features, you can create scenes that feel truly alive, so go ahead and experiment to find the perfect blend of performance and visual flair!

Exploring the Workbench renderer

The Workbench renderer is different from the photorealistic goals of Cycles and the real-time capabilities of EEVEE, serving a very practical role. Workbench is designed as a tool to help you visualize work during the modeling, layout, and animation blocking stages. It is all about speed and clarity rather than realism. If you are worried about performance, Workbench is your go-to. It is snappier than EEVEE, so if EEVEE feels sluggish or you don't need all those fancy visuals, switch over to Workbench for a faster, smoother experience.

Practical uses of the Workbench renderer

When it comes to modeling and layout, Workbench gives you a clear and straightforward view of the geometric and spatial aspects of a scene. Its simplified shading and lighting options will let you focus on form and composition without getting distracted by complex textures or lighting setups. Imagine working on a medieval castle's layout; you can easily evaluate the proportions, scales, and relationships between towers, walls, and courtyards without any unnecessary visual clutter. This is great if you are trying to lay out a medieval castle keep, and you want to make sure all the individual structures fit in well.

For animators, Workbench is a lightweight solution for blocking out animations and doing previsualizations. It has the ability to render scenes quickly, without the overhead of detailed materials or lighting simulations, as in *Figure 5.18*.

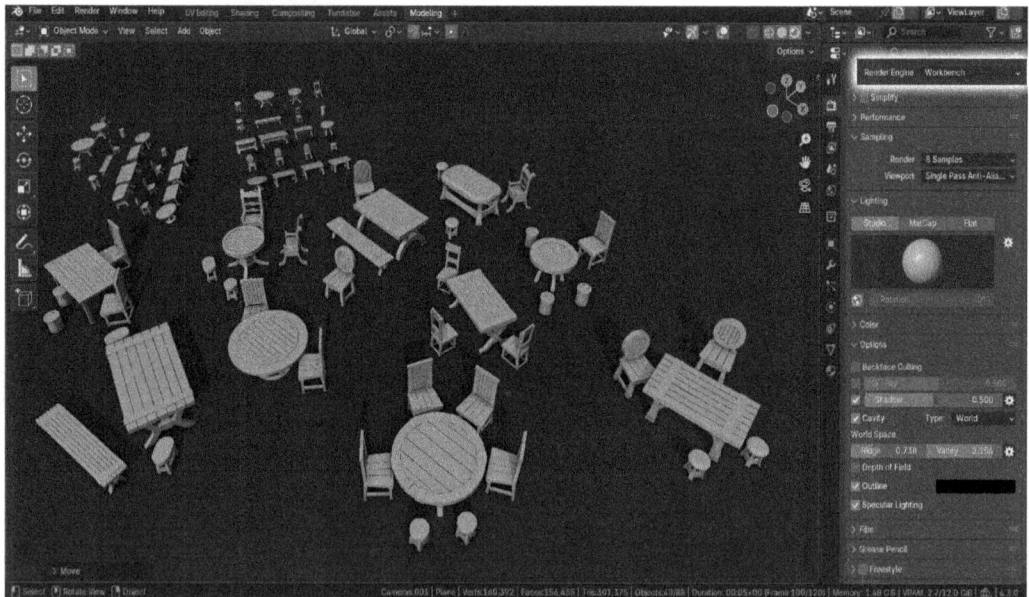

Figure 5.18: Workbench rendering a medieval tavern in Stylized Medieval Tables & Chairs Pack for Blender & Game Design | 3D Asset Pack

Flipped normals are another issue the Workbench renderer can help with. Flipped normals happen when the direction of a face's normal vector is reversed, causing shading and rendering errors. Using the **Normals** visualization mode in Workbench, you can quickly detect and fix these inverted normals to make sure your surface rendering is consistent. Last but not least, geometric anomalies are another thing Workbench is good for. These issues can include holes, overlapping vertices, or misaligned faces that can disrupt your 3D model's integrity. Workbench includes the

Curvature and **Depth** visualization modes, which help in spotting these anomalies so that you can fix your model before rendering. Outside troubleshooting functions, Workbench can also display object relationships, such as parent-child hierarchies, which is useful for organizing and debugging complex scenes.

Accessing the Workbench renderer

You can find and activate the Workbench renderer in the **Render Properties** panel in Blender. The process is straightforward. First of all, open the **Render Properties** panel. This is located on the right side of the Blender interface. Then, select **Workbench**. In the **Render Engine** drop-down menu at the top, select **Workbench**.

Using these settings and understanding the practical applications of the Workbench renderer will help streamline your workflow during the initial stages of modeling, layout, and animation. Now you can focus on design and structure without unnecessary distractions!

Summary

This chapter taught you about Cycles, EEVEE, and the Workbench renderer, so that you now understand the strengths of each engine. As you now know, Cycles is great for photorealism and EEVEE excels at fast, real-time rendering, while the Workbench renderer is perfect for quick previews and technical tasks.

As Blender evolves, it will bring new features to help you create more realistic, faster, and easier-to-use projects. That does not take away from the fact that mastering rendering in Blender is an ongoing journey of learning and experimenting. Even though, as a beginner, you still have a lot to learn, you are ready to make smart choices that improve the visual quality of your projects. For example, try making all rendering engines work together in iterative design processes. Create a detailed medieval castle, quickly model and adjust the structure in the Workbench renderer, preview it in EEVEE for immediate feedback, and finally, render it in Cycles for photorealistic results. Whether you are working on realistic visualizations, engaging animations, or efficient modeling, you have the power to create stunning visual content.

Now, brace yourself for the upcoming chapter, which will discuss the next step of your 3D artist workflow, which is light settings. There, I will guide you through mastering light linking, light portals, and **Shadow Catcher** in Blender. Whether you're aiming for photorealistic renders or stylized visual narratives, understanding how to use these lighting tools will expand your creativity.

Further reading

Looking to optimize your renders or add striking effects? Here are a few resources to guide you in adaptive sampling, max Subdivisions, compositing, and more:

- If you want to see how adaptive sampling can handle complex scenes without dragging down your system, *Blender 4: The Modular and Kitbash Environment Guide* (https://www.udemy.com/course/blender-4-the-modular-and-kitbash-environment-guide/?referralCode=D17399836E8352DFBBD2) walks you through building elaborate models while keeping render times in check.

- Curious about managing geometric detail for an ornate medieval fortress? *Building Medieval Worlds – Unreal Engine 5 Modular Kitbash* (https://www.udemy.com/course/building-medieval-worlds-unreal-engine-5-modular-kitbash/?referralCode=F936D687808F3AE55AF2) will talk you through practical tips on dialing in your max subdivisions and rendering transparent towers for easy compositing, even though it is actually an Unreal Engine 5 course.

- When you are ready to bake textures from high-poly to low-poly models without artifacts, *Stylized Medieval Tables & Chairs Pack for Blender & Game Design | 3D Asset Pack* (https://3dtudor.gumroad.com/l/stylized_medieval_tables_chairs_asset_pack) can help you understand how the **Margin** setting ensures bleed-free textures and clean UVs.

- For models to test out a real-time renderer that approximates effects such as subsurface scattering, check out *Stylized Cyberpunk Billboard Pack for Blender & Game Design | 3D Asset Pack* (https://3dtudor.gumroad.com/l/3DT_Stylized_Cyberpunk_Billboard_Pack). It highlights the differences you might see in EEVEE materials compared to Cycles, so different scenes you design can be consistent.

- If you want dramatic bloom effects in your medieval torch scene without crippling render speeds, the *Blender 20 Massive Fantasy Torches Asset Pack* (https://3dtudor.gumroad.com/l/Blender_Torches_Fantasy_Pack) is the perfect set of assets to practice adding a **Glare** node and enabling GPU compositing for smooth previews.

- Finally, for a non-photorealistic or hand-drawn vibe, the *Star-Wars AT-AT Walker Model Blender 3 File & Unreal Engine 5 Project* (https://3dtudor.gumroad.com/l/starwars-at-walker-model) render and associated YouTube video is the starting point I recommend for practicing to leverage Blender's FreeStyle engine.

Subscribe to Game Dev Assembly!

We are excited to introduce **Game Dev Assembly**, our brand-new newsletter dedicated to everything game development. Whether you're coding, designing, animating, or managing a studio, we've got insights, trends, and expert advice to help you create, innovate, and thrive. Sign up now and get exciting benefits.

https://packt.link/gamedev-newsletter

Get This Book's PDF Version and Exclusive Extras

UNLOCK NOW

Scan the QR code (or go to packtpub.com/unlock). Search for this book by name, confirm the edition, and then follow the steps on the page.

Note: Keep your invoice handy. Purchases made directly from Packt don't require an invoice.

6

Enhancing Realism in Blender: Mastering Light Linking, Light Portals, and the Shadow Catcher

Manipulating light is what breathes life into scenes and makes them look real. Lighting is not actually part of the rendering workflow, but it plays an important role since it can help you highlight details, set moods, and create depth. Blender includes a collection of lighting tools to help you along the way, with light linking, light portals, and Shadow Catcher being the key players.

Light linking lets you control which objects are influenced by specific light sources, letting you control the interplay of light and shadow. Light linking is all about picking favorites. You tell Blender which objects a light is allowed to shine on, and which ones get left in the dark. This is handy if you want control over the mood without fiddling with dozens of lights at once.

Light portals are a bit different. They are like funnels for your light, instead of light just drifting in from the world background, a portal tells Blender, "Hey, the sunlight is coming from this window, not everywhere at once." It is basically a filter, a snoot, or a spotlight for your environment's lighting. Light portals use environmental lighting to flood indoor scenes with natural light, like godrays coming through a window.

Then there is the **Shadow Catcher**, which is the sneaky trick that makes 3D objects sit convincingly in real photos or footage. It is like telling Blender, "Only grab the shadows here, nothing else," so your models do not float awkwardly on top of the background but actually belong in the shot. The Shadow Catcher effortlessly integrates 3D objects into real-world footage or images by capturing shadows and boosting the realism of the scene you created.

Whether your goal is to make photorealistic renders or stylized visual stories, this chapter will help you understand how to manipulate light linking, light portals, and the Shadow Catcher. Get ready for exciting projects such as creating a medieval marketplace at night, a sunlit medieval tavern hall, or integrating 3D models into real-world photos. You know what? Even a medieval battle scene with realistic lighting effects is not out of reach!

So, in this chapter, we will cover the following topics:

- Light linking: sculpting with light
- Light portals: guiding natural light
- Shadow Catcher: merging realities
- Creative ways to use lighting tools

Technical requirements

As for **Blender 4.5 LTS (Long-Term Support)**, the general requirements include a macOS 11.2 or newer (Apple Silicon supported natively) operating system, or a Linux (64-bit, glibc 2.28 or newer) operating system. Blender now requires a CPU with the SSE4.2 instruction set, at least 8 GB of RAM (32 GB recommended for heavy scenes), and a GPU supporting OpenGL 4.3 with a minimum of 2 GB of VRAM.

For a full list of technical requirements, please refer back to *Chapter 1* of this part.

Light linking: sculpting with light

Light linking lets you control which objects in a scene are affected by specific light sources. In Blender, light linking helps save time and can reduce noise by doing the following:

- **Cutting down light bounces on unlinked objects**: If a light is not linked to an object, **Cycles** simply skips calculating how that light bounces around it, both directly and indirectly. Less pointless maths for the computer means less noise and, in some cases, noticeably quicker render times.

- **Directly controlling object lighting**: Instead of having to constantly adjust or move lights to emphasize specific objects, light linking lets you specify which objects are influenced by which lights. This means you do not need to keep tweaking the lighting setup, and you will spend less time adjusting the overall scene lighting.

- **Enhancing textures efficiently**: You can quickly boost or reduce lighting on specific textures or surfaces by linking them to individual lights. This means you do not have to adjust texture settings or change global lighting.

- **Simplifying atmospheric adjustments**: Instead of redoing or adding new lights to change the mood or look of certain parts of your scene, you can assign lights only to objects you want affected. This means you will not need to duplicate lights or create multiple lighting setups.

By creating exclusive or inclusive relationships between lights and objects, you can also experiment with complex lighting compositions, helping you create effects that would be challenging or impossible with global lighting alone.

Note

Light linking was introduced in Blender 4.0, and it works a little differently than you might expect. By default, every object in your scene is included, which means lights will affect them unless you say otherwise. If you want to exclude something, just uncheck the little box next to its name in the **Light Link** panel. That is it, no extra include/exclude dropdowns hiding in the menu. Keep it simple: everything is lit by default, and you manually switch off what you do not want.

For example, imagine a medieval marketplace scene. You want the streetlamps to illuminate only the merchant stalls, leaving the rest of the market in a gentle shadow, as in *Figure 6.1*.

Figure 6.1: Medieval market at night in Building Stunning Medieval Worlds with Unreal Engine 5 Modular Kitbash Complete Course, by 3D Tudor

Light linking will highlight specific areas without compromising the scene's overall lighting. By dragging objects into the **Light Link** panel, you can decide which lights influence specific objects. The scene in *Figure 6.1* uses two light sources near the window; one is more intense than the other. Now, let us focus on the *why*. You want the light from the store windows to cast a soft glow on the sidewalk and ground, giving the street a warm, inviting atmosphere. At the same time, you do not want this light to affect the buildings on the opposite side of the street. Those buildings should stay dim and subtle. With light linking in Blender, this setup is easy to achieve.

You can assign the light coming from the storefront windows to only affect the ground and nearby objects, such as the sidewalk, by dragging those elements into the **Light Linking** panel for the specific window lights. The buildings on the opposite side of the street are excluded from this light, so they remain untouched. This way, the ground is lit nicely without overexposing the other buildings, keeping the lighting focused exactly where you want it.

Getting started with light linking

Light linking gives you the ultimate cheat code for control over which objects in your scene are lit by specific lights. This will save you from complex layering or compositing workflows. Essentially, light linking involves creating relationships between lights and objects.

> Tip
>
> For more complex effects, consider using multiple light links to layer lighting effects on a single object.

Using light linking, step by step

In this section, you will find a step-by-step guide to harnessing the power of light linking, along with practical examples and tips to enhance your lighting workflow:

1. Begin by arranging your scene with the objects and lights you plan to use. For this example, use a simple scene with two objects and two lights. The goal is to have each light illuminate only one of the objects.

2. In the Outliner, create two new collections by right-clicking and selecting **New Collection**. Name them according to the lights or objects they will be associated with, such as Light1_Target and Light2_Target. Then, place each object into its respective collection.

3. Switch to Blender's **Cycles** renderer.

4. Now, select one of the lights in your scene. Then, in the **Object Properties** panel, go to the **Shading** section and open the **Linking** subsection. Here, you will find options for **Shadow Linking** and **Light Linking**, as you can see in *Figure 6.2*. Expand this section.

Figure 6.2: Light linking example in Building Stunning Medieval Worlds with Unreal Engine 5 Modular Kitbash Complete Course, by 3D Tudor

5. Under **Light Linking**, you will see options for **Collection** and **Operation**. Click on the **Collection** icon and select the collection corresponding to the objects you want the light to affect.

> **Tip**
>
> In Blender, you can easily control which objects are affected by a light source using the **Light Linking** panel. Simply drag and drop items from your scene's object list directly into the **Light Linking** panel to include or exclude them from a specific light's influence.

6. Then, use the checkbox beside each object in the **Light Linking** panel to control whether the light affects it. The checkboxes beside each collection member determine whether it is included or not.

7. If you are light linking in Blender and the **Include** option is checked on, the light will only affect the items listed within the **Light Linking** panel. If the **Include** option is unchecked, the light will influence everything in the scene except for the objects listed. To do that, go to the **Light Linking** settings, and from the **Operation** drop-down menu, select **Include** to ensure that the light only affects the objects within the selected collection. Repeat this process for each light and its corresponding collection. In *Figure 6.3*, you can see where we have split the image to show both cases.

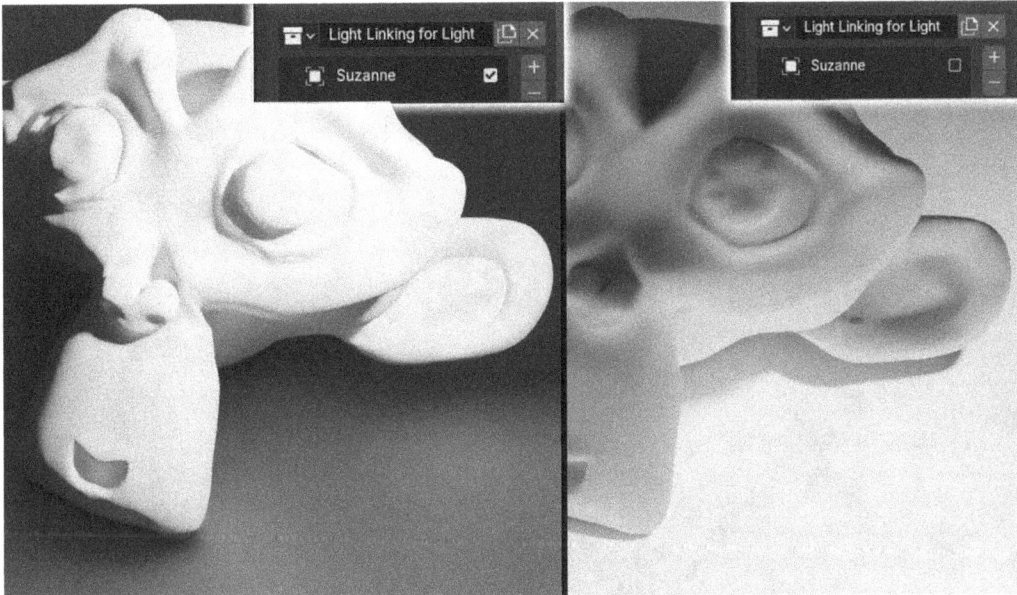

Figure 6.3: Light linking with all options checked on (left) vs. off (right)

8. This image shows how Suzanne (our example object) looks with only light affecting it (left) compared to with all other parts of the scene being affected except Suzanne (right). It is worth noting that although the light ignores the object on the right of *Figure 6.3*, the light bounces from other objects to illuminate Suzanne indirectly, resulting in a unique lighting setup.

Practical examples

Here are some practical examples of how light linking can improve your lighting setups and streamline your workflow in Blender:

- **Focused spotlight:** Use light linking to create a spotlight effect on a character in a crowded scene, where the background stays in shadow or is lit differently.

- **Selective mood lighting:** In an interior scene, link specific lamps to only shine light on certain areas or objects, creating pockets of light and shadow that will guide your viewer's eye.

Figure 6.4: Selective mood lighting (left) and focused spotlight (right) in "Stylized Graveyard Modular Pack and Cyberpunk Stylized Gas Station | Blender 3 to Unreal Engine 5 | 3D Building Guide" by 3D Tudor

Figure 6.4 shows both examples. On the left, you can see the cemetery where the lighting is coming out of the building to make the scene look eerie without affecting the darkness of the terrain and the trees. On the right, you can see a cyberpunk scene where we have used a focused spot lighting on the bar, and this enhances the volumetric effect on some of the spotlights.

With light linking, you can make it easier to highlight important elements. Now, you are ready to move on to the next powerful tool in Blender's lighting arsenal, light portals for indoor scenes.

Light portals: guiding natural light

Positioned at windows, doors, or other openings, light portals guide environmental light into interiors. One of their best pros is that they improve the accuracy and quality of indirect lighting, reducing noise and render time.

Light portals cut down noise and speed up render times by helping Blender focus on where natural light comes into a room, such as through a door or window. Without them, the software has to work harder to calculate all the light bouncing around. This can lead to grainy results and longer render times.

Consider a piano room interior. Placing light portals at the windows will allow sunlight to flood the room naturally, casting realistic shadows. This makes the room feel warm and inviting, as if real sunlight is coming through the windows, as in *Figure 6.5*.

Figure 6.5: Lighting setup in "Blender 3 Beginners Step-by-Step Guide to Isometric Rooms"
by 3D Tudor

Mastering light portals for indoor scenes

Light portals work by guiding the movement of environmental light into enclosed spaces. They make indirect lighting more accurate and reduce noise, especially when using HDRI environments or external light sources. Light portals focus global illumination calculations on areas where light naturally comes in, such as windows and doorways. This helps with rendering as well, reducing noise and render times. As they say, teaching someone how to fish is better than just giving them fish, so I will be your guide through this process.

Using light portals, step by step

Creating and positioning light portals effectively is key to getting all the benefits on offer. Follow these steps to integrate light portals into your indoor scenes:

1. Check your scene to find out where natural light comes in. This is normally a window or an open door.

2. Go to the **Add** menu, select **Light**, and then choose **Area**. Position this **Area** light at the light entry point and make sure it covers the entire opening.

3. With the **Area** light selected, go to the **Light** settings in the **Properties** panel. Check the **Portal** option to convert the area light into a light portal, as in *Figure 6.6*.

Figure 6.6: Using light portals, options, and settings in "Complete Course - Mastering the Art of Isometric Room Design in Blender 3" by 3D Tudor

4. If using an HDRI environment, rotate your scene or the HDRI itself to ensure that the brightest or most relevant parts of the environment align with your light portals. This maximizes the effectiveness of the portals.

> Note
>
> If you do not align your light portal properly, you will have less accurate lighting and potentially increased noise in your render. A light portal does not create light on its own; it directs other light rays, so it is important to ensure you have an external light source in the scene, such as a sun or HDRI. Also, correct scaling and orientation are crucial. Make sure to scale the light portal appropriately to match the window or opening and rotate it so it faces the correct direction to guide the light. Remember, portals do not emit light on their own, they only direct existing sources.

Practical examples

Here are a few practical examples of how light portals can upgrade your indoor renders in Blender:

- In a living room scene lit primarily through large windows, adding light portals can reduce noise in shadowed areas and corners and bring out texture details.

- For a studio apartment scene with a single light entry point, light portals will boost the overall lighting quality and make rendering a lot faster. This is because your computer will be focusing on the critical areas of light entry.

- In a scene with multiple light sources from overhead skylights, using light portals at each skylight entry point will make the lighting more realistic.

Directing your light will make your renders more lifelike. Think of it like a magical spell; it is not just about casting light or shadow but about finding that perfect gray area where everything looks just right. We will now learn more about Blender's Shadow Catcher to better control the darkness in a scene as well.

Shadow Catcher: merging realities

The Shadow Catcher is a feature made for compositing (which we will discuss in the next chapter); however, this feature lets 3D objects cast shadows on a transparent or invisible surface. This makes it invaluable for integrating 3D models into real-world footage or images because it renders shadows that mimic the interaction between the virtual object and the physical environment. Realistic shadows and their seamless incorporation into live-action scenes are what the Shadow Catcher is all about.

Imagine you have a 3D model of a medieval torch, and you want to place it on a real-world wall in a photo, as in *Figure 6.7*.

Figure 6.7: Full render of using the Shadow Catcher to illuminate a torch in Blender 20 Massive Fantasy Torches Asset Pack, by 3D Tudor

Without the Shadow Catcher, you would need to solve problems such as manually painting shadows and matching lighting conditions by adjusting each shadow element by hand and tweaking light settings to match the real-world photo. You might even come across problems such as your work looking like it is AI-generated by someone who did not know how to write the right prompts and forgot all about the shadows.

But with the Shadow Catcher, the tool will accurately capture the sword's shadow, making it look like the sword is genuinely lying on the table, blending seamlessly with the real environment.

Implementing the Shadow Catcher in compositing

Blender's Shadow Catcher is fantastic for making 3D models look like they are part of real-world photos or videos. It works by rendering only the shadows cast by your 3D objects onto a transparent background, letting them blend with actual footage. Both **Cycles** and **Eevee** support this feature, and I will guide you through the setup and share some advanced tips for the best results.

Note

The Shadow Catcher lets your 3D models cast realistic shadows on a real surface without rendering the surface itself. When you combine it with real-world backgrounds, the shadows from your 3D model blend naturally with the lighting and textures of the photo or video. **Cycles** and **Eevee** handle this feature a bit differently, especially in how they deal with light interaction and transparency.

Setting up the Shadow Catcher

To use the Shadow Catcher effectively, note that this feature is only available in the **Cycles** render engine. Follow these steps:

1. Import your 3D model and place it where you want it in the scene. Then, bring in your real-world background image or video as the background using the **Environment Texture** node in the **World** settings.

2. Create a **Plane** where you expect the shadows to fall. This **Plane** will catch the shadows from your 3D model.

3. Select the **Plane**, go to the **Object Properties** panel, and in the **Visibility** section, check the **Shadow Catcher** option, as in *Figure 6.8*.

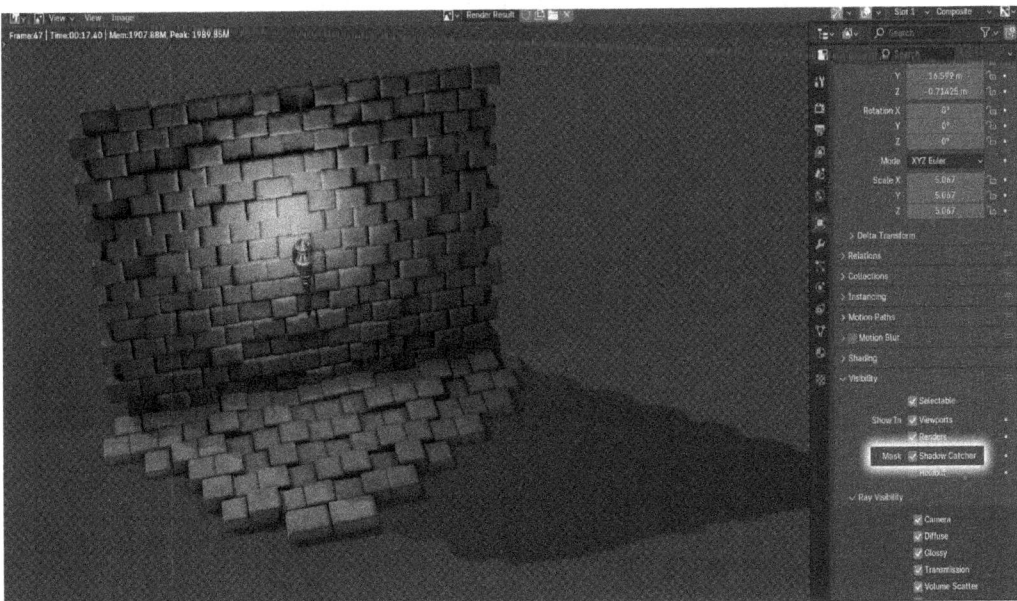

Figure 6.8: Shadow Catcher options in Blender 20 Massive Fantasy Torches Asset Pack, by 3D Tudor

4. Here's how the Shadow Catcher works in Blender, depending on the renderer you choose:

   - In **Cycles**, this makes the plane invisible in the render, except for the shadows.

   - In **Eevee**, you might need to adjust additional settings for transparency and shadow quality.

5. Make sure the lighting in your Blender scene matches the lighting in your background image or footage. Adjust the direction, intensity, and color of your lights to mimic the real-world lighting conditions.

Advanced refinement techniques for Blender's Shadow Catcher

You can make advanced adjustments to integrate your shadows better by adjusting their **Ray Visibility** settings (i.e., different types of rendering rays, such as camera, shadow, reflection, and how they interact with an object in **Cycles**). In the **Ray Visibility** tab, you decide which types of rays in **Cycles** will affect the object. The options include the following:

- **Diffuse**: Controls whether your object affects non-reflective (diffuse) shading.
- **Glossy**: Determines whether your object appears in reflections.
- **Transmission**: Sets whether your object affects transparent materials.
- **Volume Scatter**: Adjusts how your object interacts with volumetric effects.
- **Shadow**: Determines whether your object casts shadows.

Most of these options are straightforward, but note that turning off **Camera** makes the object invisible in the render while still allowing it to cast shadows and appear in reflections. This is different from disabling the *camera* icon in the Outliner because this removes the object from rendering completely, so it does not interact with light at all. This trick is especially useful in horror scenes if you want, for example, a ghostly figure to show up only in reflections or shadows, adding an eerie effect without revealing it directly in the scene.

You can also uncheck **Glossy** in the **Shadow Catcher** settings to prevent the shadows from being visible on shiny or reflective surfaces, as in *Figure 6.9*.

Figure 6.9: Glossy on (left) vs. off (right) to control Shadow Catcher effects in Blender 20 Massive Fantasy Windows Asset Pack, by 3D Tudor

In the preceding example, we show you how disabling **Glossy** removes reflections from a window, giving it a more stylized glass appearance. This technique is useful for getting a specific artistic look while keeping your control over how objects interact with light.

Practical applications

Here are a few practical examples of how you can use the Shadow Catcher in Blender to level up your renders:

- Say you are working on a **product render**, such as a sleek laptop or a phone, and you want it to sit naturally on a real desk you have photographed. With the Shadow Catcher, you can drop in the 3D model, and only the shadows will show on the desk, making it look like the product was always part of the scene, like in an *IKEA* catalog.

- If you are adding **CG elements** to a video, such as a 3D car driving down a real street, the Shadow Catcher will let you capture just the car's shadow on the road.

- For our last example, imagine placing a 3D model of a house into a photo of an empty plot of land. You can use the Shadow Catcher to get realistic shadows from the house on the ground without having to create the entire landscape in 3D.

By using the Shadow Catcher, you can blend your 3D creations into real-world scenes with much less hassle. We will now go over some creative ways to use these lighting tools.

Creative ways to use lighting tools

Blender's lighting tools, such as light linking, light portals, and the Shadow Catcher, offer endless possibilities for creativity in 3D rendering. Combining these features can lead to impressive results, and exploring different techniques will teach you even more.

By focusing light on specific objects or areas, you can highlight key elements, create dramatic contrasts, and evoke emotions in those who look at your portfolio. This approach adds depth to your narrative and makes your render more engaging because it links back to a story.

Combining tools to solve complex lighting challenges

Balancing indoor and outdoor lighting can be tricky, but combining light portals with selective light linking helps. This method balances the intensity and color of light sources, making sure that both interiors and exteriors are lit realistically, as in *Figure 6.10*.

Figure 6.10: Combining light portals, the Shadow Catcher, and light linking in "Complete Course - Mastering the Art of Isometric Room Design in Blender 3" by 3D Tudor

For scenes that need dynamic lighting changes, such as transitioning from day to night, animating light portals and linked lights can simulate the changing natural light. Going that extra mile, adding the Shadow Catcher for outdoor scenes makes the time-lapse effects more believable.

Inspiring examples from real projects

Using light portals can simulate the soft, diffused light of a cloudy day. Light linking can highlight interior design, drawing attention to textures and materials. In the same example, adding a Shadow Catcher can cast realistic shadows on the model and ground the structure in its environment. You can also use light linking to light the scene around a new gadget, emphasizing its sleek design and features. Light portals could mimic a professional studio setup. Finish it off by adding a Shadow Catcher and placing the product in various realistic settings for promotional materials.

> Note
>
> Light linking, light portals, and the Shadow Catcher can get pretty technical under the hood, but the main thing to remember is this: if your renders look noisy or your lights behave oddly, it is usually down to render engine settings rather than the tools themselves. For deeper dives into performance tweaks, noise reduction, or animation compatibility, check *Chapter 5* of this part, which is where we cover the heavy optimization tricks. Here, just focus on getting comfortable with what these tools do.

Summary

Mastering Blender's light linking, light portals, and the Shadow Catcher will help you transform ordinary scenes into immersive experiences. Through this chapter, you have learned how to control light in your scenes, make indoor lighting look natural, and seamlessly blend 3D models with real-world backgrounds.

Dive in and play around with these lighting tools in your projects. Think of yourself as a medieval wizard, but instead of casting spells, you are casting light, a bit like a discipline priest in *World of Warcraft*. By pushing the limits of what you can do with creative lighting and compositing, you can bring a whole new level of realism and storytelling to your 3D renders.

As technology keeps evolving and new tricks come out, it is like getting your hands on a brand-new spell book. It is super important to keep learning and sharpening your skills. And remember, every great scene starts with a single beam of light, kind of like how every epic quest starts with the hero forgetting their map at home!

Now, let us step into the enchanting world of compositing. In the next chapter, we will blend 3D renders with real-world footage, apply color grading to give your scenes that extra oomph, and add special effects that would make even the mightiest wizard jealous.

Further reading

Looking to refine your lighting setups or add more flexible and realistic lighting? Here are a few resources to guide you in light linking, the Shadow Catcher, light portals, and more:

- If you want to see how shadow and light linking can be used to illuminate a massive fortress without washing out every tower or doorway, our Unreal Engine 5 courses come with the pre-built model, *Building Stunning Medieval Worlds with Unreal Engine 5 Modular Kitbash Complete Course* (https://www.udemy.com/course/building-medieval-worlds-unreal-engine-5-modular-kitbash/?referralCode=F936D687808F3AE55AF2), which is where you can start.

- Curious about creating dramatic spotlights for a character reveal, or a moody cemetery with just the right pockets of shadow? *Stylized Graveyard Modular Pack* (https://3dtudor.gumroad.com/l/Blender-stylized-grave-yard) and *Cyberpunk Stylized Gas Station | Blender 3 to Unreal Engine 5 | 3D Building Guide* (https://3dtudor.gumroad.com/l/cyberpunk_stylized_3D_gas_station) will let you try out focused spotlight techniques and selective mood lighting setups.

- When you are ready to bring a sunlit glow into a cozy isometric interior, *Blender 3 Beginners Step-by-Step Guide to Isometric Rooms* (https://www.udemy.com/course/blender-3-beginners-step-by-step-guide-to-isometric-rooms/?referralCode=AB7E2519D26525F1320A) shows you how to place light portals at windows so that sunlight floods a room naturally.

- For a deeper dive into combining light portals with various lighting sources, *Complete Course - Mastering the Art of Isometric Room Design in Blender 3* (https://www.udemy.com/course/blender-3-mastering-the-art-of-isometric-room-design-in/?referralCode=663C5F3BD974A0124FB7) details how to balance indoor and outdoor lighting without blowing out your highlights.

- If you want to practice casting clean shadows for torches in a fantasy environment, *Blender 20 Massive Fantasy Torches Asset Pack* (https://3dtudor.gumroad.com/l/Blender_Torches_Fantasy_Pack) will let you try out using a Shadow Catcher for seamless compositing.

- Finally, if your scene involves shiny windows or reflective surfaces, *Blender 20 Massive Fantasy Windows Asset Pack* (`https://3dtudor.gumroad.com/l/blender_fantasy_windows_asset_pack`) can show you how disabling **Glossy** in the **Shadow Catcher** settings keeps unwanted reflections at bay.

Subscribe to Game Dev Assembly!

We are excited to introduce **Game Dev Assembly**, our brand-new newsletter dedicated to everything game development. Whether you're coding, designing, animating, or managing a studio, we've got insights, trends, and expert advice to help you create, innovate, and thrive. Sign up now and get exciting benefits.

`https://packt.link/gamedev-newsletter`

Join the 3D Tudor Channel Discord Server!

Join the 3D Tudor Channel Discord Server, a creative hub for learning Blender, Unreal Engine, Substance Painter, and 3D modeling, for discussions with the authors and other readers:

`https://discord.gg/5EkjT36vUj`

7

Guiding You through Compositing in Blender

You might have thought that, by this point, we have covered pretty much everything that has to do with 3D modeling in Blender. However, Blender also includes strong **compositing** tools, which we have not talked about yet. These tools help you combine different visual elements in one scene, helping you add depth, realism, and special touches to your projects.

The core of post-processing in Blender is its **compositor**. It will help you with detailed visual effects, blending **computer-generated (CG)** elements with real footage, and telling visual stories. Blender's compositor is node-based, which means that you have a lot of control and flexibility, letting you tweak images and footage without permanently changing them.

Chapter 7 of this part is here to help you explore Blender's compositing, from the basics to more advanced techniques, making sure you get a good understanding of this powerful post-production tool, as shown in *Figure 7.1*.

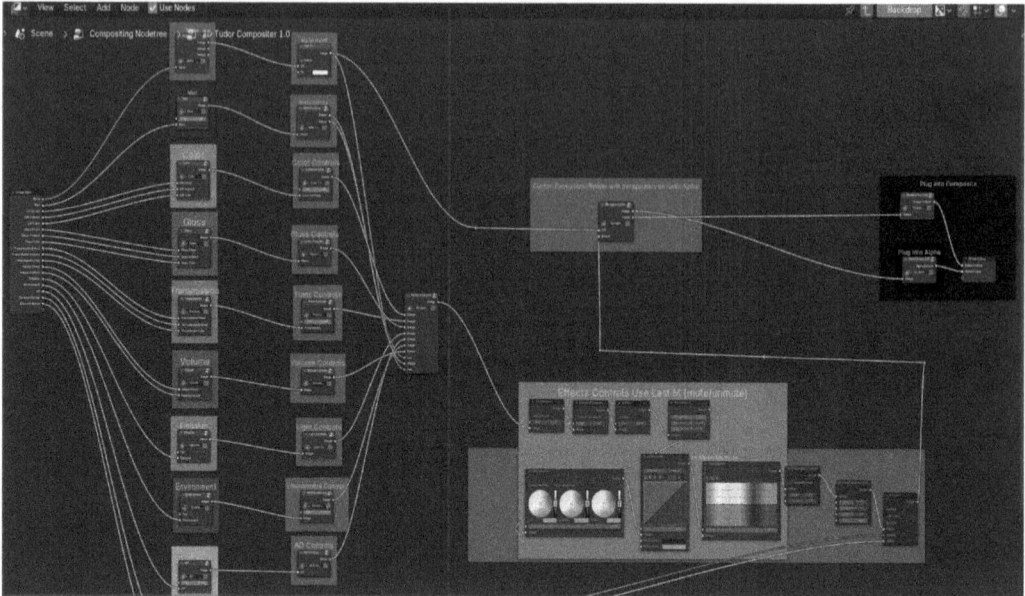

Figure 7.1: Node setup of the Blend Craft Compositor Blender Plugin by 3DT in Blender's compositor

When you render in Blender, you can use the compositor to fine-tune how your image looks by mixing different passes such as color, mist, and lighting. This setup is part of a custom node group called *Blend Craft Compositor Blender Plugin by 3DT* (https://3dtudor.gumroad.com/l/blend_craft_3DT_compositor), which gives you lots of control over your final render. Even though we will not go through exactly how it works in this chapter, you will learn all about the components it is made up of here.

You will learn how Blender's node-based workflow gives you full control over effects such as **Color Correction**, **Depth of Field**, and **Motion Blur**. We will also explore how to blend CG elements with real footage using keying and masking techniques, making it easier to create seamless visual effects. Along the way, you will get hands-on experience with render layers and passes, master Blender's **Node Wrangler** for a smoother workflow, and compare how **Eevee** and **Cycles** handle compositing.

So, in this chapter, we will cover the following topics:

- Getting started with Blender compositing
- Understanding render layers and passes
- Mastering Node Wrangler for enhanced Blender compositing

- The power of nodes in Blender compositing
- Leveling up your node setups for advanced compositing in Blender
- Eevee versus Cycles in compositing: maximizing Blender's rendering engines
- Compositing for visual effects in Blender

> **Note**
>
> As we talked about in *Chapter 5* of this part, Blender uses two main rendering engines: Eevee and Cycles. Eevee is a real-time render engine that is fast and efficient, perfect for quick previews and projects with tight deadlines. Cycles is slower but known for its highly realistic results. Knowing the differences between these engines and how they work with compositing is important for getting the most out of your Blender projects. So, if you have not done so already, go back to *Chapter 5* for a refresher!

Technical requirements

As for **Blender 4.5 LTS (Long-Term Support)**, the general requirements include a macOS 11.2 or newer (Apple Silicon supported natively) operating system, or a Linux (64-bit, glibc 2.28 or newer) operating system. Blender now requires a CPU with the SSE4.2 instruction set, at least 8 GB of RAM (32 GB recommended for heavy scenes), and a GPU supporting OpenGL 4.3 with a minimum of 2 GB of VRAM.

For a full list of technical requirements, please refer back to *Chapter 1* of this part.

Getting started with Blender's compositor

Jumping into Blender's compositing tools is like diving into a kitchen where Bob Ross and a mad scientist are working together. Compositing combines creativity and technical know-how, allowing you to blend, enhance, and tweak visual elements to create scenes that are beautiful and impressively detailed. In this section, we will start with Blender's compositor, setting up a workspace that makes compositing easier, and going over some key terms you will need to know. When you are comfortable with these basics, you will build your first composite.

Navigating to the compositor

You can access the Blender compositor through the **Compositing** tab at the top of the workspace menu. Blender's **Node Editor** is the specific area within the compositor workspace where you actually arrange and connect the individual nodes for compositing. I would compare **nodes** to factory workers in the manufacturing industry. Each one has a job, whether it is tweaking colors, adding a blur, or mixing images together. You connect them in a chain, and they pass the information along to build up your final image.

The **Node Editor** has several key areas, as shown in *Figure 7.2*.

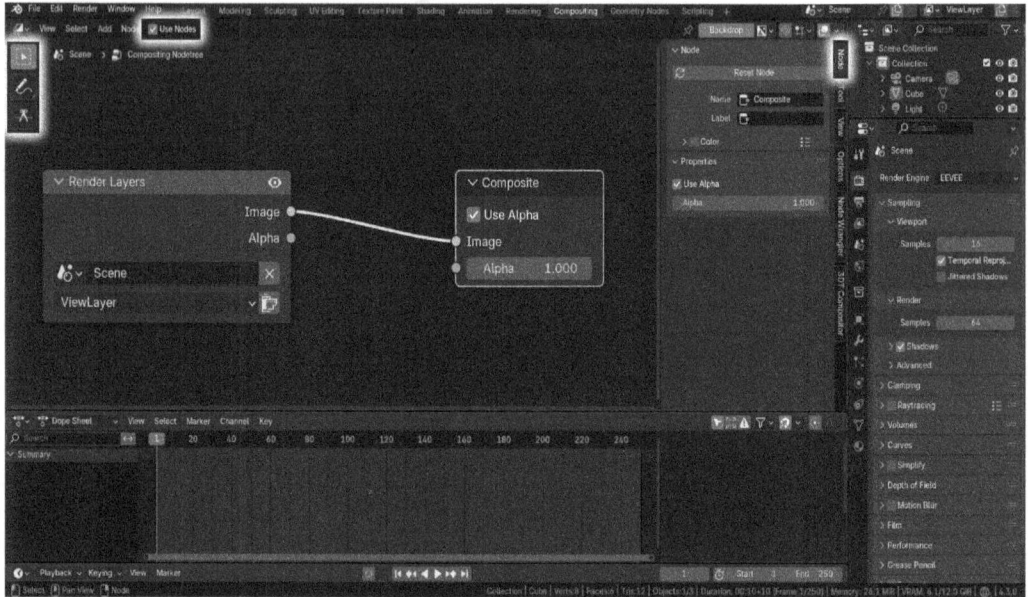

Figure 7.2: Navigating Blender's Compositor tab

Once you enable **Use Nodes** at the top, you will see a graph where you can build your composite. The main area is where you drag in nodes and connect them to control your final image. On the left is the toolbar for selecting, moving, and linking nodes, and on the right is the **Properties** panel, which shows detailed settings for the selected nodes.

Customizing the workspace for efficient compositing

Blender lets you customize your workspace to make compositing more efficient. A well-organized workspace helps you work faster and focus better. When you start a render in Blender by pressing *F12*, a new window will open, showing the rendered image from the active camera's viewpoint. This is your render result. Once the render is complete, you can make adjustments in the compositor.

As you tweak nodes, such as adding color corrections, applying filters, or combining render passes, you will get real-time feedback on how your compositing adjustments impact the final output.

A large **Node Editor** for building and tweaking your nodes and a dedicated **Image Editor** for previews will give you all the tools you need at your fingertips. You can use the **Node Editor** to blend different layers of computer-generated buildings, streetlights, and atmospheric effects such as fog and rain. With the **Image Editor** set up for real-time previews, you can instantly see how changes to the lighting or the addition of special effects impact the overall scene.

Basic concepts and terminology

To use Blender's compositor well, you need to understand some key concepts and terms, as shown in *Table 7.1*:

Key Concepts and Terms in Compositing	Function
Nodes	These are the basic parts of your composite. Each node does a specific job, such as color correction, blurring, or combining images.
Node Trees	This is the layout of connected nodes that shows how your composite is built. It controls the flow of data from one node to the next.
Sockets	These are the input and output points on a node. They are color-coded to show the type of data they handle, such as images, values, or vectors.
Data Flow	This is how information moves through your node tree, from one node's output socket to another node's input socket, creating a sequence of operations that leads to your final composite.

Table 7.1: Compositor terminology

Executing your first composite with rendered output

After customizing your workspace for **compositing**, the next step is to create a composite from rendered output. Here is how to set up your first composite using a rendered image:

1. Set up a simple scene and render it by going to the **Render** menu and selecting **Render Image** or using the shortcut *F12*. Choose the rendering engine (Eevee or Cycles) that best fits your project. Refresh your knowledge and double-check in *Chapter 5* of this part.

2. Switch to the **Compositing** workspace with the **Node Editor** and **Image Editor**. Your rendered scene should appear in the **Image Editor** set to **Render Result**.

3. In the **Node Editor**, enable **Use Nodes**. You will see two default nodes: **Render Layers** (inputs your rendered scene) and **Composite** (i.e., the endpoint of your node tree).

4. Add a **Brightness/Contrast** node between the **Render Layers** node and the **Composite** node by pressing *Shift + A*, then selecting **Color | Brightness/Contrast**. Adjust the brightness and contrast to your liking.

5. If you want to preview the output of a specific node in real time, especially in larger, more complex node trees, connect the output of your **Brightness/Contrast** node to a **Viewer** node. This lets you isolate and see exactly what that node is doing in the **Image Editor** set to **Render Result**, without viewing it through other nodes in the chain.

6. When you are happy with your composite, save the final image by going to the **Image** menu in the **Image Editor** and selecting **Save As**.

I am sure that these steps have helped you grasp the basics of Blender's compositing workflow. Experimentation also sets the stage for more advanced techniques. Now, to take your skills further, it is important to understand render layers and passes.

Understanding render layers and passes

In compositing, render layers and passes are like your secret weapons. They let you break down scenes into parts, apply effects to specific elements, and combine everything with precision. Instead of working with one big, flat render, you can break your scene into separate layers, such as foreground, background, lighting, or effects, and adjust each one on its own. This makes it much easier to fine-tune details, fix problems, or add creative touches without re-rendering the whole scene.

Let us go through the basics of render layers and passes to see how they work and how to set them up.

Introduction to render layers

Render layers let you divide your scene into smaller, manageable chunks. This is super helpful for complex scenes where working with everything at once would be too difficult or slow.

Note

When working with Eevee and Cycles in Blender, it is important to understand that each rendering engine handles render passes differently. Cycles, as a path-tracing engine, supports more detailed passes such as **Indirect Lighting**, **Volume Scatter**, and **Transmission**, which help create complex, photorealistic scenes. Eevee, on the other hand, is a real-time engine designed for speed, focusing on simpler passes such as **Diffuse**, **Glossy**, and **Emission**. If you need physically accurate lighting and reflections, Cycles is often the better choice, while Eevee is perfect for quick previews or stylized projects that do not require highly detailed lighting.

The **View Layer** panel is your control center for managing render layers and passes in Blender. In the **View Layer** panel, you can turn specific objects, collections, and effects on or off for each layer.

The panel also lets you choose which passes to include in your render, such as diffuse color, specular highlights, or volumetrics. Each selected pass becomes a separate channel in the compositor, ready for integration into your composite.

By mastering render layers and passes, you gain powerful tools to dissect and reassemble your scenes. With these basics in place, it's time to explore tools that streamline your workflow. To do that, you will need **Node Wrangler**. With its suite of shortcuts, visualization enhancements, and organizational tools, **Node Wrangler** simplifies the management of complex node trees.

You can manage render layers in the **View Layer** panel in the **Properties** window. In the **View Layer** panel of the **Properties** window, open the **Shader AOV** tab to create a new custom channel. Click the + button and Blender will add an AOV with a default name, which will now appear as an output option in your **Render Layers** node inside the compositor.

To put it to use, pick the object you want to isolate, in this example, the tent, and in **Shader Editor**, add an **AOV Output** node with the same name as the channel you created. By feeding a pure white RGB value into this node, you generate a clean mask for that object, ready to use later in the compositor.

For example, in *Figure 7.3*, a white AOV has been added to a camping tent material.

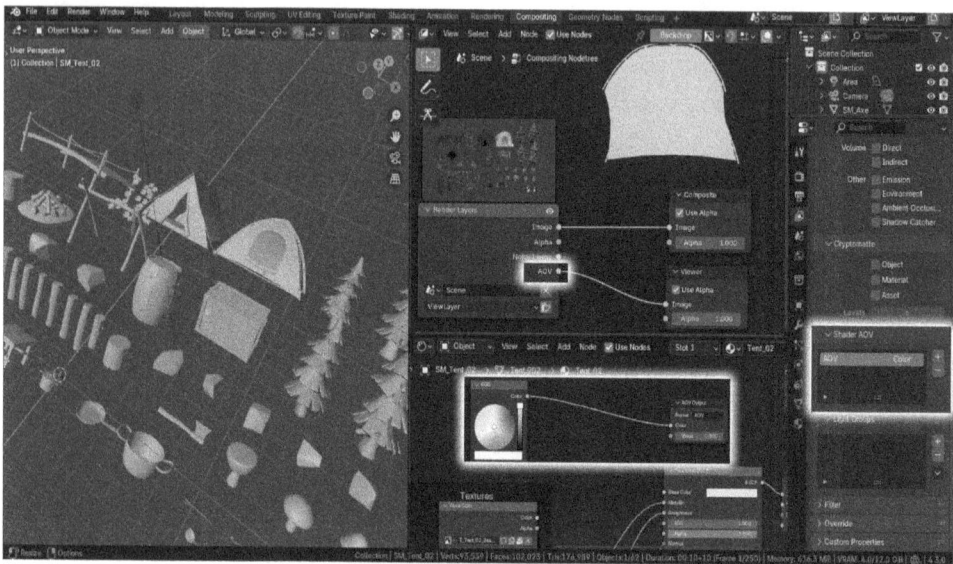

Figure 7.3: Creating a shader AOV mask for a specific object in 3DT Fantasy Forest Camp
Environment Pack for Blender & Game Design | 3D Asset Pack by 3D Tudor

This acts like a mask, so you can boost its color or tweak just that tent in **Composite**.

In *Figure 7.4*, that same AOV is used to change the tent's color from blue to red.

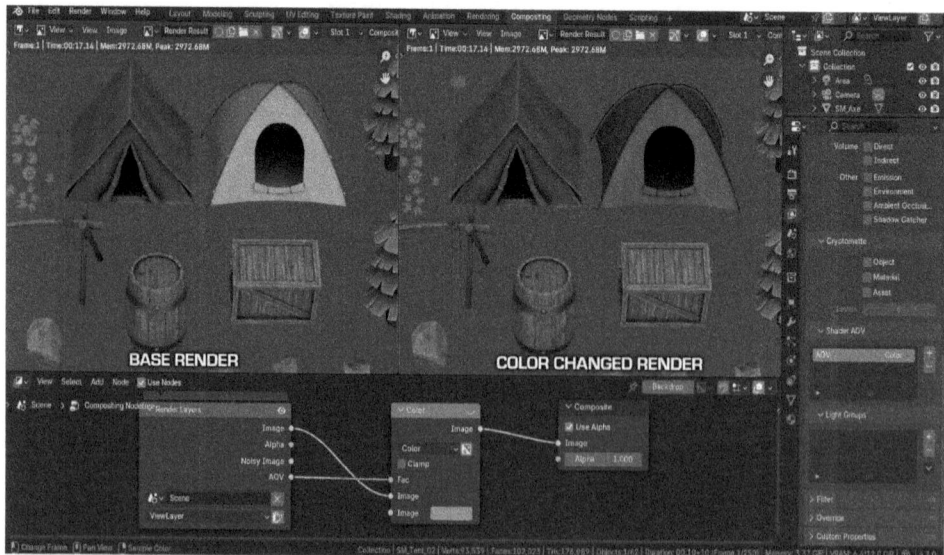

Figure 7.4: Using the AOV mask in the compositor to change an object's color in 3DT Fantasy
Forest Camp Environment Pack for Blender & Game Design | 3D Asset Pack by 3D Tudor

You can try this too by doing the following:

1. Add a **Color Mix** node.

2. Plug the original image into the first input.

3. Connect the **AOV** render into the **Fac** input to use it as a mask.

4. Set the mix mode to **Color Blend**.

5. Use the second color input to choose a new color, such as red.

6. Then connect the output to the **Composite** node to see your final result.

This method gives you a lot of flexibility and control, especially when you want to adjust specific parts of your render without affecting the whole scene.

All in all, by splitting your scene into layers, you can work on specific parts separately, such as foreground objects, background scenery, or special effects. This makes compositing easier and more flexible, letting you tweak and improve each part of your scene individually.

Utilizing render passes

Render passes break down the rendering process into different elements such as color, shadows, reflections, and depth. Each **pass** captures specific data about the scene, giving you detailed control over the compositing stage. The main types of render passes can be seen in *Table 7.2*:

Render Pass	Function	Notes
Z-depth	This pass measures how far objects are from the camera and records it in grayscale. Darker shades mean objects are closer, while lighter shades mean they are further away.	This pass is useful for adding effects such as depth of field (blurring based on distance) and atmospheric effects such as fog. Use to simulate camera focus effects post-render, such as depth of field, where you can blur elements based on their distance from the camera.
Shadow	This pass isolates shadows so you can adjust their color, intensity, and softness without affecting the rest of the image.	This pass is great for matching shadows in CG elements with those in live footage.

Render Pass	Function	Notes
Ambient Occlusion (AO)	AO captures the soft shadows in tight spaces where objects are close together.	It adds depth and realism to your scene by emphasizing details and textures.
Shadow Catcher	This special pass allows objects to receive and render shadows from other objects without being visible themselves.	This pass is perfect for integrating 3D objects into live-action scenes, making the shadows match the lighting of the real-world footage.
Diffuse, Glossy, and **Transmission**	These passes separate the contributions of different materials to the scene for targeted adjustments. • **Diffuse:** Handles the basic color and shading, without any reflections or see-through stuff. • **Glossy:** Focuses on shiny surfaces, so you can control reflections and highlights. • **Transmission:** Deals with how light passes through transparent materials such as glass.	These passes are super handy when you want to fine-tune specific materials in your scene. For example, if you are working on a glass object and need to adjust the reflections separately from how light passes through it, you can tweak the **Glossy** and **Transmission** passes without messing with the rest of the image.
Emission	This pass isolates light emitted by materials.	You can use it to enhance light sources.
Vector and **Speed**	The **Vector** and **Speed** passes are involved in adding motion blur in post-production.	The **Vector** and **Speed** passes are incredibly useful if you are adding motion blur to moving objects in your scene during post-production. Instead of rendering motion blur directly (which can slow down your renders), you can use these passes to add it later in compositing.

Table 7.2: Types of render passes

Render passes can help you break your scene into parts that you can fine-tune on their own. For example, in a project with an ancient Aztec temple environment, like in *Figure 7.5*, I would use the **Z-depth** pass to create atmospheric effects such as mist or fog that add a sense of mystery and depth to the scene, blurring distant trees and mountains.

Figure 7.5: Aztec temple environment at night in Blender 4: The Modular and Kitbash Environment Guide by 3D Tudor

The **Shadow** pass would make sure that the shadows cast by the temple and the surrounding jungle match perfectly. Then, **Ambient Occlusion** would highlight the intricate carvings and textures on the temple walls. Finally, the **Shadow Catcher** pass would be used to seamlessly integrate any added 3D elements, such as animated animals or additional vegetation, making sure their shadows match the natural lighting of the environment.

Now that you have got a handle on the basics of compositing, let us take it a step further by exploring how different passes work together in the **Node Editor**.

Connecting and disconnecting sockets

In Blender's **Node Editor**, linking sockets is simple. Just click the small circle (socket) on a node's output, drag the line to another node's input socket, and let go. This way, data (e.g., color or shader info) travels from one node to the next. If you need to remove a connection, *click and drag* the line away from the socket until it disconnects, or hold *Alt* and *left-click* on the line to instantly detach it.

Layering different rendered data

When you want to combine different passes in Blender (e.g., **Diffuse**, **Glossy**, or **Ambient Occlusion**), it is all about stacking them on top of each other, like in *Figure 7.6*.

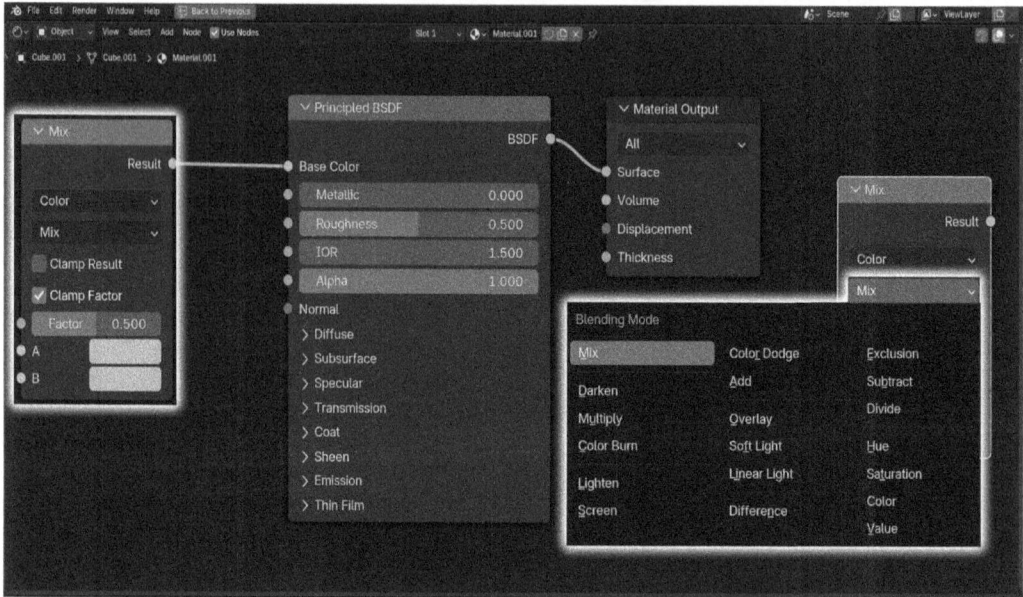

Figure 7.6: Changing blend modes in the Color Mix shader node

> **Note**
>
> When you change the blend mode on a **Color Mix** node, the name of the node changes too. By default, it is called **Mix**, but if you switch it to something such as **Overlay**, the name at the top of the node updates to match, just so you always know what blend mode you are using.

Each pass carries color information, so the **Color Mix** node is your go-to tool for merging them, for example. Blender's **Color Mix** node takes two images (or passes) and blends them in a controlled way, letting you decide how they interact.

Blending modes in the Color Mix node

Inside the **Color Mix** node, you'll find multiple blending modes, each affecting how the images combine:

- **Add**: Great for boosting brightness or adding light, such as an emission pass.
- **Multiply**: Ideal for darkening or applying shadows, such as **Ambient Occlusion.**
- **Overlay**: A mix of darkening and brightening, depending on the base image.
- **Subtract**: Useful for removing light or making parts of the image darker.

Picking the right blend mode lets you dial in how shadows, highlights, and color mix together in your scene.

Using the Fac slider

The **Fac** (factor) value in the **Color Mix** node controls how much each image influences the final result. At 0, you will only see the first image; at 1, you will only see the second. Anything in between mixes both images, which gives you precise control over the end look.

Input order

It also matters which image you plug into the top or bottom socket. The top input usually works as the base, while the bottom input modifies it. For example, if you are using **Multiply** and want to darken the base with **Ambient Occlusion**, connect **AO** to the bottom input.

> Note
>
> If you swap where you input **AO**, things might get weird. For example, if you put **AO** on top and the base image on the bottom, you could end up brightening the scene instead of darkening it, making shadows look washed out.

Clamp option

Turning on **Clamp** in the **Color Mix** node caps your color values between 0 and 1. This is handy if you have very bright lights or strong emission passes, and it helps you stop parts of your image from getting overexposed or "blown out."

Layering and hierarchy of render layers

The order in which you stack your passes also makes a big difference. For example, if you apply **Bloom** before **AO**, your bloom might get darkened. But if you add **AO** first, then apply **Bloom**, you will end up with a properly shaded scene that still shows off bright, glowing areas.

In *Figure 7.7*, you can see what happens if you apply glare before **AO** on the left (i.e., the wrong way) and glare after **AO** on the right (i.e., the right way).

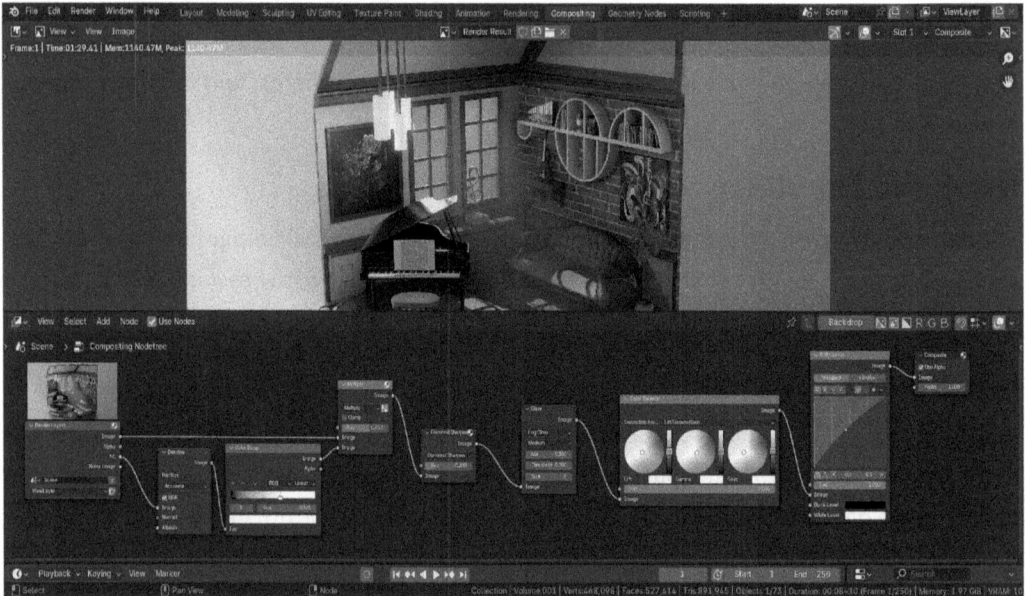

Figure 7.7: Layering and hierarchy of render layers example in "Blender 3 Beginners Step-by-Step Guide to Isometric Rooms" by 3D Tudor

In the following example, in *Figure 7.8*, the difference in how the glare looks is all about the order in which you put things together. On the left side, the glare is added *before* **Ambient Occlusion**, so **AO** darkens everything, including the glare. That makes the light look more dull and less punchy. On the right side, the glare comes *after* the **AO**, so it stays bright and really stands out over the shadows. It looks more balanced and natural, and the lighting has more impact.

This shows how important it is to think about the order of your nodes when you are compositing. By using tools such as the **Color Mix** node, tweaking **Fac** values, and layering your passes smartly, you get full control over how your lighting and effects come together. That means you can create a look that is super realistic, totally stylized, or anything in between.

Figure 7.8: Glare placement before versus after ambient occlusion in Blender's compositor in "Blender 3 Beginners Step-by-Step Guide to Isometric Rooms" by 3D Tudor

Without these compositing techniques, getting a polished final render would be much more challenging.

Mastering Node Wrangler for enhanced Blender compositing

Node Wrangler is a Blender add-on that completely changes how artists work with the compositor. It makes workflows smoother, simplifies managing nodes, and boosts efficiency, especially when dealing with complex node setups. You can activate **Node Wrangler** by simply going to **Preferences**, then **Add-ons**.

This section explores what **Node Wrangler** can do, focusing on how it improves compositing with shortcuts, better visualization, and features such as framing, naming, and coloring nodes to keep everything organized.

Node Wrangler supports framing, naming, and coloring nodes to keep complex composites organized, like in *Figure 7.9*.

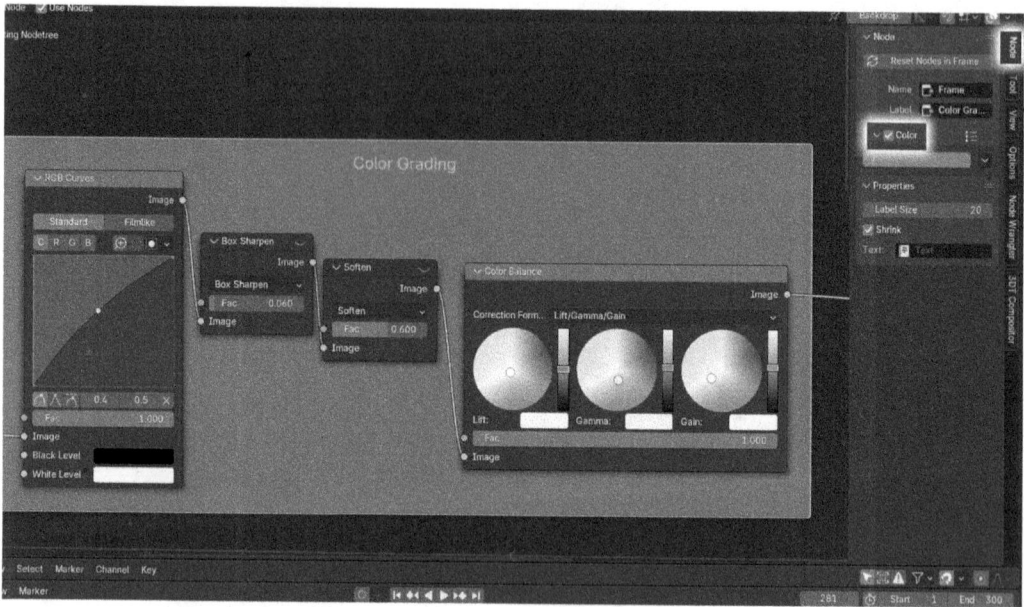

Figure 7.9: Using node comments and color coding for better organization in the compositor

Here, you can see how easy it is to keep things organized in your node setup. Just select a bunch of nodes, press *Ctrl + J* or *F* to group them into a comment box, then hit *F2* to give it a name. If you need to separate nodes from the frame, select them and press *Alt + P*.

Using **Node Wrangler**, you can group nodes into frames to make segmentation better. You can also use naming to clarify each node's function and connections, and apply color coding to make things visual.

> Tip
>
> With the frame selected, open **N-panel**, go to the **Node** tab, and enable the **Color** checkbox to change the color of frames or nodes, making it easier to visually organize your setup.

Essential features for compositing

Node Wrangler makes connecting and duplicating nodes quick and easy. All you have to do is drag and drop to link nodes and duplicate them without disrupting your workflow. You know what? You can instantly preview any node's output by selecting it and pressing *Ctrl + Shift + Click*. This connects it directly to a **Viewer** node, as shown in *Figure 7.10*.

Figure 7.10: Lazy Connect in Blender 4: The Modular and Kitbash Environment Guide by 3D Tudor

Another powerful feature is **Lazy Connect**, which helps you build your node tree faster by automatically linking nodes with a **Color Mix** node, like in *Figure 7.10*. Just hold *Ctrl + Shift* and drag the right mouse button across two nodes, and Blender will instantly drop in a **Color Mix** node between them. If you just want to connect an output socket to an input socket directly, you can use *Alt + RMB* (they should be highlighted in red) instead.

To see what it looks like, just *Ctrl + Shift + left-click* on the mix node to hook it into the **Viewer** mode. Now, it will show up in the background. Just make sure the **Backdrop** is turned on, or you will not see the preview behind your nodes.

All in all, **Lazy Connect** speeds up the process of checking how different parts of your composite look, making it easier to refine your work.

Node Wrangler also helps you interact with your scene's backdrop better. You will find tools for fitting, zooming, and panning within the **Node Editor**. This improved control is crucial for fine-tuning your composites. Creating and managing node groups is also made simpler by **Node Wrangler**.

For example, in a project with a medieval well scene with overgrown foliage and a flower meadow, I would use **Node Wrangler** to connect and adjust nodes for things such as the lighting, shadows, and textures of the well and surrounding plants. This would also give me some flexibility with experimenting with different times of day, such as a bright sunny morning or moody twilight.

In *Figure 7.11*, you can see a setup using four key effects: **Ambient Occlusion Overlay**, **Bloom Effect**, **Background Image**, and **Color Grading**.

- **Ambient Occlusion Overlay** is added on top of the base render using a **Multiply Color Mix** node. This helps darken small creases and corners to make the shapes pop more. A **Denoise** node and **Color Ramp** node help smooth it out and control how strong it looks.

- **Bloom Effect** is added with a **Glare** node and tweaked using curves. It is applied to both the image and its alpha channel, so the glow still shows up even if the background is transparent.

- **Background Image** is added using an **Alpha Over** node, which lets it blend nicely into the scene without harsh edges.

- **Color Grading** is done with **Color Balance** and **RGB Curves** nodes, giving you control over brightness, contrast, and overall color mood.

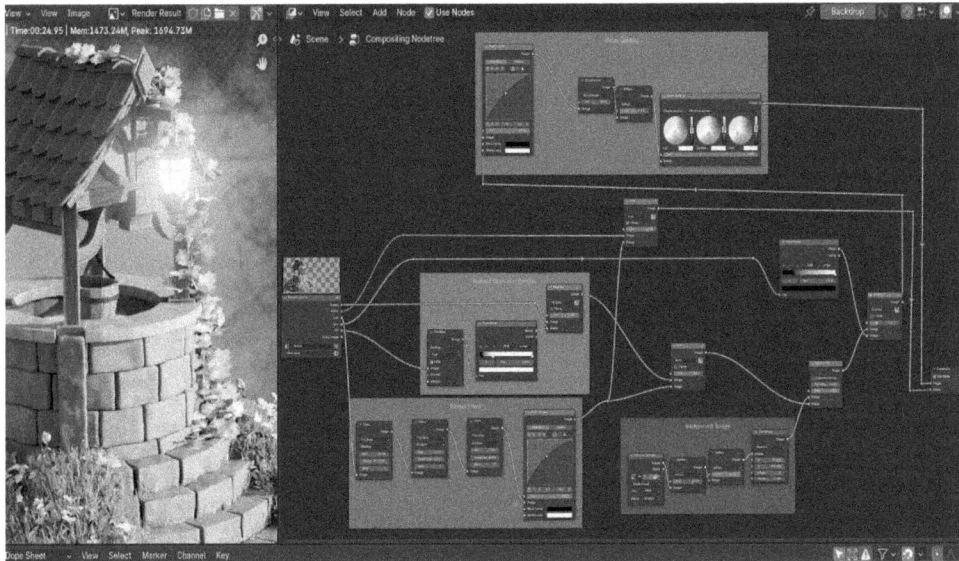

Figure 7.11: Post-compositing render of a medieval well in Stylized Environments with Blender 4 Geometry Nodes by 3D Tudor

With this setup, when you go to save your render, you can pick **RGB** (just the image) or **RGBA** (image + transparency). The *A* stands for **Alpha**, which lets you include or leave out the background, just like you see in *Figure 7.12*.

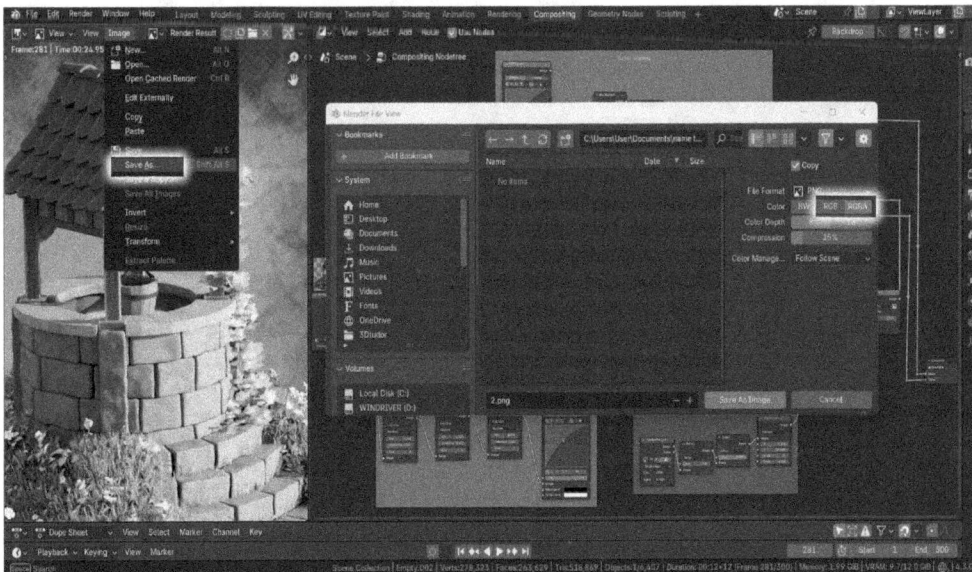

Figure 7.12: Saving the final render with or without transparency using the RGBA option in Stylized Environments with Blender 4 Geometry Nodes by 3D Tudor

To wrap things up, the **Node Wrangler** add-on is a real game-changer when it comes to working efficiently in Blender's compositor. Whether you are tweaking lighting, adjusting colors, or layering effects such as **Bloom Effect** and **Ambient Occlusion**, **Node Wrangler** helps you move faster and stay in control.

Reroutes for a tidy setup

Another trick for keeping your workspace neat is using reroutes. By holding *Shift + right-clicking* and dragging across a connection between two nodes, you create a small reroute point. This helps you steer multiple connections without crisscrossing lines everywhere. Reroutes are easy to move around. Just select them (by clicking or using a selection box) and press *G* to grab and move, so you can organize the flow however you like, keeping your compositor layout clear and clutter-free.

Next, we are going to dive into the cool stuff you can do with nodes in Blender compositing. We will check out some must-know nodes, such as **Color Ramp** and **RGB Curves**, that can transform your work. Plus, we will look at using node groups and advanced techniques, some of which you can see in *Figure 7.13*.

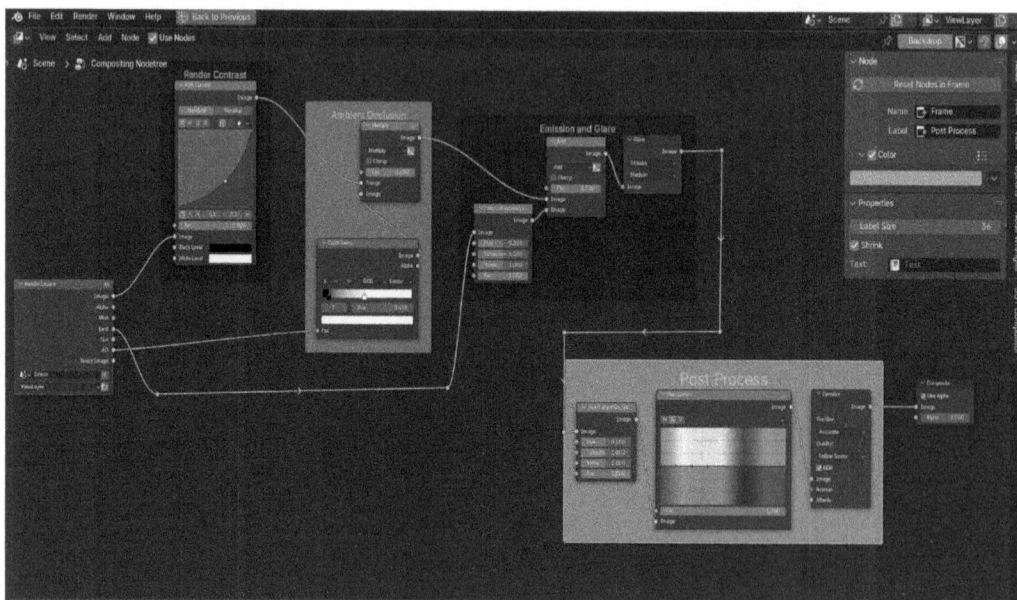

Figure 7.13: Clean compositor setup with grouped nodes, reroutes, and N-Panel open for frame settings

This Blender compositor setup showcases organized group panels for clarity, such as **Ambient Occlusion**, **Emission and Glare**, and **Post Process**, with reroutes helping to keep the noodle connections clean. **N-panel**, on the side, is open, showing the node frame settings for the selected group.

Reviewing the power of nodes in Blender compositing

Blender's node-based compositing system is a dynamic and flexible approach to enhancing visual content. It lets you manipulate images, integrate CG elements with live footage, and create complex visual effects. We have talked about some of these nodes before, but this time, we will focus on their role in compositing. Take a look at *Table 7.3*.

Node Name	Role in Compositing
Mix	The **Mix** node is essential for layering images or render layers. It blends two inputs based on selected blending modes, giving you control over how elements combine visually.
Color Balance	The **Color Balance** node adjusts shadows, mid-tones, and highlights, making sure you get a cohesive final image by unifying the color palette of your composite.
Blur	The **Blur** node adds realism and depth, whether simulating depth of field, motion blur, or softening edges. You can choose between **Gaussian** (i.e., a smooth, evenly distributed blur) and **Fast Gaussian** (i.e., a quicker version of Gaussian with lower computational cost) blur types, with adjustable size and quality settings.
Color Ramp	The **Color Ramp** node is super useful for working with **Ambient Occlusion** passes or creating gradient effects. It maps input values across a gradient, dramatically enhancing the depth and realism of shadows in a scene.
RGB Curves	There is nothing better than the **RGB Curves** node for precise control over color and luminance. It lets you make intricate adjustments to the contrast, brightness, and color balance of an image.
Denoise	If your renders are looking grainy or noisy, especially in low-light or low-sample situations, the **Denoise** node can really help. It cleans up your image by smoothing out unwanted grain while keeping all the important details intact. This is a lifesaver if you are working in Cycles, where noise can be a common issue.

Node Name	Role in Compositing
Diamond Sharpen	The **Diamond Sharpen** node is all about making your images pop by sharpening edges and fine details. It does this with a special diamond-pattern filter, giving clarity to areas that might look soft or blurry.

Table 7.3: List of Blender nodes

After this brief node overview, I am sure you can understand the power of nodes and how they play a crucial role in Blender's compositing system. It is time to dig deeper. In the upcoming sections, we will explore how to use these nodes in real-world scenarios, from simplifying complex node trees with **node groups** to advanced color grading with **Vector Curves** and **Hue/Saturation**.

Creating node groups

As your compositing projects become more complex, you will need to pay more attention to node groups so that you can manage and reuse node configurations. Grouping nodes simplifies complex node trees by grouping related nodes (*Ctrl + G*). This creates a single node group that can be edited, reused, or shared.

Reusing node groups can be added to any node tree within your project. This is a non-destructive and modular approach to compositing, and it is what I prefer.

You can also share node groups to work better in bigger groups of artists. I encourage you to go the extra step and create a personalized library of effects and tools that can be easily accessed and implemented.

> **Note**
>
> To enter a node group, select the group and press *Tab*. To exit the group, press *Ctrl + Tab*. There is an additional button at the upper right (a curved arrow) that you can use to exit as well.

Advanced node techniques

Blender includes nodes such as **Vector Curves** and **Hue/Saturation** to correct color in a targeted way. These nodes are your best friend when it comes to color grading and correction. If you are compositing CG elements over live footage, keying nodes such as **Chroma Key** and **Keying** remove backgrounds based on color.

It is a bit like when you are trying to create clipart. Without the right tools or knowledge of how to make image backgrounds transparent, your age-long battle is to make the individual image backgrounds work with each other.

Leveraging nodes such as **Noise** and **Voronoi** can be another ace up your sleeve since they generate procedural textures and patterns directly within the compositor. For example, you could use these nodes to create a stylized blacksmith workshop or take it a step further than what we have done in *Figure 7.14*.

Figure 7.14: Stylized blacksmith workshop in "Blender 3 Animated Stylized Blacksmith House | 3D Modelling Guide | Pack Blender file" by 3D Tudor

Start by using the **Noise** node to add rough textures to the anvil and forge, giving them a worn, realistic look. The **Voronoi** node can then generate patterns for the stone walls and floor, adding a unique, handcrafted feel. Finally, combine these with the **Color Ramp** node to adjust the hues and contrasts.

Understanding the power of nodes in Blender opens up a world of possibilities for compositing. From adjusting color and luminance with the **RGB Curves** node or enhancing depth with the **Color Ramp** node, there is no end of post-processing modifications you can make. Next, we will look into how these nodes work in more detail and explore advanced techniques to take your compositing skills to a professional level.

Integrating custom backgrounds with the Alpha Over node in Blender: a step-by-step guide

Blender's **Alpha Over** node is super handy for blending CG elements with custom backgrounds to create awesome scenes.

To start, you need to make sure that everything blends smoothly once you bring your elements together. Follow my lead:

1. Before you render your CG elements, make sure you have transparency enabled so you keep the **Alpha** channel.

2. Go to the **Render Properties** panel, find the **Film** section, and check the **Transparent** box. This step is key for the **Alpha Over** node to overlay your elements onto the background properly.

3. Design a custom background in Blender or import an external image that fits your scene's style. For example, if you are creating a magical forest with shiny runes, ensure your background matches the lighting and perspective of your CG elements.

Next, you need to set up the **Alpha Over** node in Blender's compositor to integrate your CG elements with the background seamlessly. Let us do this together step by step as well:

1. With transparency enabled, render your scene. This makes sure your CG elements are saved with an **Alpha** channel, keeping their transparency intact. You can see what it looks like to have an **Alpha** channel in *Figure 7.14*.

2. Switch to the **Compositing** workspace and activate **Use Nodes**. You will see the default setup with the **Render Layers** node connected to the **Composite** node.

3. Add an **Image** node by pressing *Shift + A*, then go to **Input** and click on **Image** to import your custom background. If your background is another Blender scene, use a **Render Layers** node to bring it in.

4. Insert an **Alpha Over** node by pressing *Shift + A*, going to **Color**, followed by **Mix**, and then selecting **Alpha Over**. Connect the **Render Layers** node (i.e., your CG elements) to the **Alpha Over** node's top input and the background image to the bottom input. The **Alpha Over** node will overlay your rendered elements onto the background, using the **Alpha** channel for transparency.

5. Link the **Alpha Over** node to both the **Composite** and **Viewer** nodes to finalize and view your composition. In the **Compositor** backdrop, you will see your integrated scene, with your CG elements perfectly blended with the custom background.

You might want to make a scene with a floating island surrounded by magical mist, a bit like what we made in *Figure 7.15*.

Figure 7.15: Stylized floating island in "Blender 3D Modelling & Animating A Stylized Oriental Scene" by 3D Tudor

First, enable transparency and render the island. Then, import a mystical sky as your background. Use the **Alpha Over** node to combine them, ensuring the floating island looks like it is part of the sky.

By carefully preparing your scene with a transparent background and using the **Alpha Over** node, you can seamlessly integrate CG elements into any backdrop. This not only makes your projects look better but also gives you more chances to tell a story through scene creation in Blender.

Leveling up your node setups for advanced compositing in Blender

Blender's compositor is packed with nodes that you can mix and match to create all sorts of cool visual effects. We will look at enhancing **Ambient Occlusion** with **Color Ramp** and **Denoise** nodes, as in *Figure 7.16*, creating glowing effects with **Emission** and **Glare** nodes, and achieving volumetric lighting effects with **RGB Curves**. Each setup includes step-by-step instructions to help you get the hang of these techniques in your projects.

Enhancing ambient occlusion with Color Ramp and Denoise

To start, let us see how you can enhance **Ambient Occlusion** to add more depth and detail to your scenes. This technique is great for making shadows look more realistic and detailed:

1. Make sure your scene is rendered with an **Ambient Occlusion** pass. In the compositor, add the **Ambient Occlusion** pass by selecting it from the **Render Layers** node.

2. Insert a **Color Ramp** node by pressing *Shift + A*, navigate to **Converter**, and select **Color Ramp**. Insert it between the **Ambient Occlusion** pass and the **Composite** node. This lets you adjust the intensity and spread of the **Ambient Occlusion** effect by moving the color stops closer or further apart.

3. To reduce noise in the **Ambient Occlusion** pass, especially in dark areas, add a **Denoise** node (*Shift + A*, go to **Filter** and select **Denoise**) before the **Color Ramp** node. Connect the **AO** pass to the **Denoise** node, then from the **Denoise** to the **Color Ramp** node. You will have something like *Figure 7.16*.

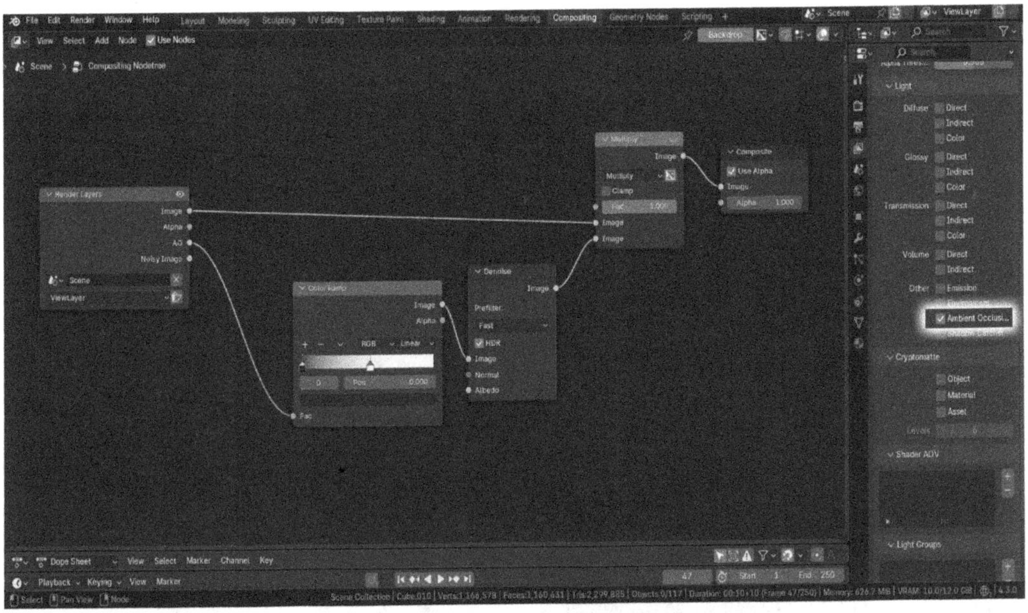

Figure 7.16: Compositing Ambient Occlusion for surface detail enhancements

4. Play around with the **Color Ramp** sliders to get the **Ambient Occlusion** effect you want. A tighter gradient creates more defined shadows, while a broader gradient gives a softer look. For example, this can help create deep, dramatic shadows for a mystical cave scene.

5. Use **Color Mix** and set **Blend** mode to **Multiply**, apply the render image from the **Render Layers** node to the upper image socket of the **Color Mix** node. Then apply the denoised **Ambient Occlusion** to the lower **Image** socket.

Creating glowing effects with Emission and Glare

Next, we will look at how to create cool glowing effects, perfect for magical objects or futuristic scenes:

1. In your 3D scene, apply an **Emission** shader to the objects you want to glow. Make sure **Emission Strength** is high enough to be noticeable.

2. Include an **Emission** pass in your **Render** layers. In the compositor, add this pass from the **Render Layers** node.

3. To add the glow effect, insert a **Glare** node (press *Shift + A*, navigate to **Filter**, and select **Glare**) after the **Emission** pass. Choose the **Fog Glow** preset for a soft glow effect.

4.   Adjust the **Glare** node settings, such as the **Threshold**, **Size**, and **Mix** values, to control the glow's intensity and spread, like in *Figure 7.17*.

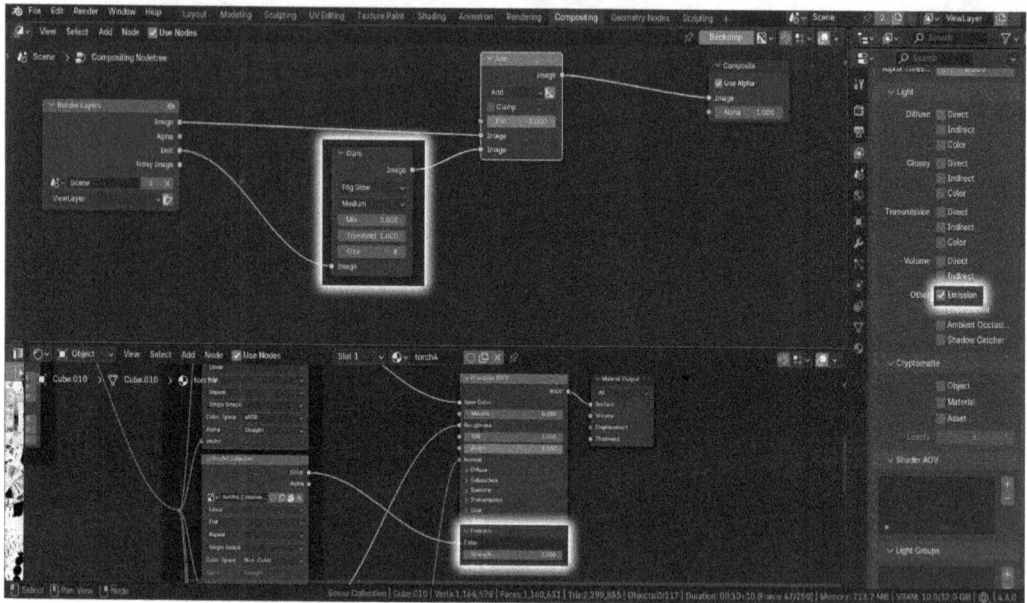

Figure 7.17: Adding Emission glow with a Glare node in the compositor

Combining multiple **Glare** nodes with different settings can create more complex glowing effects, such as for a glowing enchanted sword in a fantasy scene.

5.   Before you plug everything into the **Composite** node, add a **Color Mix** node and set the blend mode to **Add**. Make sure to turn on **Clamp**; this keeps the brightness from going too high and stops weird artifacts or blown-out spots from showing up in your final render. It is a small step, but it helps keep your image looking clean and balanced.

Achieving volumetric lighting with RGB Curves

Finally, let me help you create stunning volumetric lighting effects to add atmosphere and depth to your scenes:

1.   Ensure your scene has a volumetric element, such as a **Volume Scatter** shader applied to a domain object. Render your scene with a **Volume** pass included.

2.   In the **View Layer Properties** panel, go to **Passes**, followed by **Light**, **Volume**, and then **Direct**. Check the box to enable **Volume Pass**. Then, in the compositor, add the **Volume** pass from the **Render Layers** node. This pass captures the volumetric lighting effects in your scene.

3. Insert an **RGB Curves** node (press *Shift + A*, go to **Color**, and pick **RGB Curves**) between the **Volume** pass and the **Composite** node. Adjust the curves to enhance the contrast and brightness of the volumetric lighting, making it more pronounced.

4. If the volumetric effect looks a bit noisy, you can clean it up by adding a **Blur** or **Denoise** node. You can also bump up your render samples for a smoother result.

5. Then, drop in a **Color Mix** node and set the blend mode to **Lighten**. This will layer the volumetric effect nicely over your main render, helping the lighting blend in naturally and feel more realistic, like in *Figure 7.18*.

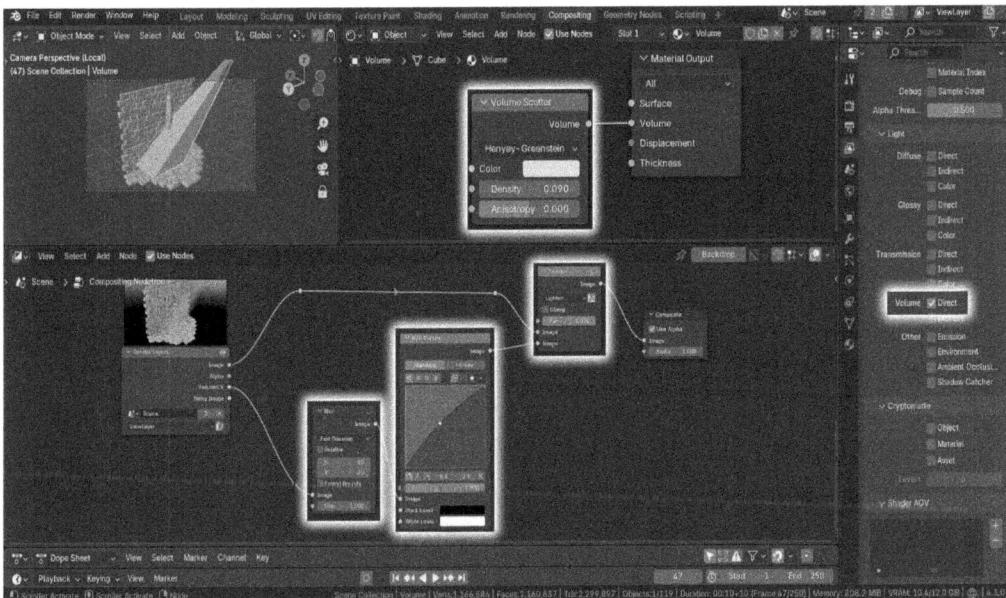

Figure 7.18: Compositing volumetric effects with Blur, RGB Curves, and Lighten blend mode

6. Experiment with different curve adjustments. Slight adjustments can significantly impact the mood and depth of your scene. For example, in a scene with a haunted forest, you can create eerie lighting, giving you a sense of something evil hiding in the darkness.

Whether you are enhancing shadows with **Ambient Occlusion**, creating those magical glowing effects, or making your lighting feel more realistic with volumetrics, it is all about playing around with the nodes and fine-tuning them. Don't worry, each technique has step-by-step instructions, so you will be able to follow along easily.

Next, we will look at different ways of maximising Blender's render engines for compositing.

Eevee versus Cycles in compositing: maximizing Blender's rendering engines

Blender is amazing at 3D modeling and animation, thanks to its two powerful rendering engines, Eevee and Cycles. Each engine has its own strengths, and knowing the differences can help you get the best results in your projects. You can read more about them with a direct comparison in *Chapter 5* of this part. We will break down what makes Eevee and Cycles unique, giving you tips on how to use each one for awesome compositing results. We will also look at some cool project examples to show when each engine works best.

Optimizing for each engine

Each render engine in Blender works a bit differently, so it helps to know what each one's good at. Here are some simple tips to get the best out of Eevee and Cycles:

Eevee

- To make the most of Eevee in compositing, focus on its real-time capabilities.
- Use features such as **Ambient Occlusion**, **Bloom**, and **Screen Space Reflections** to improve your composites directly in the engine.
- For complex lighting setups, think about baking the lighting into your scenes. This keeps Eevee fast and makes your scene look dynamic.
- **Example**: In a project with a stylized fantasy village, you can quickly adjust the lighting and effects to get the right atmosphere—without long render times.

Cycles

- Take advantage of the detailed render passes to fine-tune your images in Cycles.
- Use passes such as **Indirect Light**, **Reflection**, and **Shadow** to composite with greater precision.
- Since Cycles takes longer to render, optimize your scenes by reducing samples where you can.
- Apply denoising to keep your image quality without overinflating your render times.

   Example: Picture a detailed mythical blacksmith's workshop: you will need realistic metal textures and lighting. Cycles gives you that realism, but you will want to manage the render time carefully.

Note

Effects such as **Bloom**, **Glare**, or **Glow** may use the same compositor nodes in Eevee and Cycles, but they do not always look the same, and that is mostly due to how each engine handles light and post-processing. In Eevee, **Bloom** is a screen-space effect applied in real time, so it can sometimes look more stylized or exaggerated, especially around bright areas such as lamps or glowing signs. In Cycles, effects like that often feel softer and more natural because Cycles simulates light more physically. **Bloom** tends to blend more smoothly with the surrounding lighting and materials, and you get a more photographic result. Basically, even though the nodes you use might be identical, the final look and feel can be quite different. It is worth adjusting your settings depending on which engine you are using: what works in Eevee might need dialing back in Cycles, and vice versa.

Understanding the pros and cons of Eevee and Cycles is crucial if you want to excel in compositing. We will now look at combining different nodes to upgrade your compositing game to new heights using simple creative thinking!

Compositing for Visual Effects in Blender

Blender's compositing capabilities go beyond simple image tweaks. They let you mix CG imagery with live footage. We will explore Blender's tools and techniques that will help you create effects such as fire and smoke, and use motion tracking for realism.

Integrating CG with live footage

The key to blending CG elements into live footage is matching the lighting and perspective. For example, in a scene featuring a mystical forest, use Blender's environment textures to mimic the lighting of your live footage. Focus on the direction, color, and intensity of light sources so that CG elements, such as glowing mushrooms, appear naturally lit. Match the perspective by carefully placing the virtual camera in Blender to mimic the real camera's viewpoint and lens.

For dynamic scenes, such as a battle in an enchanted castle, you need to synchronize camera movements between your CG and live footage. Use Blender's motion tracking to track your live-action camera's movement and apply it to the virtual camera. This way, CG elements such as animated creatures or magical effects move naturally with the footage, maintaining the illusion that it is all part of the same single scene.

Creating visual effects

You can use the compositor with Blender's simulation tools to create realistic effects such as fire, smoke, and explosions. Imagine a scene where a sorcerer casts a spell, causing a fiery explosion. Start by generating the fire and smoke using Blender's physics-based simulations. Then, fine-tune the look and blend these bits into your live footage using the compositor. Use color correction, blending modes, and masking to make everything look seamless.

Motion tracking and stabilization

Blender's **motion tracking** can do more than just track the camera. It can track objects in the scene too. For example, if you are adding a glowing rune to a warrior's sword, track the sword's movement to ensure the rune stays in place. This integration will make sure that your CG elements move and orient correctly with their real-world counterparts.

> Tip
>
> Use motion tracking to stabilize shaky footage, especially in scenes shot with hand-held cameras. Imagine you are filming a scene in a street market and the camera shakes. Stabilize the footage in Blender before adding CG elements.

Compositing visual effects in Blender is a complex process. We have definitely not covered it all. But for now, you can push the limits of visual storytelling with what you have learned in this chapter already. Integrate CG with live footage, create convincing visual effects, and use motion tracking and stabilization in your next project. Remember, the key to successful compositing lies in experimentation, continuous learning, and a keen eye for detail.

Summary

Compositing is key for adding depth, realism, and special touches to your projects. We have covered a lot of ground, from getting to know the compositor's interface and basic node operations to diving into advanced techniques with render layers, passes, and node setups. Compositing is versatile and transformative, as the practical exercises and examples in this chapter showed you.

By learning how to manipulate render layers and passes, you can control different parts of your scene down to pinhead accuracy. Key nodes such as **Mix**, **Color Balance**, and **Blur**, along with the powerful **Node Wrangler** add-on, open up possibilities for color correction, keying, and creating cool procedural effects.

We also stressed the importance of integrating CG elements with live footage. Apply your compositing skills in different scenarios. Try exercises such as day-to-night scene conversions, blending 3D models into real photos, and creating dynamic visual effects.

This chapter focused on the core skills of compositing, getting comfortable with render layers, AOVs, and the fundamental mix-and-match workflows. Once you have those nailed, you can step into more advanced techniques such as rotoscoping, multi-pass compositing, or green-screen removal. Those belong in the "bigger toolbox" of compositing, but for now, think of this as laying the groundwork so those more complex effects will actually make sense when you get there.

As we approach the final chapter of this book, we focus on Blender optimization. In *Chapter 8*, we will go over essential techniques to streamline your workflow, enhance Blender's and your hardware's performance, and optimize your settings to their fullest.

Further reading

- If you are just starting out with compositing in Blender and want a solid overview of key tools and techniques, the *Blend Craft Compositor Blender Plugin by 3DT* is a good pre-built custom framework to start with (`https://3dtudor.gumroad.com/l/blend_craft_3DT_compositor`).

- If you want to explore custom shader outputs and create masks directly in your materials, Shader AOVs are a great place to start; this technique is used effectively in the *3DT Fantasy Forest Camp Environment Pack for Blender & Game Design* (`https://3dtudor.gumroad.com/l/fantasy_forest_camp_asset_pack`).

- If you are curious about render passes such as Z-depth and how they can be used to add atmospheric effects such as mist or fog, take a look at the *Blender 4: The Modular and Kitbash Environment Guide* (`https://3dtudor.gumroad.com/l/blender_modular_kitbash_environment_guide`).

- To see how layering impacts your final composite, such as applying **Glare** before or after **Ambient Occlusion**, try *Blender 3 Beginners Step-by-Step Guide to Isometric Rooms* (`https://3dtudor.gumroad.com/l/Blender3-isometric-room`).

- If transparent backgrounds are giving you trouble, and you want clean control using **RGBA** output and **Alpha Over** nodes, this technique is also covered in *Stylized Environments with Blender 4 Geometry Nodes* (`https://3dtudor.gumroad.com/l/Stylized_Environments_with_Blender_4_Geometry_Nodes`).

- To dive into procedural looks created entirely in the compositor using nodes such as **Noise**, you can check out our setup in the *Blender 3 Animated Stylized Blacksmith House | 3D Modelling Guide | Pack Blender file* (`https://3dtudor.gumroad.com/l/blender-particles`).

Subscribe to Game Dev Assembly!

We are excited to introduce **Game Dev Assembly**, our brand-new newsletter dedicated to everything game development. Whether you're coding, designing, animating, or managing a studio, we've got insights, trends, and expert advice to help you create, innovate, and thrive. Sign up now and get exciting benefits.

`https://packt.link/gamedev-newsletter`

Get This Book's PDF Version and Exclusive Extras

UNLOCK NOW

Scan the QR code (or go to packtpub.com/unlock). Search for this book by name, confirm the edition, and then follow the steps on the page.

Note: Keep your invoice handy. Purchases made directly from Packt don't require an invoice.

8

Optimizing Blender for Success

Welcome to the grand finale of our Blender adventure! We spent an entire book diving into Blender and all it can do. By now, you have concluded that optimization is super important. This is what *Chapter 8* is there for, to help you streamline your projects.

This last chapter is here to guide you through the many aspects of Blender optimization, covering everything from setting up your scene and modeling to rendering and animating. You will also get practical tips and advanced techniques that will help you use Blender to its full potential, saving you time and making your scenes more interactive.

Think of this chapter as your ultimate toolkit for making Blender sing. As we go through it, you will learn how to spot and fix common performance issues, streamline your modeling and texturing, and get the most out of Blender's rendering.

By the end, you will be an optimization wizard, ready to make Blender do your bidding faster and better than ever before. So, let us wrap this up with a bang!

In this chapter, we will cover the following topics:

- Understanding Blender's performance bottlenecks
- Making Blender's viewport faster (and more fun)
- Streamlining your modeling workflow in Blender
- Optimizing materials and textures in Blender
- Optimizing lighting and rendering in Blender
- Streamlining animation and rigging in Blender

- Making Blender projects awesome with optimized physics and simulations
- Streamlining your workflow with effective scene management in Blender
- Fine-tuning hardware and software for Blender optimization

Technical requirements

As for **Blender 4.5 LTS (Long-Term Support)**, the general requirements include a macOS 11.2 or newer (Apple Silicon supported natively) operating system, or a Linux (64-bit, glibc 2.28 or newer) operating system. Blender now requires a CPU with the SSE4.2 instruction set, at least 8 GB of RAM (32 GB recommended for heavy scenes), and a GPU supporting OpenGL 4.3 with a minimum of 2 GB of VRAM.

For a full list of technical requirements, please refer back to *Chapter 1* of this part.

Understanding Blender's performance bottlenecks

Being efficient is just as important as being creative when you are 3D modeling. Blender is not an exception to that. To keep your workflow smooth, you often have to deal with performance bottlenecks that can slow you down. This section will help you understand the common bottlenecks in Blender, how they affect your projects, and ways to fix these issues.

Identifying common bottlenecks

Performance bottlenecks in Blender impact how quickly and effectively you can work. Some of the most common problems include high polygon counts, using too many high-resolution textures, and running complex physics simulations.

Here is an easy-to-follow way to identify those three main bottlenecks:

- **High polygon counts**:
    - **What it is:** When your models have more vertices and faces than necessary, Blender has to work overtime to render and manipulate them.
    - **How to spot it:** If your 3D Viewport starts lagging or your system's memory usage spikes whenever you zoom or move around your model, you might be dealing with a high polygon issue.
    - **Why it's a problem:** The more polygons you have, the harder your computer has to work, leading to longer render times.

- **How to fix it**: Use modifiers such as **Decimate** or **Remesh**, and try to keep your models as low-poly as possible. For detailed areas, you can use techniques such as normal maps, textures, or Blender's **Displacement** modifier to fake extra detail without ramping up the poly count.

- **Too many high-resolution textures:**

  - **What it is**: Large texture files, especially when you stack multiple 4K or 8K textures in your scene, can quickly eat up memory.

  - **How to spot it**: You will notice slow texture loading, viewport lag, or even crashes if your graphics card cannot handle the massive data.

  - **Why it's a problem**: These big files can choke your system, slowing down your workflow and increasing both load times and render times.

  - **How to fix it**: Resize textures to a reasonable resolution (for instance, 2K instead of 4K if you're not zooming in super close). Blender's **Image Editor** or external tools can help you scale them down. You can also use a **texture atlas** to combine multiple textures into one file.

- **Complex physics simulations:**

  - **What it is**: Simulations such as fluids, cloth, or rigid body dynamics can be processor-heavy, since Blender has to calculate all the physical interactions and collisions in your scene.

  - **How to spot it**: Your timeline playback might freeze or crawl, and bakes for simulations can take ages to complete.

  - **Why it's a problem**: Heavy simulations can dominate your CPU usage, slowing down everything else you're doing in Blender.

  - **How to fix it**: Use lower-resolution or simplified proxies during setup (for example, a lower collision quality in **Cloth** or **Fluid** modifiers). Bake simulations in parts and only go for higher-quality settings when you're ready for final output. You can also hide or mute simulations you are not currently working on to keep the scene running smoothly.

Although high polygon counts, high resolution textures, and complex physics simulations are needed to create detailed and dynamic scenes, they can slow down your 3D Viewport performance and increase render times. Spotting these bottlenecks early in your workflow is the first step to optimizing your projects.

Scene complexity and its effects

Performance slowdowns in Blender often happen when a scene is too complex. Scenes filled with millions of polygons, multiple light sources, and volumetric effects can challenge even the most powerful computers. For example, you can use modifiers such as **Decimate** to reduce polygon counts without losing much detail and employ techniques such as **level of detail (LOD)** to adjust the complexity of models based on their distance from the camera, as in *Figure 8.1*.

Figure 8.1: LOD 0 with most topology and closest to the camera vs. LOD 2 with least topology and furthest from the camera

Blender's **Decimate** modifier helps you reduce the number of polygons in your models without changing how they look too much. It is perfect for making scenes less heavy on your computer.

For example, think of a detailed fairy castle. The **Decimate** modifier can simplify the bricks and towers without making the castle look any less magical.

Here are the steps to use it:

1. Select your fairy castle model in **Object Mode**.
2. Go to the **Modifiers** tab and add a **Decimate** modifier.
3. Adjust the **Ratio** value to reduce polygons as needed.

LOD systems automatically change how detailed a model is based on how far they are from the camera, which is great for real-time applications such as games.

For example, when the camera is far from a magical forest, the trees look simpler, but as you move closer, you see all the tiny leaves and branches.

By cutting down on polygons, using LOD systems, and streamlining your lights and effects, you can keep even the wildest scenes from slowing you down. Now that your scene is running smoother, let's see how a few smart hardware tweaks and software tricks can give you an extra speed boost. On to the next section, let's make your Blender experience even more fun and fast!

Optimization and hardware

Optimizing your software settings will improve Blender's performance; however, you cannot ignore the hardware you are running it on. Different hardware setups can greatly affect how Blender performs, from the speed of modeling operations in the 3D Viewport to the time it takes to render a final image.

A smooth Blender experience starts with using your hardware correctly, especially the **graphics processing unit (GPU)** and **video random access memory (VRAM)**.

Blender loves a powerful GPU. It can be used for both viewport rendering and final renders, speeding things up a lot. Head to **Preferences**, find the **System** tab, and select your beefiest GPU for **Cycles** rendering. For **Eevee**, make sure Blender is not slumming it with an integrated GPU.

VRAM is like gold for rendering complex scenes. High-res textures, detailed meshes, and heavy lighting all eat up VRAM. Keep an eye on your VRAM usage to avoid crashes. Tools such as **GPU-Z** or Blender's status bar can help you manage VRAM effectively.

Upgrading components such as the CPU, GPU, and RAM can significantly boost performance:

- A faster CPU can speed up simulation calculations and render times.
- A powerful GPU can improve the interactivity of your 3D Viewport and support more efficient rendering with Cycles.
- Increasing your **RAM** capacity will help your computer handle larger scenes and more complex simulations without slowing down.

When you are thinking about your next trip to the store to get those hardware upgrades, make sure you think about your needs and the types of projects you typically work on. For example, if you often do GPU rendering with Cycles, investing in a high-end GPU will be more beneficial than upgrading the CPU. On the other hand, if your tasks rely more on CPU power, such as physics simulations and certain types of rendering, a faster CPU would be better.

Getting through Blender's performance bottlenecks takes a mix of software optimization techniques and smart hardware choices. By identifying common bottlenecks, managing scene complexity, and understanding how hardware affects Blender's performance, you can create a more efficient workflow. Remember, the goal of optimization is not just to speed up your processes but to avoid throwing your computer out the window in a fit of rage. More speed means more time to create, explore, and maybe even sneak in a snack break without Blender crashing!

Now that you know how to spot and tackle Blender's biggest bottlenecks, let us jump into the next section and discover some simple tricks to speed up your 3D Viewport, while keeping things fun, of course!

Making Blender's viewport faster (and more fun)

Keeping things smooth and snappy in Blender's 3D Viewport is super important. It keeps you efficient and lets your creativity flow without hiccups. Blender has some neat tricks to help you out, so let us break them down.

Keeping it simple

One of the best ways to speed things up is by simplifying your scene. Think of it like decluttering your workspace, but for Blender.

To do this, head over to the **Render Properties** panel and look for the **Simplify** option and select **Texture Limit**. This magical button lets you dial down the detail in the 3D Viewport.

> Note
>
> This option only works in **Rendered Viewport** mode, and it is a tab that lets you pick between different resolutions.

Less detail means your computer does not have to work as hard, so you can move around your scene without feeling like you are wading through sticky mud, as in *Figure 8.2*.

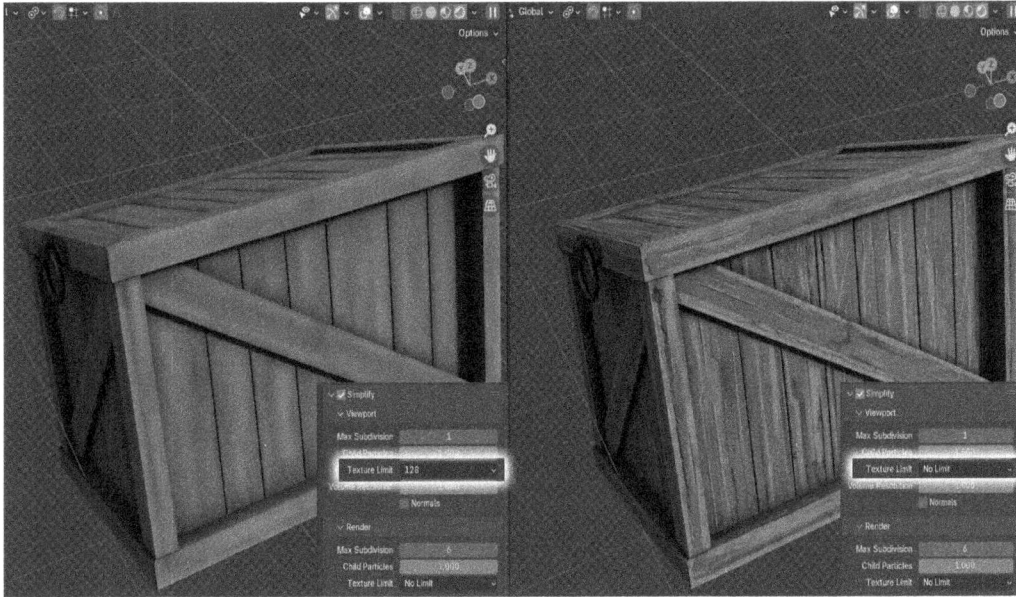

Figure 8.2: Texture Limit parameter adjustments and resulting texture detail

To find these options and more, just go to the **Properties** window, click on the **Render Properties** tab, and voila, there is the **Simplify** section. Here, you can tweak settings such as reducing how detailed your meshes are, lowering the resolution of shadows and textures, or adjusting **Culling** options (i.e., controlling when items disappear based on distance). Trust me, your computer will thank you.

Simplifying your 3D Viewport for the win

Besides the global **Simplify** settings, Blender gives you even more control with viewport-specific **Simplify** options. After all, **Simplify** is a tab that has multiple options, as shown in *Figures 24.2* and *24.3*. This lets you dial down the detail in the 3D Viewport without messing with your final render quality.

To tweak these settings, go to the **Render Properties** tab and find the **Simplify** section, as shown in *Figure 8.3*.

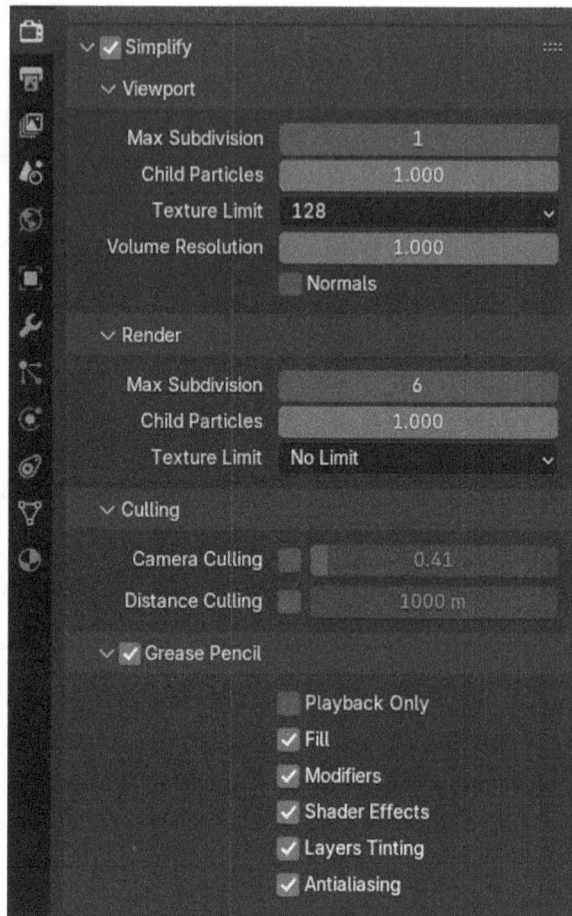

Figure 8.3: Simplify settings in Blender

You can adjust things such as how detailed your meshes are in the 3D Viewport and the shadow resolution. Lower these settings to make navigating and editing your scene a breeze.

But why use the viewport **Simplify** option?

- **Smoother navigation**: When you lower mesh detail, shadow resolution, or other heavy-lifting features just in your 3D Viewport, Blender stops chugging along, kind of like Flash the sloth from *Zootopia* processing a joke in slow motion at the DMV. **Simplify** does not affect your final renders, so it is a free performance boost for day-to-day work.

- **Focused editing**: If you are refining shapes, blocking out animations, or testing materials, high detail in the 3D Viewport can be overkill. **Simplify** settings let you concentrate on your 3D Viewport experience and needs without wasting computer power.

- **Avoid surprises**: Global **Simplify** changes what you see and what you render. But if you only want to speed up the 3D Viewport, using global **Simplify** makes sure your final render still shows every little detail, shadow, and texture.

Imagine you are chatting with a friend about Blender, and they mention *global Simplify*. It might sound like some completely separate feature, but it is really just the **Simplify** panel in the **Render Properties** tab; there is not a separate tool by that name. The whole idea behind these settings is to cut down on scene complexity so your computer does not struggle too much.

> Note
>
> The global **Simplify** panel only shows up if you are using the **Cycles** render engine. If you switch over to **Eevee**, poof, it disappears, and none of those settings do anything at all. Most of the performance-related settings (e.g., texture resolution and culling) are not available in **Eevee**. However, some core viewport options, such as reducing subdivisions, are still there. So do not worry if you make changes there and switch to **Eevee**, and it feels like nothing is happening. That is normal.

Inside the panel, you will notice two sections: **Viewport** and **Render**. The **Render** part is pretty obvious: it affects your final renders. The **Viewport** section can be a little confusing, though. It only matters if you are in **Cycles** and **Viewport Shading** is set to the **Rendered** mode. If you are using **Solid** or **Material Preview** shading, these settings will not change anything in your 3D Viewport.

Once you get how **Simplify** works, and remember that it is tied to both **Cycles** and the **Rendered** mode for viewport previews, you will avoid a lot of headaches. That way, you will only tweak those settings when they will actually help speed things up.

Even lowering something such as **Shadow Resolution** a notch can really help smooth out your workflow, especially with bigger scenes or more modest hardware. And remember, these settings will not compromise the final image or animation you crank out of Blender later on: they are only there for you to have a breezier 3D Viewport experience.

By keeping your scenes simple, picking the right shading mode, and using Blender's **Simplify** options, you can make your 3D Viewport experience more fun. Now, on to shading.

Choosing your shading adventure

Blender has different shading modes, kind of like different lenses you can use to look at your scene. Each mode has its pros and cons:

- **Solid**: This is your go-to for basic work. It shows the bare bones of your scene without any fancy textures. It's super fast and great for modeling:

  - *Pros*: The **Solid** mode displays your mesh in its simplest form: no textures and no fancy lighting calculations. It is super-fast and perfect for quickly modeling, sculpting, or blocking out scenes.

  - *Cons*: It does not show you how materials and textures will actually appear, so it is not the best choice for fine-tuning colors or surface details.

  - *Performance boost*: Because the **Solid** mode uses fewer resources to display your scene, you will have less lag.

- **Material Preview**: Want a sneak peek at your materials and textures without going all out? This mode gives you a nice balance between detail and performance:

  - *Pros*: **Material Preview** is like a middle ground. It gives you a decent idea of your materials and textures without fully simulating all the final render effects. This is great for quickly adjusting colors, roughness, and other material properties without waiting for a complete render.

  - *Cons*: It is a bit heavier on your system than the **Solid** mode, and if you have a lot of complex materials, you might still see some slowdown in heavier scenes.

  - *Performance boost*: The **Material Preview** mode is not as snappy as the **Solid** mode, but it still keeps things relatively quick. It is a good go-to for checking on and improving texturing and material setups without crashing your 3D Viewport.

- **Rendered**: The big guns. This mode shows you exactly how your final render will look, with all the bells and whistles. It is awesome for fine-tuning, but it can slow things down, especially with complex scenes:

- *Pros*: The **Rendered** mode shows your scene exactly how it will look once it is fully rendered, lighting, shadows, materials, and all. This is perfect for final tweaks to your lighting or textures because you are seeing the end result in real time.

- *Cons*: Because the **Rendered** mode calculates everything in real time, it can be slow or choppy. You will see that more if you are working with complex scenes or advanced render engines such as **Cycles**.

- *Performance boost*: The easiest way to speed things up here is to switch to a less demanding render engine (e.g., **Eevee**) or drop the sampling rate when previewing. You can also try toggling off certain effects (e.g., **Volumetrics**) or lowering the sample count until you're ready to commit to a final render.

By picking the right shading mode for the job, **Solid** for raw modeling speed, **Material Preview** for a nice balance, and **Rendered** when you need the real deal, you will keep Blender's 3D Viewport working like a well-oiled car engine, no matter how intense your project gets.

Streamlining your modeling workflow in Blender

Creating detailed 3D models is fun, but managing complex meshes can slow you down. To keep Blender running smoothly without sacrificing detail, you need some handy tricks. This section is all about modeling optimizations that can speed up your workflow. By using tools such as the **Decimate** modifier, retopology, and instancing, you can keep your projects detailed and performing well.

Using the Decimate modifier

The **Decimate** modifier is like magic for reducing the polygon count of complex meshes without changing how they look too much. This is super useful for models from sculpting apps or 3D scans that have way more geometry than you need.

To use the **Decimate** modifier, follow these steps:

1. Select your mesh in **Object Mode**.

2. Go to the **Modifiers** tab in the **Properties** panel, and click **Add Modifier**. Choose **Decimate** from the list.

3. Adjust the **Ratio** slider to reduce the polygon count, as shown in *Figure 8.4*.

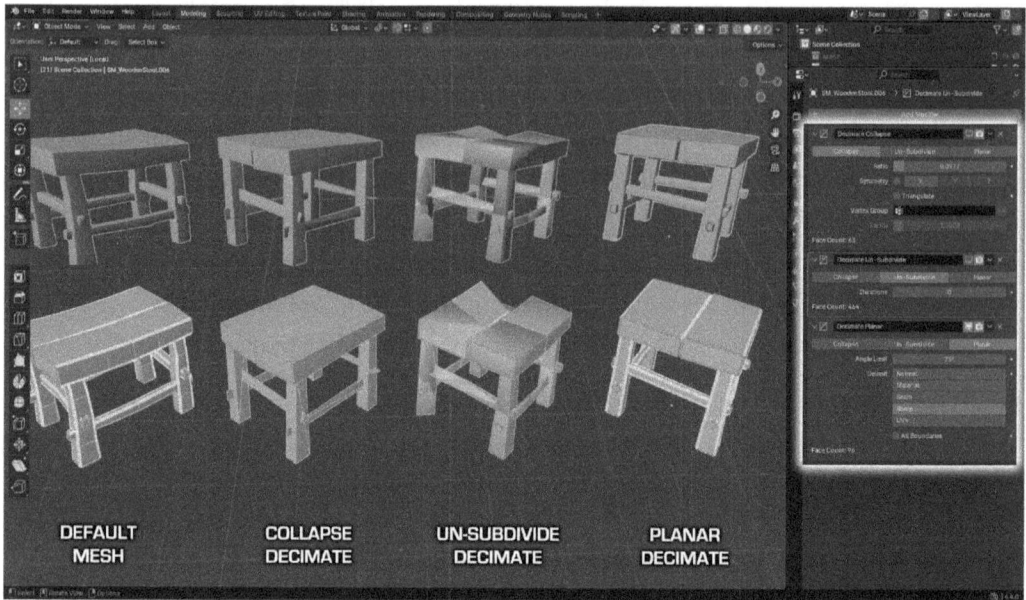

Figure 8.4: Decimate modifier options in Blender

The **Decimate** modifier has different modes, such as **Collapse**, **Un-Subdivide**, and **Planar**, each for different types of mesh simplification. Let us learn a little bit about each one in *Table 8.1*:

Decimate modifier type	What it does	When to use it
Collapse	This mode reduces your mesh's polygon count by merging vertices together based on the ratio you set. It looks at your geometry and starts removing polygons while trying to keep the overall shape the same.	**Collapse** is your go-to option for most high-poly models (e.g., sculpts or 3D scans). It is flexible enough to handle lots of detail without completely destroying your silhouette.

Decimate modifier type	What it does	When to use it
Un-Subdivide	**Un-Subdivide** reverses subdivisions in your mesh. If you have subdivided a mesh several times and later decide you need a lower-polygon version, **Un-Subdivide** can help you backtrack, like the typical undo shortcut function.	Use **Un-Subdivide** if you are dealing with models that were initially created using **Subdivision Surface**. It is especially handy when you want to remove some subdivision levels but keep a cleaner, more even topology than **Collapse** might give you.
Planar	**Planar** reduces polygons by merging faces that are nearly coplanar (i.e., faces lying on roughly the same plane). It is great for simplifying flat or gently curved surfaces without messing up the areas that actually need more detail.	If you have mechanical or architectural models with large flat surfaces, **Planar** is perfect for shaving off unnecessary polygons at the same time as keeping your crisp edges and planes intact.

Table 8.1: Decimate modifier types and their uses

Play around with these settings to get the best balance between detail and performance for your model.

Revisiting retopology

Retopology is about making a new, more efficient mesh over an existing high-poly model. This is crucial for animation because it makes sure the mesh deforms correctly while keeping the polygon count low.

Blender has several tools for retopology, such as the **Shrinkwrap** modifier and **Snap to Faces**. These features let you create a new mesh that sticks closely to the high-poly model's surface. For detailed retopology, try Blender's **Poly Build** tool and the **F2** add-on to manually refine the mesh. *Table 8.2* will tell you a bit more about each one of these tools:

Retopology tool	What it does	When to use it
The **Shrinkwrap** modifier	**Shrinkwrap** projects one mesh onto the surface of another. You can create a low-poly mesh in the shape of your high-poly model by literally wrapping it onto the detailed surface.	It is ideal for quickly conforming a simpler mesh to a complex form, great for characters or organic models where you want a manageable topology that hugs the details of your sculpt.
Snap to Faces	The **Snap to Faces** feature lets you move, place, or create vertices and edges directly onto the surface of another object, similar to **Shrinkwrap** but in a more manual, per-vertex approach.	Use **Snap to Faces** if you prefer hands-on control over where each vertex goes. It is especially helpful for detailed retopology jobs where you need to carefully place loops around muscles, joints, or hard edges.
Poly Build	The **Poly Build** tool is a nifty, interactive modeling feature that allows you to create and manipulate polygons on the fly. You can quickly extrude edges, merge vertices, or fill gaps just by clicking around your model.	Use this when you want more direct control over every polygon you are creating. It is perfect for organic retopology where you need to draw loops over tricky areas such as faces or hands.
The **F2** add-on	The **F2** add-on speeds up the process of adding faces between vertices. You can build out geometry by pressing *F* to fill gaps intelligently, rather than creating multiple edges and faces manually.	If you find yourself frequently building new faces one by one, **F2** can drastically cut down the time you spend on manual face creation. This is a must-have tool for finishing off your retopology work.

Table 8.2: Additional retopology tools and their uses

Now that you have got a handle on using the **Decimate** modifier, retopology techniques, and other handy modeling optimizations, it is time to explore another major performance booster in Blender by making multiple copies of your objects without ballooning your scene size.

Looking at instancing/duplication

Instancing is like making multiple copies of the same object without actually duplicating all the data. If you place an instance in different spots, they are all tied back to the original. That means when you edit the original, all those instances update automatically.

If you need multiple copies of an object in a scene, instancing or duplication is the way to go. This replicates the object without blowing up the file size or memory usage.

Instancing is great for objects such as trees, furniture, or background elements. By using a single mesh data block for all instances, Blender can render many copies of an object more efficiently than if each copy were unique.

Blender has several methods for creating instances, such as pressing *Alt + D* (i.e., **Duplicate Linked**) and using the **Array** and **Particle System** modifiers for more complex duplication patterns. When you use **Duplicate Linked**, you create an instance. From there, you can go straight into **Edit Mode** and adjust the mesh, and the instances will be adjusted automatically, as in *Figure 8.5*.

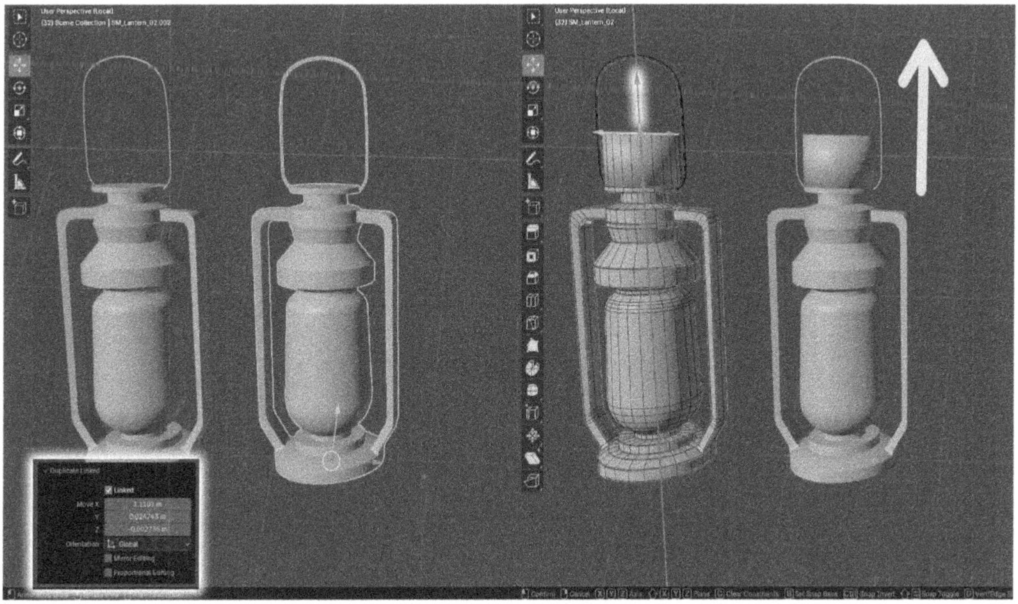

Figure 8.5: Duplicate Linked in action

As you can see, *Table 8.3* includes an expanded explanation of the different instancing methods you can use in Blender, and why they matter for keeping your scenes both detailed and efficient:

Instancing method	What it does	When to use it	Good to know
Alt + D (**Linked Duplicate**)	When you duplicate an object using *Alt + D*, Blender references the same mesh data block for both the original and the duplicate. This means any edits to one object's geometry automatically show up in the other.	If you need multiple copies of an object that all share the same shape but perhaps differ in position, scale, or rotation, linked duplicates are perfect. Using *Alt + D* keeps file size low and performance high, because Blender does not store separate data for every copy.	If you later decide you need to make a change to just one of the duplicates, you can always make it a single-user copy by essentially unlinking it from the others.
Array	The **Array** modifier creates a sequence of duplicates of your mesh in a specific direction or in multiple directions. There are many **Offset** controls, and this helps you offset distance, number of copies (i.e., with **Count**), and even add a bit of randomness if you use additional modifiers or constraints.	This is ideal for repeating patterns: think fences, stairs, pillars, or anything that lines up nicely in a row. You can stack multiple **Array** modifiers to duplicate along different axes, which is super handy for creating grids or large structures.	Because **Array** references just one mesh data block, it significantly reduces memory usage compared to manually copying an object multiple times.

Instancing method	What it does	When to use it	Good to know
Particle System	**Particle System** can scatter instances of an object across a surface. For example, you can have a single rock or tree mesh and use particles to place it dozens or hundreds of times across a terrain.	This is perfect for random distributions, such as forests, fields of rocks, or crowds of characters, without clogging up your 3D Viewport with hundreds of duplicate objects.	You can control **Density, Scale, Rotation**, and **Randomness** of the scattered objects. Because it is all instanced, you can tweak the original mesh and see the updates applied across all your particles.

Table 8.3: Instancing methods and their role in 3D modeling efficiency

By integrating these modeling optimizations into your Blender workflow, you can create detailed and complex scenes that look amazing and run smoothly. The **Decimate** modifier and retopology techniques are a huge help when you are creating larger scenes or working with detailed objects such as foliage, furniture, or set decorations. We will now move on to talking about different ways you can optimize your textures and materials.

Optimizing materials and textures in Blender

Alright, let us talk about how to make your 3D models look awesome without turning Blender into a sluggish mess. Materials and textures are key to making your models pop, but they can eat up memory and slow down renders. This section will be your comprehensive guide to keeping things running smoothly without sacrificing quality.

Keeping texture sizes in check

Textures are like the makeup for your models, but high-resolution textures can bog things down. Think about what needs to be detailed. For example, if you are working on a stylized building project, the bricks on a far-off castle wall do not need to be super high-resolution. You can use Blender's Image Editor to resize textures on the fly, following these steps:

1. Open the Image Editor:

    a. Open your Blender project.

b. In any editor window (e.g., **3D Viewport** or **Shader Editor**), go to the top-left corner.

c. Click the **Editor Type** icon (a little cube or graph icon).

d. From the dropdown, choose **Image Editor**.

2. Load the image:

a. In the Image Editor, click **Open** (located on the top bar) to browse and load your texture.

b. If your image is already in your scene (i.e., if it is being used in a material), click the image icon dropdown and choose it.

3. Use the **Resize** option:

a. With the image open in the Image Editor, go to the top-left menu bar.

b. Click **Image** and then **Resize**, as in *Figure 8.6*.

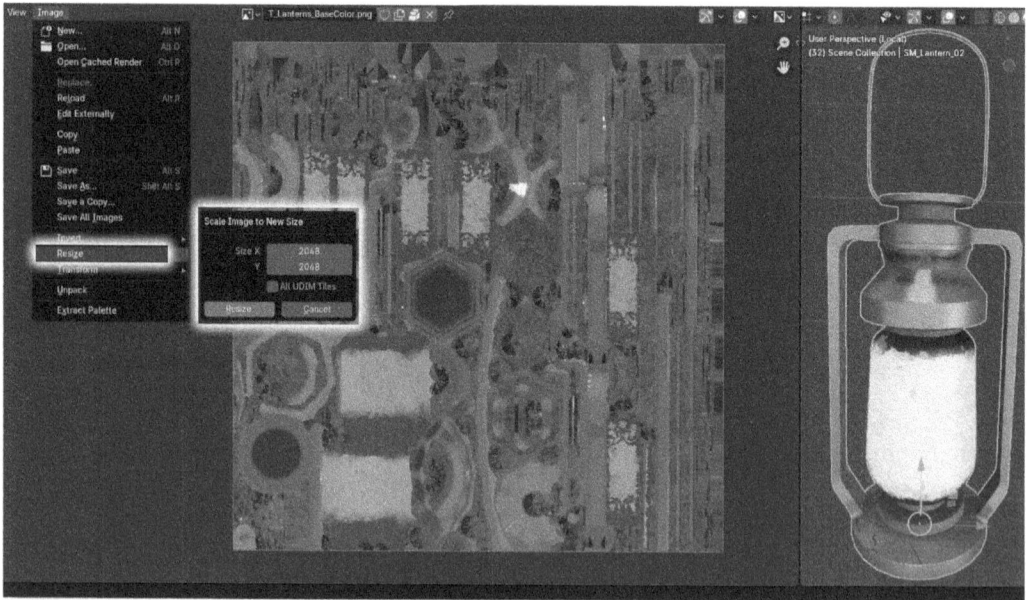

Figure 8.6: Resizing textures in Blender's Image Editor

4. Set new dimensions:

   a. A popup will appear or a field in the bottom-left corner of the screen, called the **Adjust Last Operation** panel.

   b. Enter your new **Width** and **Height** values in pixels (e.g., reduce from 4096×4096 to 1024×1024).

   c. Press **OK** or hit *Enter*.

5. Save the resized image:

   a. Go to **Image** and select **Save As.**

   b. Choose a file location, name, and format (e.g., PNG or JPEG).

   c. Click **Save As Image.**

Once you have made your image textures smaller, try something even better that helps your project run faster. Another trick to save memory and stay flexible is procedural textures. They do not take up space like image files do, and still give you loads of detail to play with.

Making procedural textures your best friend

Procedural textures are like the magic spells of Blender. They are generated within the software, saving memory and giving you a ton of flexibility. For example, imagine you have a wood texture covering both the red railings and the wooden base. It keeps everything looking consistent, but you can still swap around details whenever you want. Here is the quick rundown:

1. Start with a base PBR wood material using **Node Wrangler** (check *Chapter 13* in *Part 1* of this book for a full how-to).

2. Scale the seamless texture in the shader if you need a sharper look; in this example, we used a scale of 4 (for more on this trick, see *Chapter 15* in *Part 1* of this book).

3. Add a red overlay just for the railings, using a **Mix** shader or **Color Overlay** node.

4. Use an edge wear mask to bring out the edges without having to paint on the UV map.

This setup makes life easier because you are using a single seamless texture for everything, which speeds things up and cuts down on extra materials. You still get nice, crisp details, plus the freedom to tweak different parts of the model. *Figure 8.7* shows how it all comes together!

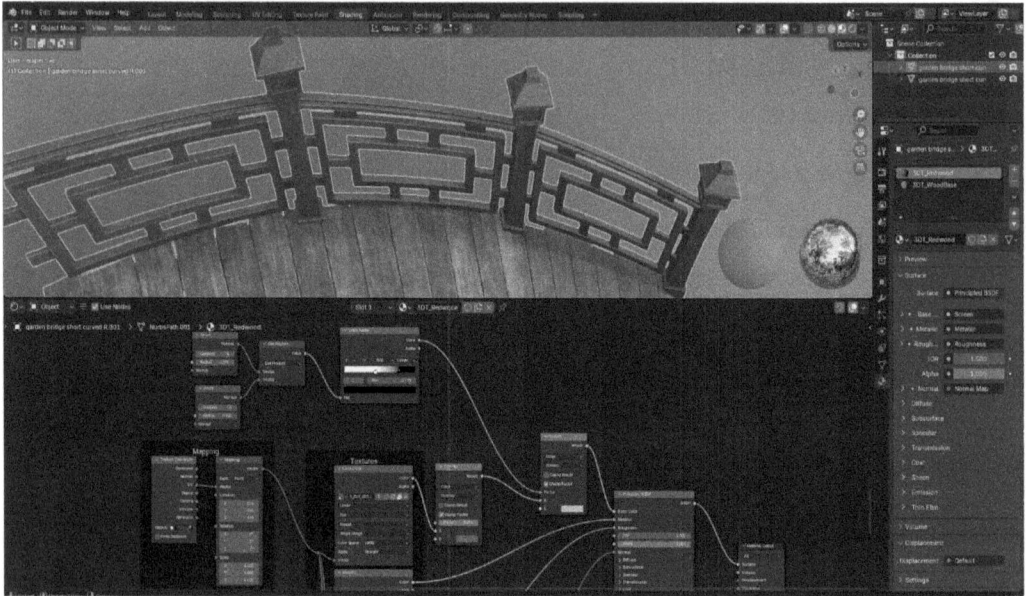

Figure 8.7: Setting up a node wood edge wear texture in stylized Japanese-style fencing

Packing and compressing textures

Packing textures into your `.blend` file is a lifesaver. It keeps everything together, so you do not end up with missing textures when you move your project around. Just go to **File**, **External Data**, and **Pack All Into .blend**. Easy peasy.

And do not forget compression. Convert your textures to efficient formats such as JPEG for **Diffuse** maps. This is especially handy for funky projects such as a stylized cityscape, where you have a ton of different surfaces, a bit like in *Figure 8.8*.

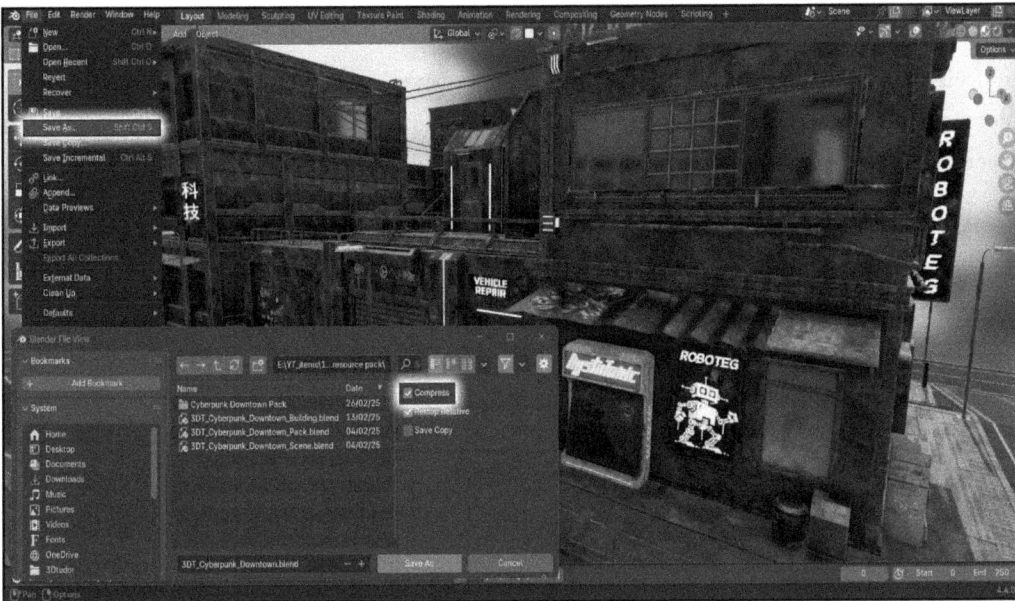

Figure 8.8: Stylized city building in Stylized Cyberpunk Downtown Modular Kitbash Pack for Blender & Game Design | 3D Asset Pack by 3D Tudor

When you save your project using **Save As**, select the **Compress** option. It squeezes your file size down, including any packed textures.

Optimizing lighting and rendering in Blender

I am dying to talk to you about getting those jaw-dropping visuals in Blender without turning your computer into a potato. Lighting and rendering can be super demanding, but with a few tricks, you can get high-quality renders faster and easier.

Denoising: your new best friend

Denoising is a game-changer. It smooths out the noise in your renders, so you can use lower sample rates and still get clean images. Blender has a few denoising options: the built-in **Denoiser**, NVIDIA's **OptiX AI-Accelerated Denoiser**, and **OpenImageDenoise**. You can read more about them in the *Blender Manual* (https://docs.blender.org/manual/id/2.93/render/layers/denoising.html).

You can find these under the **Render Properties** panel in the **Denoising** section. Play around with them to see which one gives you the best balance between quality and speed.

Tweaking those sample rates

In **Cycles**, the sample rate is like how many times Blender checks each pixel for light. More samples mean better quality but longer renders. So, if you do not want to grow old waiting for your scene to render, you need to find a sweet spot.

Head over to the **Render Properties** panel and look for the **Sampling** section. Here, you can set the **Render** and **Viewport** sample rates. If your lighting is not too crazy, you can lower the **Render** samples and still get great results without taking forever.

For a simple scene, and having a denoiser enabled, using 40 samples is more than enough to get great results while making the render process fast.

Trying out the indoor lighting hack

Light portals are awesome for indoor scenes, especially when using environment lighting such as **HDRI maps**. They tell Blender where to focus its lighting calculations, which reduces noise and speeds up render times.

To use light portals, place an area light where your windows or openings are. Then, go to the **Light Object Data** properties and check the **Portal** option. This lets **Cycles** know that this light is a guide for environmental light, not a direct source. To find out more about light portals, go back to *Chapter 6* of this part.

By tweaking sample rates, using denoising, and adding light portals, you can make Blender render faster and better. This means you can spend more time being creative and less time waiting for your computer to catch up. Now that you have rendering down to a science, let's shift gears and explore how to streamline animation and rigging.

Streamlining animation and rigging in Blender

Animating and rigging are the magic tricks that bring your characters and scenes to life. But we need to be honest: complex rigs and animations can make your animation feel like you are watching a slideshow, especially during playback.

Unlike static props, characters need proper edge flow to deform well during animation. That is why **Decimate** is (usually) a bad idea; it can trash the loops your rig relies on. A **Remesh** modifier is sometimes safer for sculpted models, but keep an eye on tricky spots such as joints and facial features where detail matters most.

Bone count is another silent performance killer. Every bone adds extra maths per frame, so cutting rigs down to the essentials can really speed up playback and rendering without hurting animation quality.

And do not forget frame count. High-FPS or long animations eat resources quickly. If you are working with dense mocap or keyframe-heavy data, thinning or resampling the keys will lighten the load while keeping the motion natural. The result? Animations that still look good but do not grind your machine to a halt.

Here is how to keep things easy-going while working on your animations.

Simplifying those rigs

For background characters or those not stealing the spotlight, simplify the rigs. This might mean fewer bones, less intense constraints, or even simpler deformation methods for characters chilling in the background.

Start by figuring out which parts of the character need detailed movement and which parts can do without. For example, background characters do not need super detailed facial rigs. You can also use Blender's **Decimate** modifier to cut down the geometry being deformed by the rig. Another trick is lowering the frame rate for secondary characters: even if you are animating at 60 FPS for the main action, playing them at 15 FPS with motion blur often hides the difference. Trust me, your computer will thank you.

Boosting animation playback

Got a busy scene with lots of characters and animations? Blender's **Simplify** option in the **Scene Properties** panel will let you dial down the detail during playback so you can see things moving smoothly.

How to use VAT in Blender with OpenVAT

VAT—what a scary word for any business owner with tight purse strings and overstretched budgets! Good thing that VAT does not have the same connotations in Blender. **OpenVAT** is an awesome (and free!) add-on that bakes your vertex animations into textures, making it super easy to bring complex Blender animations into real-time engines such as Unreal, Unity, or WebGL. Here is the short and sweet version of how to get started:

1. Install OpenVAT: If you're using Blender 4.2 or later, you can install OpenVAT directly inside Blender, no separate download needed:

    a.   Go to **Edit**, select **Preferences**, and choose **Extensions**.

   b. Click **Get Extensions** to open Blender's official extension browser.

   c. Look for **OpenVAT**, click **Install**, and then make sure it is enabled.

2. Prepare your animated mesh:

   a. Check that your object is actually animated (for example, with cloth, soft body, or rig animations).

   b. Apply all transforms (*Ctrl + A*) and scrub through the timeline to make sure everything is working as expected.

3. Bake the **Vertex Animation Texture** (**VAT**):

   a. Select the mesh you want to bake.

   b. In the N-Panel (i.e., the sidebar), go to the **OpenVAT** tab and find the **Encoding** panel.

   c. Choose the animation type (**Rigid**, **Soft Body**, **Skinned Mesh**, etc.).

   d. Set your **Start Frame** and **End Frame** values.

   e. Click **Bake VAT**. OpenVAT will then create the following:

     • A position texture (tracks how each vertex moves in each frame)

     • A normal texture (for proper shading)

     • A UV-ready mesh with a special layout

   f. Export data (FBX/GLTF) if you need it for a specific engine.

4. Export to a game engine:

   a. Export your baked mesh and textures (FBX or GLTF works great).

   b. In Unreal or Unity, load up a **VAT** shader that reads the texture data and applies the animation on the GPU, no rig or physics required.

Why use VAT?

Using VAT can help with the following:

- **Performance boost**: Perfect for real-time apps since it offloads animation to the GPU

- **No bones needed**: All your animation data is stored in textures

- **Great for complex simulations**: Works wonders for cloth, destruction, fluid, or any fancy procedural motion

In *Figure 8.9*, you can see how the OpenVAT add-on is set up in **Preferences**.

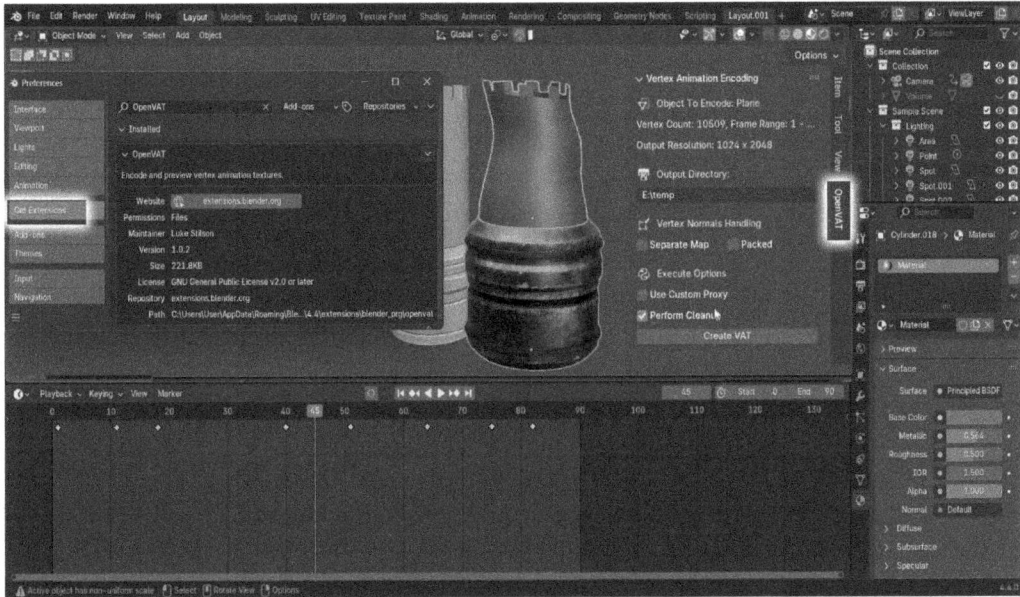

Figure 8.9: Setting up the OpenVAT add-on in Blender Preferences

Then, as shown in *Figure 8.10*, the add-on automatically generates a VAT. In this example, a piece of metal foil is attached to a heat pipe, using the VAT to drive its animated motion in the scene.

Figure 8.10: Generated VAT for the metal foil attached to the heat pipe

With OpenVAT, you can turn your most detailed Blender animations into assets that look amazing in real time, all while keeping things light and fast!

Also, use **Local View** or hide parts of the scene to focus on what you are currently animating.

By simplifying rigs and optimizing playback settings, you can keep your animation workflow responsive at every step. This way, you get real-time feedback to fine-tune movements and nail the emotional impact of your scenes. Remember, it is all about balancing performance with the level of detail you need to tell a convincing story. Now, let us move on to optimizing physics and simulations!

Making Blender projects awesome with optimized physics and simulations

Physics simulations and particle systems are Blender's secret sauce for adding realism and action to your scenes. But let us be honest, they can turn your computer into a snail if you are not careful, a bit like too much sriracha sauce could burn your throat. I will guide you through how to keep things fast and fun while using these powerful tools.

Using Bake physics simulations

Baking physics simulations turns all those complex calculations into a pre-made sequence, so Blender does not have to figure it out every single frame. This makes everything faster and more predictable.

To bake a physics simulation in Blender, follow these steps:

1. Go to the **Physics Properties** panel of the object with the simulation.

2. Find the **Bake** section under the **Cache** options of your **Physics** tab. Choose your **Bake** option based on the **Simulation** type (such as **Cloth**, **Fluid**, or **Smoke**):

   - **Cloth:** Ideal for fabrics and flexible materials. Think of fluttering banners or curtains, or clothing realistically moving on characters.

   - **Fluid:** Perfect for water or liquids. Use it to simulate realistic flowing rivers, pouring drinks, or splashes in fountains.

   - **Smoke:** Great for creating atmospheric effects such as smoke rising from a chimney, steam escaping pipes, or thick fog drifting through a scene.

3. Click **Bake** to precalculate the simulation. For more complex setups, consider **Bake All Dynamics** or try using **VAT**.

Once baked, you can easily scrub through the timeline, making fine adjustments to timing and interactions. Baking the **Cloth** simulation ensures that banners move smoothly every time you hit **Play**.

Optimizing particle systems

Particle systems can be performance hogs if you are not careful. But with a few tweaks, you can keep the visual impact high without slowing things down. Try the following strategies:

- Lower the number of particles. For example, if you are creating falling leaves around a house, hundreds of particles might look just as good as thousands, especially in the background.

- Instead of cranking up the particle count, use **Children** particles. These are like particle babies generated from parent particles, reducing the load. Adjust **Display Amount** and **Render Amount** in the particle settings to find the sweet spot between performance and quality. Think of the sweet spot as the point where you get just enough variety in each particle (e.g., different sizes or rotations) without totally crushing your computer's performance. The more you crank up **Display Amount** and **Render Amount**, the more unique each particle becomes, but Blender also has to do more work, especially if the **Children** settings are really detailed. So, the best approach is to gradually bump those numbers up while keeping an eye on how smoothly your scene still runs.

- Just like with physics simulations, baking particle systems turns their behavior into a pre-made sequence. In other words, Blender figures out all the particle movements and actions once and then remembers them. So, every time you play your animation or move through your timeline, Blender does not need to redo all those complicated calculations. This keeps things running smoothly and makes it easier to see exactly what is happening, really handy if you've got things such as leaves falling gently around the bottom of your house.

More practical tips

Here are some extra tips to keep things stress-free when baking and optimizing your particle systems and simulations:

- For scenes with multiple simulations or particle systems, bake them individually. This keeps things flexible if you need to make changes later.

- Save your project regularly before baking simulations. Baking can take time and might need a few tries to get right.

- Use Blender's **Simplify** settings to tone down the detail during playback.

By managing physics simulations and particle systems with these baking and optimization tricks, you can make your Blender projects more realistic and complex. So, whether it is fluttering banners or falling leaves, your stylized building scenes will look fantastic without the frustration of lagging performance. In the next section, go through some of the scene management ideas, but try not to overdo it! Too much management can make things more complicated than they need to be.

Streamlining your workflow with effective scene management in Blender

Keeping your Blender projects organized is key, especially when you are juggling a ton of elements. Good scene management makes everything easier to navigate, edit, and render. Here is how to use layers, collections, and the **Outliner** to keep things neat and boost your productivity.

Using layers and collections

Blender ditched the old layer system for collections. Collections let you group things logically, so you can easily hide, lock, or exclude them from renders; we talked about them before in *Chapter 4* in *Part 1* of this book. This is a lifesaver for complex scenes where you need to focus on specific parts without getting distracted.

This is a quick walkthrough of how to make the most of collections:

1. Group related objects by selecting them and pressing *M* to move them to a new or existing collection. For example, if you are working on a cyberpunk project, as in *Figure 8.11*, you could have one collection for walls, another for neon signs, and so on.

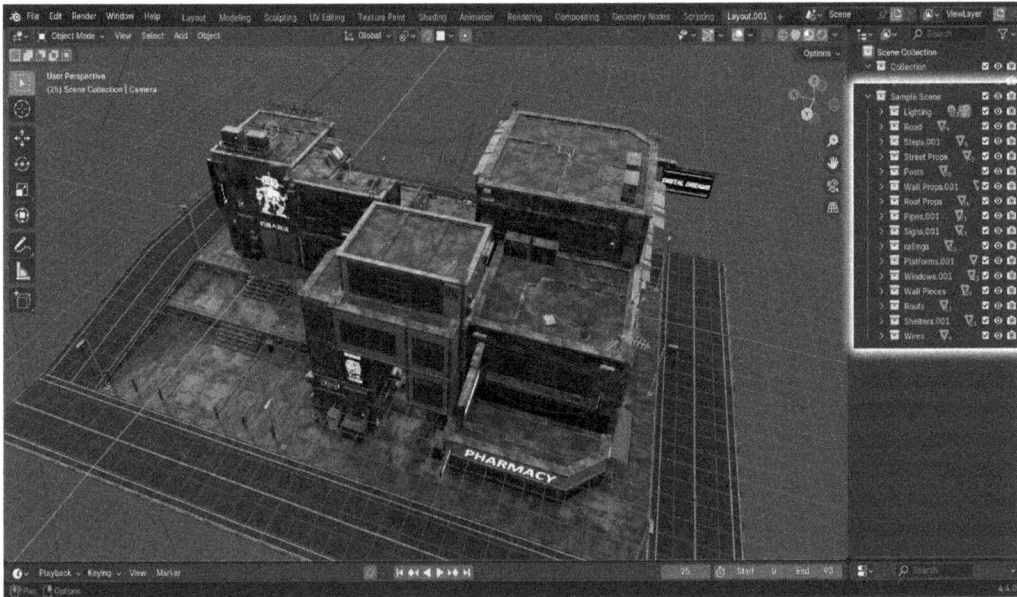

Figure 8.11: Collections in Stylized Cyberpunk Billboard Pack for Blender & Game Design | 3D Asset Pack by 3D Tudor

2. You can create collections within collections (i.e., **nested collections**) for even more organization. Maybe your pyramid collection has sub-collections for individual blocks and interior chambers.

3. Use the eye icon in the Outliner to toggle visibility and the camera icon to control whether they are included in renders.

4. Blender's collection system is basically the modern version of the old layer system, but way more flexible and useful. Back in the day (before version 2.8), you had those basic layers you could toggle on and off, but now, with collections, you can organize your scene in a much smarter way. It is super helpful when you are working on more complex projects and need to keep things neat and easy to manage.

Organizing the Outliner

The Outliner is your project's map, showing all the elements in a neat hierarchy. It is great for quick selection, visibility toggling, and organizing objects, collections, and data blocks.

To optimize your Outliner, follow these steps:

- Use the filter options at the top to show only what you need, such as objects, collections, or animation data. This is super handy when your kitbash project is bursting at the seams.

- Quickly find objects or collections with the search bar, perfect for densely packed scenes. Lost your pharaoh statue? Type it in and find it instantly.

- Reorganize by dragging objects or collections around in the Outliner. Need to move all your tomb artifacts into one collection? Just drag and drop.

> Tip
>
> The **Simple Renaming** add-on is a super handy tool in Blender that makes it easy to rename a bunch of objects or collections all at once. Once you have installed it, you will find it in the N-Panel (i.e., the side toolbar in the 3D Viewport). From there, you can quickly add prefixes, suffixes, numbers, or totally rename things, no need to do it one by one. It is a real time-saver, especially when your scene gets crowded with stuff that all has messy or default names. With Simple Renaming, you can keep your Outliner clean and organized, which makes finding and managing things way easier, especially in bigger projects.

You can preview **Simple Renaming** and its options in *Figure 8.12*:

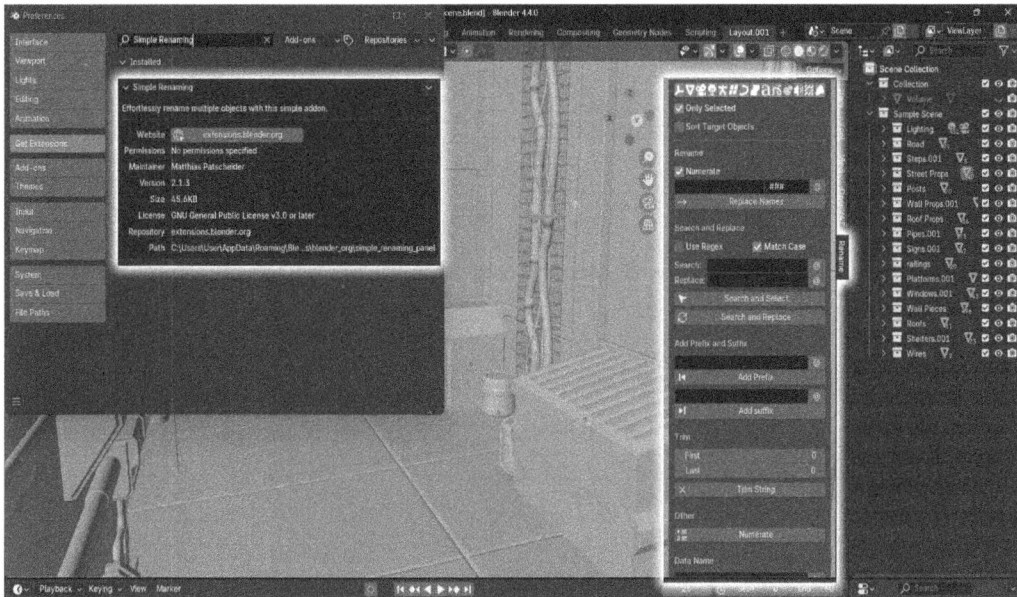

Figure 8.12: Simple Renaming options in Blender

Getting comfortable with the Outliner can seriously level up your Blender workflow. It is like having a control panel for your whole scene, making it easier to find stuff, stay organized, and keep things tidy as your project grows.

More practical tips

Here are a few extra tips to help you keep your scenes tidy, organized, and easy to navigate:

- Regularly review and organize your scene into collections before it gets out of hand. Trust me, *future you* will thank you.

- Use color coding in the Outliner to visually separate different parts of your scene. Right-click on a collection and pick a color. Your Egyptian obelisks can be yellow, while hieroglyphics are green.

- For multiple versions of an object (e.g., high-poly and low-poly versions of a pharaoh character model), use collections to easily switch between them for rendering or viewing.

By mastering layers, collections, and the Outliner, you will make managing your Blender scenes a breeze. These tools streamline your workflow and lighten the mental load of navigating complex scenes. Now, let us move on to optimizing hardware and software in the next section.

Fine-tuning hardware and software for Blender optimization

Getting Blender to run smoothly is not just about tweaking the software settings. It also involves making the most of your hardware. Here is how you can optimize both for the best 3D modeling and rendering experience.

Tweaking Blender's software settings

Blender's user preferences offer more ways to boost performance. Under **Preferences** in the **System** tab, you can tweak settings to enhance performance. For example, reducing the number of undo steps saves memory in complex scenes. Adjusting the **Memory Cache Limit** size for the Sequencer and tweaking audio settings can also help in certain projects. As the popular British supermarket chain Tesco says, "Every little helps!"

Blender's **Preferences** panel is full of little tweaks that can speed things up. Head to the **System** tab, and you'll find a bunch of options:

- **Undo Steps**: Blender usually keeps a high number of undos (e.g., 32), which can use a lot of memory in big scenes. If you are dealing with heavy projects, lowering this number, or even turning off **Global Undo** when you do not need it, can help free up RAM and make things run smoother.

- **Memory Cache Limit** and **Disk Cache**: If you are doing video editing (using the Sequencer), adjusting these settings can help with playback and scrubbing. You can set a higher **Memory Cache Limit** size if you have extra RAM or enable/disable **Disk Cache** depending on your needs.

- **Garbage Collection Rate** and **Texture Time Out**: These control how Blender manages memory. A higher **Garbage Collection Rate** value frees memory more aggressively, while lowering the **Texture Time Out** value keeps your textures loaded longer, which is handy in texture-heavy scenes.

- **VRAM Usage**, **VBO Time Out**, and **Max Shader Compilation Subprocesses**: These settings handle GPU memory usage. This is super important if your graphics card does not have a lot of VRAM.

The status bar at the bottom of Blender's interface shows real-time information about your scene, such as object counts, memory usage, and VRAM consumption. Keep an eye on these numbers to know when to simplify your scene or optimize assets.

More practical tips

Here are a few practical tips to help you keep Blender running at its best, from updates and VRAM management to tailoring the interface just the way you like it:

- Regular updates are your friend. Keeping Blender and your graphics drivers updated gets you the latest performance boosts and bug fixes. As with all software, you need to keep everything in top shape.

- Managing VRAM is also crucial. If your project is pushing your VRAM limits, try texture baking to reduce the real-time load or use simpler shaders for background objects. Your detailed spaceship interiors will look just as impressive without overloading your system.

- As you well know, Blender lets you change its interface and settings to your workflow. Customize keymaps, adjust the layout, and set up quick access to frequently used tools to speed up your modeling and animation process.

By fine-tuning both your hardware and software, you can make Blender run more efficiently. With that smoother workflow, you can dive into creating detailed and imaginative scenes, such as forests or magical castles, without interruption.

Summary

In this last chapter, have taken the training wheels off and tuned the engine. We looked at Blender optimization, uncovering all the tricks and tools that make the 3D creation process smoother and more efficient.

We talked about using the **Decimate** modifier and LOD systems to keep our scenes light without losing quality. You found out about organizing scenes with collections and instancing to keep everything tidy. And you should not forget the magic of Python scripting—it automates the boring stuff so you can focus on being creative. By tweaking user preferences and system settings, you can make Blender even more responsive to your needs.

As we wrap up, mastering these optimization techniques is not just about faster renders or smoother viewports. It is about giving you, the artist, the freedom to focus on creativity and innovation. By knowing that, with these strategies, I have your back, you can push your projects further.

Farewell for Now — The Whole Journey

Congratulations everyone! We have reached the grand finale of our Blender journey, and what a ride it has been. Across *Part 1* of *Blender for Beginners*, you built the essentials: clean modeling habits, UVs that behave, principled materials, scene hygiene, and your first confident steps in animation. In *Part 2*, you added the systems that make work reliable at scale: rigs that pose without drama, weight painting that holds its shape, beginner-friendly **Geometry Nodes**, lighting and rendering that read clearly, compositing that adds finish, and optimization that keeps everything moving briskly.

Together, the two parts of *Blender for Beginners* form one complete loop: plan, build, animate, present, optimize. That is a workflow you can trust on every project, from a game-ready hero to a portfolio short that makes people stop scrolling.

Remember, the journey through Blender does not end here. Every new project will bring fresh challenges and opportunities to hone our skills. So, keep exploring, optimizing, and 3D modeling. Here's to making Blender sing and dance, faster and better than ever before!

Until next time, happy modeling, everyone!

Neil and Vanessa

Further reading

- If you want to make sure your textures stay linked and travel safely with your project, *Stylized Cyberpunk Downtown Modular Kitbash Pack for Blender & Game Design* (`https://3dtudor.gumroad.com/l/stylized_cyberpunk_downtown_modular_kitbash`) shows how packing everything into the `.blend` file avoids broken links.

- If you want an easy way to organize your scene and keep your Outliner clean, *Stylized Cyberpunk Billboard Pack for Blender & Game Design* (`https://3dtudor.gumroad.com/l/3DT_Stylized_Cyberpunk_Billboard_Pack`) lets you practice grouping related assets into collections, such as walls, signs, or props.

Subscribe to Game Dev Assembly!

We are excited to introduce **Game Dev Assembly**, our brand-new newsletter dedicated to everything game development. Whether you're coding, designing, animating, or managing a studio, we've got insights, trends, and expert advice to help you create, innovate, and thrive. Sign up now and get exciting benefits.

```
https://packt.link/gamedev-newsletter
```

Join the 3D Tudor Channel Discord Server!

Join the 3D Tudor Channel Discord Server, a creative hub for learning Blender, Unreal Engine, Substance Painter, and 3D modeling, for discussions with the authors and other readers:

```
https://discord.gg/5EkjT36vUj
```

9

Unlock Your Exclusive Benefits

Your copy of this book includes the following exclusive benefits:

- ☁ Next-gen Packt Reader
- 📄 DRM-free PDF/ePub downloads

Follow the guide below to unlock them. The process takes only a few minutes and needs to be completed once.

Unlock this Book's Free Benefits in 3 Easy Steps

Step 1

Keep your purchase invoice ready for *Step 3*. If you have a physical copy, scan it using your phone and save it as a PDF, JPG, or PNG.

For more help on finding your invoice, visit https://www.packtpub.com/unlock-benefits/help.

> **Note:** If you bought this book directly from Packt, no invoice is required. After *Step 2*, you can access your exclusive content right away.

Step 2

Scan the QR code or go to `packtpub.com/unlock`.

On the page that opens (similar to *Figure 9.1* on desktop), search for this book by name and select the correct edition.

Figure 9.1: Packt unlock landing page on desktop

Step 3

After selecting your book, sign in to your Packt account or create one for free. Then upload your invoice (PDF, PNG, or JPG, up to 10 MB). Follow the on-screen instructions to finish the process.

Need help?

If you get stuck and need help, visit `https://www.packtpub.com/unlock-benefits/help` for a detailed FAQ on how to find your invoices and more. This QR code will take you to the help page.

Note: If you are still facing issues, reach out to `customercare@packt.com`.

‹packt›

www.packtpub.com

Subscribe to our online digital library for full access to over 7,000 books and videos, as well as industry leading tools to help you plan your personal development and advance your career. For more information, please visit our website.

Why subscribe?

- Spend less time learning and more time coding with practical eBooks and Videos from over 4,000 industry professionals
- Improve your learning with Skill Plans built especially for you
- Get a free eBook or video every month
- Fully searchable for easy access to vital information
- Copy and paste, print, and bookmark content

At www.packtpub.com, you can also read a collection of free technical articles, sign up for a range of free newsletters, and receive exclusive discounts and offers on Packt books and eBooks.

Other Books You May Enjoy

If you enjoyed this book, you may be interested in these other books by Packt:

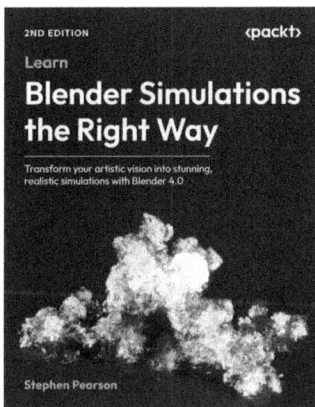

Learn Blender Simulations the Right Way

Stephen Pearson

ISBN: 978-1-83620-005-5

- Create a realistic campfire simulation with sparks and motion blur
- Simulate a chaotic explosion using smoke, fire, and particle effects
- Implement Fluid simulation for a waterfall with waves and foam
- Use the Soft Body system to simulate a sphere moving through obstacles
- Apply Cloth physics to animate a waving flag attached to a pole with ropes
- Master the Rigid Body system to create a Rube Goldberg machine-like animation
- Animate painting effects and raindrops using Dynamic Paint
- Combine multiple simulation effects to create a burning effect animation

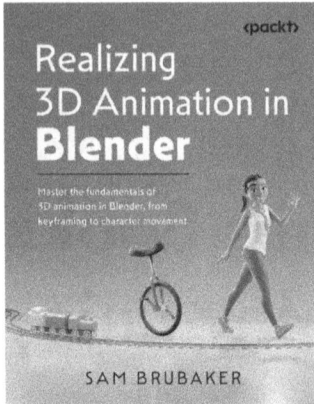

Realizing 3D Animation in Blender

Sam Brubaker

ISBN: 978-1-80107-721-7

- Become well-versed with the simple rules of keyframing and interpolation
- Understand the function and behavior of Blender's animation curves
- Bring a character to life with Blender 3D character animation
- Utilize multiple cameras and the video sequence editor for advanced shot composition
- Get to grips with Blender's mysterious non-linear animation tool
- Explore advanced features such as physics simulation and camera techniques

Packt is searching for authors like you

If you're interested in becoming an author for Packt, please visit authors.packt.com and apply today. We have worked with thousands of developers and tech professionals, just like you, to help them share their insight with the global tech community. You can make a general application, apply for a specific hot topic that we are recruiting an author for, or submit your own idea.

Share your thoughts

Now you've finished *Blender for Beginners, Part 2*, we'd love to hear your thoughts! Scan the QR code below to go straight to the Amazon review page for this book and share your feedback or leave a review on the site that you purchased it from.

https://packt.link/r/1806381990

Your review is important to us and the tech community and will help us make sure we're delivering excellent quality content.

Index

www.ingramcontent.com/pod-product-compliance
Lightning Source LLC
Chambersburg PA
CBHW061806210326
41599CB00034B/6898